GW00854201

A PILGRIM'S GUIDE TO FORTY-SIX TEMPLES

A Pilgrim's Guide to Forty-Six Temples

by Shiro Usui

translated by Stephen D. Miller

New York · WEATHERHILL · *Tokyo*

First Edition, 1990

Published by Weatherhill, Inc., New York, with editorial offices at
Tanko-Weatherhill, Inc., 8–3 Nibancho, Chiyoda-ku, Tokyo 102, Japan.
Copyright © 1982, 1989 by Shiro Usui; all rights reserved. Printed and
first published in Japan.

Library of Congress Cataloging-in-Publication Data: Usui, Shirō, 1920–
. / A pilgrim's guide to forty-six temples. / Translation of: Selected
chapters of Koji junrei hitoritabi. / 1. Temples, Buddhist—Japan—Kinki
Region. / I. Title. / BQ6353.K45U8813   1987   294.3′435′09521864
86–32473 / ISBN 0–8348–0211–2

ABOUT THE AUTHOR

SHIRO USUI was born in 1920 in Gifu Prefecture. Graduated from Otani University, where he majored in Eastern philosophy and religion, he became Editorial Director and is presently Vice-President of Tankosha, Ltd., a Japanese publisher based in Kyoto. He has published many books in Japanese.

The bird's-eye view illustrations of the forty-six temples are drawn by Toshinori Takemura, a scholar well known for his studies of Japanese temples and shrines.

Contents

Preface

If I were to claim that Japan is a country teeming with gods and Buddhas, the burden of a great deal of explanation would be mine to bear, since the most common image of Japan in the world today is not as a religious nation but as a great economic power.

The Japanese have at the same time a pantheistic and a practical view of religion. The Buddhist and Shinto views of man and the world are alive together in their minds and hearts, without the least contradiction. The enormous number of shrines and temples in Japan are testimony to this. According to the latest statistics of the Japanese Ministry of Education, there are more than 123,000 Shinto shrines and 100,000 Buddhist temples across the land. In fact, instead of a country teeming with gods and Buddhas, it may be more accurate to describe Japan as a country teeming with shrines and temples.

Hōryūji and Shitennōji, two of the oldest surviving temples, were built at the start of the seventh century, soon after Buddhism was first introduced to Japan. In many ways, the story of Japanese history is the story of the construction of temples and pagodas. Over the centuries, the Japanese have prayed to the Buddhas, carved their hallowed images, and constructed grand and impressive halls to house those precious images.

There are many different religious sects in Japan as well. Though a simple sketch can trace the introduction of the Six Nara sects, followed by the founding of Tendai and Shingon in the ninth century, and the appearance of the new sects of the twelfth through fourteenth centuries—the Pure Land sects, Zen, and Nichiren's Buddhism—in fact the whole story is ever so much more complex.

While the earliest years of Japanese Buddhism were centered in Nara and Kyoto, gradually the religion spread throughout the islands, to all corners of the nation. Now it is impossible to visit all of the temples in Japan. Instead, I have chosen just forty-six. These I have taken from the heartland of Japanese Buddhism, the Nara and Kyoto region, and I have selected well-known temples that claim both ancient grace and a long history of fervent support from the populace.

My book is based on my travels and observations for the series *Koji Junrei*, which included sixty-six temples. I supervised the publication of that series, and later I employed my notes from my visits to the temples in writing the Japanese book, *Koji Junrei Hitori Tabi*, upon which this English version is based.

A friend, Stephen Miller, translated my book into English. Mr. Miller is now studying medieval Japanese literature at UCLA. I thank him for the great pains he took with the translation, for the original included many difficult passages and quotations from ancient Japanese literature, and he did a fine job in finding the proper English for them.

> The beautiful, the eternal
> Lies hidden deep inside the ancient temples
> To find the truth of human existence
> I make my pilgrimage—utterly alone.
> Seeking to ease my troubled mind
> And to experience for myself the heart of prayer.

I will be greatly pleased if this little book can serve as a gentle guide to those who wish to make their own visit to the ancient temples of Kyoto in the same spirit, the spirit of a pilgrim.

Shiro Usui

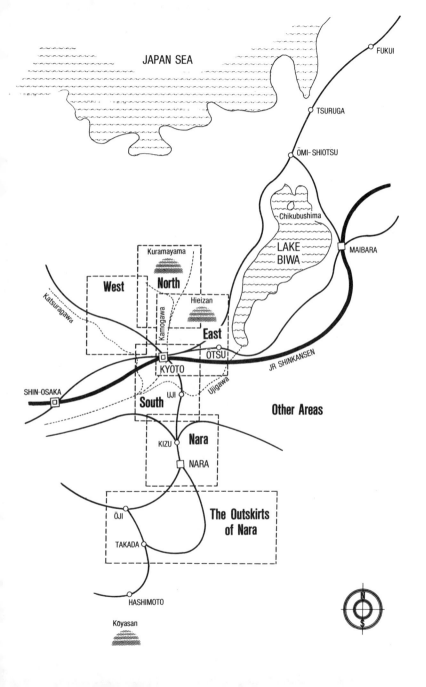

EASTERN KYOTO

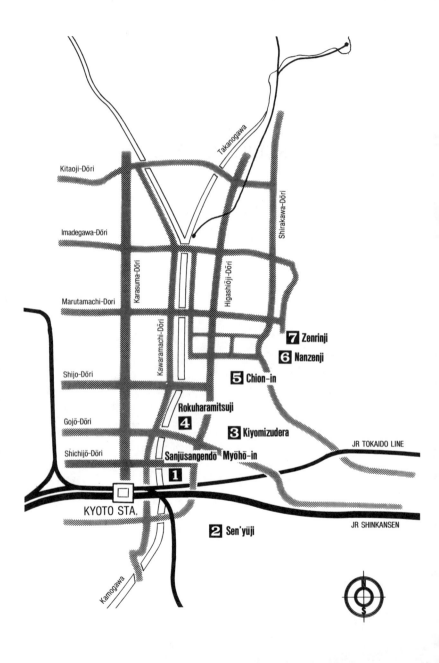

1. Myōhō-in and Sanjūsangendō

On a pilgrimage to Kyoto it is not permissible to pass by Sanjū-sangendō without stopping. Elementary school children almost always begin their school excursions here.

There is a song about Sanjūsangendō that Kyoto children sing, trying to say it three times in one breath:

> *"Kyō no Sanjūsangendō no hotoke no kazu wa*
> *Samman sanzen sanjūsan tai aru to ina*
> *Ō makoto ni sō kai na."*

(They say Sanjūsangendō in Kyoto
Has 33,333 statues of the Buddha.
Oh, could this really be true?)

This song shows how close Kyoto people feel to Sanjūsangendō.

Sanjūsangendō is the longest temple in Japan. It used to be the main Hall of Rengeō-in, a subsidiary temple of Myōhō-in. Up until the time of the movement to rid Japan of Buddhist influences (Haibutsu Kishaku) at the beginning of the Meiji era in the late nineteenth century, Rengeō-in occupied a section of Myōhō-in's grounds, which covered 86,900 square yards. Sanjūsangendō now gives the impression of being a separate temple, because the

妙法院

御座ノ間

庫裡 **5**

寺務所 **6**

横翠園庭園

東大路通 **9**

東山区役所

京都国立博物館

1. Karamon
2. Ōgenkan
3. Shinden
4. Daishoin
5. Kuri
6. Jimusho
7. Hondō
8. Chishaku-in
9. Higashiōji Dōri

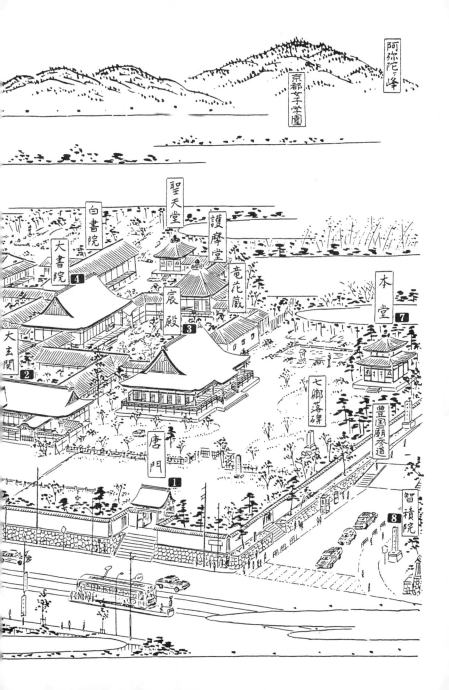

阿弥陀ヶ峰

京都女子学園

聖天堂

護摩堂

白書院

大書院 ④

竜花蔵

宸殿 ③

大玄関 ②

本堂 ⑦

七郷落碑

唐門 ①

豊国廟参道

智積院 ⑧

grounds of Myōhō-in were split up and eventually intersected by Shichijō and Higashiyama streets.

It is impossible not to feel the powerful allure of the 1,000 Kannon statues that stretch out on either side of the Thousand-armed Kannon in the center. This National Treasure was sculpted by Tankei (1175–1256), a famous Kamakura-period sculptor, when he was eighty-two years old. There are actually 1,001 statues altogether and they are collectively known as the Thousand-armed Thousand-eyed Kannon. Each statue was individually carved. Their very number as well as their ethereal quality evoke a mixture of fear and wonder, producing a strangeness that seems to close in on the observer with incredible energy. It's as if they are a chorus singing for all sentient beings an extraordinary song that descends all the way from the Pure Land to this defiled realm. What could be more moving than standing in front of these legions of Kannon?

Suddenly I recalled the twenty-fifth chapter of the Lotus Sutra, where Kannon vows to save all sentient beings:

> The Buddha's spotless, pure wisdom-light
> Shines into every dark corner of our lives
> Subduing the winds and fires of misfortune
> And illuminating the entire world.
> Coming to this place of the gods
>   to appeal for divine sympathy
> If we are enveloped by fear
>   as if we are surrounded by a hostile army,
> Invoking the power of Kannon
> Dispels our myriad resentments.
> Mystifying sounds, sounds of contemplation,
> The voice of the Buddha and the words of his sermons
> Are the extraordinary sounds of this world.
> For these reasons, we should invoke his name.

I often wonder why these large statues were made. Who planned the project and why? What joy were they in quest of? There is more to this legacy than just the sense of awe we experience when we are looking at them.

The Tendai monk Gisen Misaki wrote about the origin of these statues: "Retired Emperor Goshirakawa had extraordinary faith in the Thousand-armed Kannon. During a retreat at Kumano Shrine in 1162, he was chanting an abbreviated form of the Kannon Sutra when he became overwhelmed with devotion for this bodhisattva. On a certain night he could be heard singing a popular verse, continuing until morning: 'The Thousand-armed Kannon's vow to save all sentient beings is more reliable than our faith in the myriad buddhas. The true teaching will cause withered grasses and trees to suddenly bloom.'" The emperor's devotion was certainly ardent.

We can't reflect on the sacred power of the Thousand-armed Kannon without considering the age, the conditions, or the ideas in which this faith existed and upon which, in large part, it depended. The world at the time of its creation seemed to be on the brink of complete extinction after the unrest that Japan experienced in the late twelfth century. The Heike clan that had so proudly ruled Japan in the eleventh century had been completely defeated and the rival Genji had triumphantly established the new shogunate, or military government, in Kamakura. The turbulent seas of upheaval were rougher than they had ever been before. Values and beliefs were shifting and the only thing upon which one could depend seemed to be Kannon's saving grace.

There was a great drive to try to symbolize that power on earth, and there was also a strong belief that devotion could be most earnestly expressed by extremes of religious activity, so that both quality (ever-more luxurious religious ceremonies) and quantity (repetition of religious acts) were thought to be necessary to gain religious merit in this dark age. To erect a Buddhist image was a long-sanctioned sign of devotion. In the new age, the emphasis was on erecting great numbers of images: if one Kannon image was efficacious, how much more so would a hundred or a thousand be! This also held true for the chanting of sutras or the nembutsu (repetition of the Buddha's name): a thousand or several thousand repetitions expressed a higher degree of devotion—and was a means of proving that devotion to others.

What would happen if I tried prostrating myself just once right now in front of this legion of Kannons? Above all else I would probably feel the strange and awesome power with which we infuse our religious beliefs.

The poet Eiji Usami has described this experience: "After a while, the one thousand and one Kannons would turn to the prostrating pilgrim and begin to play mysterious, strange music —the same music heard by all believers throughout history.

"Suddenly I felt as if the bosatsu had begun to overlap vividly with a group of schoolgirls dressed in white.

"Sometime after that, whenever I listened to the last movement of Beethoven's Ninth Symphony—the section where a large chorus is standing behind and singing along with the orchestra—I would see rows of bodhisattvas lined up like a chorus on the stairs at Rengeō-in."

I am thankful, for they have awakened these same feelings of joy in me.

SECT   Tendai.

ESTABLISHMENT   Myōhō-in was founded by Saichō, and San-jūsangendō, originally known as Rengeō-in, was built in response to an imperial edict by Retired Emperor Goshirakawa in 1164.

PRINCIPAL IMAGE   Fugen is the main image at Myōhō-in and the Thousand-armed Kannon is the main image at Sanjūsangendō.

CULTURAL PROPERTIES   The Kitchen (Kuri) at Myōhō-in, the Main Hall (Hondō) at Sanjūsangendō, and the Kannon images inside the Main Hall are all National Treasures.

VISITING INFORMATION   Sanjūsangendō is open to the public all year long, but Myōhō-in is only open for one week during the first part of November. The most famous yearly event at Sanjū-sangendō is called Tōshiya. Held on January 15, this is an archery competition in which participants shoot their arrows from one end of the Main Hall to the other, a distance of 118 meters. Tōshiya dates from the Edo period (1600–1868), and the record of arrows successfully shot is 8,133, set in 1686.

OF SPECIAL INTEREST   Sanjūsangendō's huge Main Hall is the main architectural attraction here, and the 1,001 images of Kannon in the Main Hall at Sanjūsangendō are great works of Japanese sculpture.

LOCATION AND TRANSPORTATION   The address of Myōhō-in is Maegawa-chō, Myōhō-in, Higashiyama-ku, Kyoto. Sanjūsan-gendō is at Meguri-chō, Sanjūsangendō, Higashiyama-ku, Kyoto. Take city bus 16, 206, or 208 and get off at Higashiyama-Shichijō Bus Stop, or take the Keihan train line to Shichijō Station and walk east about five minutes. Both temples are located near the Kyoto National Museum, about a twenty-minute walk from Kyoto Station.

妙法院　　　京都市東山区妙法院前側町
三十三間堂　京都市東山区三十三間堂廻町

2. Sen'yūji

Sen'yūji is located on Mount Tsukinowa in the Higashiyama Mountains just a little south of Toribeno. Here the gently sloping mountains extend on out to the Uji River to the southeast.

In the spring Kyoto's temples and shrines once again become dusty and dirty with the onslaught of the tourist season. Sen'yūji is different, though. Perhaps in part this is due to its location. The temple is not particularly inconvenient, but it is situated outside the city center. These days, however, that does not guarantee peace and quiet: no matter how far removed a place might be from the hustle and bustle, cars and crowds will still make their way there and turn it into a noisy scene.

Still, Sen'yūji is different. It is out of the way, tranquil, and its overall environment makes it seem elegant. It does not seem like the kind of temple that would permit just anybody to enter.

Sumie Tanaka, author and essayist, wrote the following about Sen'yūji: "Kyoto residents do not call Sen'yūji a temple with the usual honorific prefix o- (o-tera), but instead call it mi-tera. The prefix mi- is also honorific, but it imparts more of a feeling of respect and veneration."

Why is it that Kyoto people respect and venerate Sen'yūji? One reason may be that there are many imperial tombs here that

recall Kyoto's long and sad history. The tomb of Sen'yūji's founder, Shunjō (d. 1227), is here, as well as the tombs of emperors
Shijō (r. 1232–42), Gohorikawa (r. 1221–32), Gomizunoo (r. 1611–
29) and Kōmei (r. 1847–66). In all there are some thirty tombs and
cremation grounds, all a testament to the long imperial history of
Kyoto. In many ways, it is a sad testament.

> If, like the luxuriant reeds,
> Your evil power should prosper,
> Then let it be thus.
> A world ruled by self-seekers
> Is a world without reason.

This poem by Emperor Gomizunoo clearly expresses his indignation, which at times nearly reached despair, toward the
despotic Kamakura military leadership that had usurped imperial
power.

> Oh, how wretched!
> How truly pitiable!
> Like the reeds bent in the breeze
> The rulers in Musashino
> Yield their trustworthiness for power.

Hundreds of years later, Emperor Kōmei too felt anger and grief
toward the military government in Edo (Tokyo) as we can see in
the poem above.

Sen'yūji is a temple of respect and adoration, a *mi-tera,* where
these quiet feelings of sadness about the struggles between the
imperial family and the military government can drift through the
temple grounds like a breeze. It brings to mind the irreversible
destiny of history. That is why Sen'yūji is a temple of sadness.

History is merely the record of human rivalries and victories

月輪山 **6**

仙遊石

孝明帝陵

李明后陵

後堀河帝陵

開山堂

月輪陵

妙応殿

庫裡 **4**

小方丈 **3**

御座所

海会堂

霊明殿

舎利殿 **2**

仏殿

清少納言歌碑

泉涌水

雲竜院

1. Butsuden
2. Shariden
3. Shōhōjō
4. Kuri
5. Raigō-in
6. Mount Tsukinowa

and defeats. As Emperor Gomizunoo said in his poem, it is "a world without reason." It always has been and it always will be, and "wretched" as well.

Shunjō founded Sen'yūji because he felt that religious faith was important. The temple was built in 1218 at the beginning of the Kamakura period (1185–1333). Shunjō had experienced the tragedy of the struggle between the Genji and Heike clans for power in all of its gruesomeness. He had lived amidst upheavals of all kinds and had experienced the antagonisms between the imperial family and the military government in Kamakura. Surrounded by all of these uncertainties and so much violence, he still lived his life according to the Buddhist path: "It is difficult to regard life and death as different. The cycle of death and rebirth is unending. If you do not practice with one-pointed devotion, how will you be able to attest to your own realization?" Shunjō spent thirteen years in China practicing and studying, returned to Japan, and received this temple as a contribution to his efforts. He changed its name and embarked on a campaign to collect money to repair and refurbish the temple buildings.

There is a document written by Shunjō called *Sen'yūji Kan'enso*, which is a National Treasure and is kept at the temple even today. Evidence of Shunjō's thirteen years of practice in China seems to exude from this magnificent document. Its characters are written in the carefree style of the Kōzankoku school of calligraphy, but out of that carefreeness comes a rigorousness that reflects Shunjō's discipline. The document itself concerns Shunjō's reasons—inspired probably by grief—for establishing a temple in which the Buddhist discipline could be put into practice. "Honorable Emperor, please give your consent to this project. These buildings will surely reach to the heavens. Allow me to build this monastery."

Shunjō was filled with an incredible vitality that reached out in all directions when he was seeking donations for his temple. Sen'yūji was completed with the financial assistance of people as high-ranking as Retired Emperor Gotoba (r. 1183–98) and Emperor Gotakakura father as well as from the nobility and the samurai who formed the foundation of the government in Kamakura.

It it is true, as they say, that the words we write or speak can move another person, how greatly people must have been moved by the eloquent text of the *Kan'enso*. It says in the temple records that Retired Emperor Gotoba and Emperor Gotakakura's father were so deeply impressed by Shunjō and his appeals that they each donated ten thousand rolls of woven silk.

People from all different stations of life, regardless of rank and religion, gathered around Shunjō, forming a strong foundation for the construction of a *mi-tera*.

Sen'yūji is quiet and invites its visitors to consider its past and the people in it. There is no end to the historical fancies one can revel in here. Sen'yūji has walked the course of Japanese history quietly without proclaiming its status as a temple of the imperial court.

SECT   Headquarters of the Sen'yūji branch of the Shingon sect.

ESTABLISHMENT   Founded by Shunjō in 1218.

PRINCIPAL IMAGES   Shakamuni, Amida, and Miroku.

CULTURAL PROPERTIES   Volumes of ancient Buddhist texts in the possession of Sen'yūji have been declared National Treasures. The Main Hall (Butsuden) and numerous images are Important Cultural Properties.

VISITING INFORMATION   The Main Hall, Reliquary Hall (Shariden), Kannon Hall (Kannondō), and the Imperial Hall (Gozasho) are open to the public. From March 14 to March 16 the Buddha's nirvana is commemorated. Paintings depicting this event were a popular genre in Buddhist art and were called nirvana paintings (*nehan e*). Sen'yūji has the largest nirvana painting in Japan. It measures sixteen meters by eight meters and is on view during the celebration. On the second Sunday of October at So-kujō-in, a subtemple of Sen'yūji, a ceremony called Nijūgo Bosatsu Nerikuyō is held in which twenty-five people wearing masks form a procession of bodhisattvas who have come to this world from the Pure Land paradise.

OF SPECIAL INTEREST   The temple buildings can best be viewed by following the approach that leads you to the Main Hall and the Reliquary Hall and eventually to a spot above the temple from where you can look down upon the whole area. There are numerous Buddhist images here in addition to the Shakamuni, Amida, and Miroku images that make up the principal trinity.

LOCATION AND TRANSPORTATION   Yamanouchi-cho, Sen'yūji, Higashiyama-ku, Kyoto. The temple can be reached by city buses 16, 202, 207, or 208. Get off at the stop called Sen'yūji Michi.

泉涌寺　　京都市東山区泉涌寺山内町

3. Kiyomizudera

Minako Ōba, the novelist, wrote about Kiyomizudera and its significance to the Japanese: "Kiyomizudera, one of Kyoto's most famous temples, is a place where we can take a brief respite from the burdens of our worldly, everyday concerns. Always lively and bustling with visitors, it is a place where we suddenly feel we can idle away some time merrily or where we can presume to avail ourselves upon its friendly and trustworthy environment.

"This friendliness or trustworthiness is the foundation of Japanese culture. More than that, though, it is the kind of dependency Japanese people throughout history have dreamed about. Whenever there was suffering or nowhere to turn, they would rely on some power greater than themselves. They have always believed that this power would extend the hand of salvation to them."

Kiyomizudera is the head temple of the Kyoto branch of the Hossō sect. Hossō was one of the original six sects of Nara-period Buddhism, along with the Kegon, Sanron, Kusha, Jōjitsu, and Ritsu sects. Each of these relied greatly on Buddhist philosophical theory and, because of that, were difficult for most people to understand.

The previous abbot of Kiyomizudera, Ryōkei Ōnishi, (1876–1983), who at 107 years of age was still active in propagating the teachings of the Buddha, wrote the following about the philoso-

清水寺

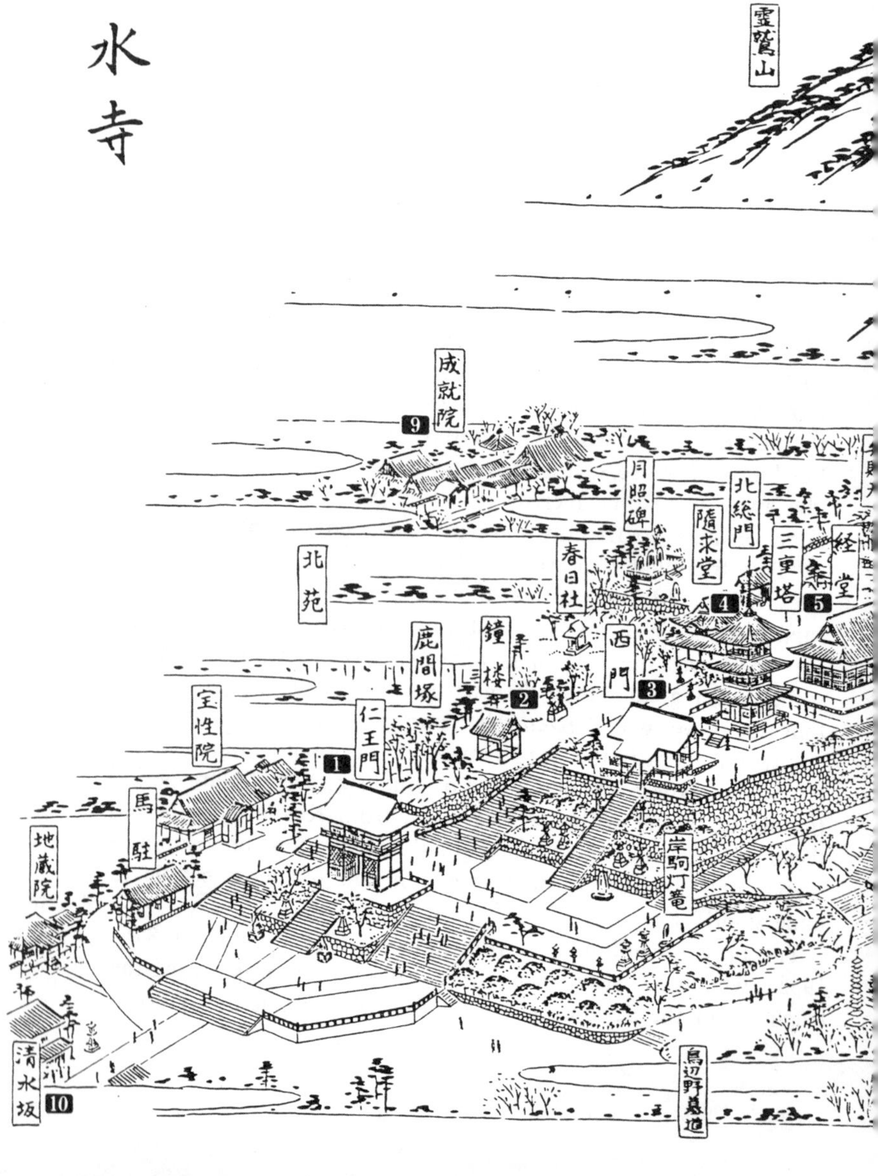

霊鷲山

成就院 **9**

月照碑

北総門

北苑

隨求堂

経堂 **5**

三重塔

春日社

室性院

鹿間塚

鐘楼 **2**

西門

4

馬駐

仁王門 **1**

3

地蔵院

岸駒灯竜

清水坂 **10**

鳥辺野墓道

音羽山

地主神社 **8**

本堂 **6**

釈迦堂

阿弥陀堂 **7**

奥ノ院

朝倉堂

田村堂

轟門

泉水

音羽ノ滝

清水寺路

子安塔

南苑

延命院

1. Niōmon
2. Shōrō
3. Nishimon
4. Sanjū no Tō
5. Kyōdō
6. Hondō
7. Shakadō
8. Jishu Shrine
9. Jōju-in
10. Kiyomizuzaka

phical foundations of the Hossō sect: "Dharma (*hō*) comes from basic laws and it is what gives form to a thing's essential characteristics (*sō*). We cannot see air with our eyes, but when the atmosphere becomes cold, rain turns to snow. This is dharma. Because there is dharma, things have their own form. This is why this sect is called Hossō (*hō* plus *sō*)." This is a difficult theory for the average lay person to follow, certainly.

For the boys and girls here on their school trips or the devout who come to pay their respects, Hossō theory is rather remote. But still, there is something unseen which calls forth a response from the hearts of the people. There is a feeling of wanting to depend on something beyond ourselves and a hope that this will serve as the hand of salvation. That is probably what Ōnishi meant when he was speaking of dharma, or *hō*.

The manifestation of that power at Kiyomizudera is the Kannon with eleven faces, a thousand arms, and a thousand eyes. It is because of this bodhisattvas's compassion that salvation can be granted. In order to get close to the Buddha here, people come by bus and car and push their way into the Hall where this manifestation of compassion is enshrined.

Kiyomizudera is a temple where faith in Kannon's compassion is supreme. Because of this, it surpasses any attempts to classify it by sect or religious dogma. It is also the sixteenth temple on the pilgrimage to the thirty-three sacred temples in western Japan. It is not a place for austere religious practices nor to escape from the world while searching for truth. It is Kannon's sanctuary, and that is why people can come as they are without any pretensions. Austerities and purifications are unnecessary.

Kannon does not discriminate between the young and the old or those of humble social position and those of high standing. Each and every pilgrim comes hoping to be blessed with Kannon's spiritual powers or virtues. This is why people make pilgrimages to Kiyomizudera, and have done so ever since the eighth century. Perhaps the significance of a visit here lies within this stability.

The prayers of the people who come here are simple. There is no determination to attain complete liberation as one might find at a Zen temple. Worshipers bring an ingenuous delight with them. Kiyomizudera caters to all of these people, providing a kind of social environment infused with religion for the sake of peace and quietude.

All of the tales and legends about pilgrimages to Kiyomizu are tales of miracles performed by Kannon. They originated in the simple prayers of the people. These prayers were invocations of salvation from suffering, the suffering we all must bear during our lifetimes. There is nothing more beautiful than the prayers of the people. And all of those prayers germinate and bloom like flowers at Kiyomizudera. Scholarship has nothing to do with religious faith; on the contrary, it can alienate faith. Faith, on the other hand, is nothing other than action. Many people make a morning pilgrimage to Kiyomizu daily, come rain or shine. They are the ones who keep the light of faith burning for us all. Or, as Abbot Ōnishi said, "When you climb this mountain, you are approaching the Buddha. If you come every day, you come even nearer."

The following words are those of one of Kiyomizu's daily pilgrims. Their simplicity is particularly beautiful: "My relationship to Kiyomizu goes all the way back to the time of my mother, who is now dead. For more than thirty years I've been coming here every morning. I wake up early and walk here from the Gion by way of Ninenzaka (Two-Year Slope) and Sannenzaka (Three-Year Slope). I walk up the stone steps from the spice shop on the corner. Usually I'm still sleepy as I begin my climb up Kiyomizu Slope, lined with souvenir shops on either side. When I look up at the large stone steps, the two-storied gate, and the three-storied pagoda rising up out of the mist, I always feel like I've come home. I feel revived as I stop in front of Otowa Waterfall, worship Fudō, and scoop up some of the water and drink it. That water seems to wash away any lingering bad feelings from the day before. Then

I gather my strength, climb the eighty-three stone steps up to Kannon Hall and give thanks for another safe day. The warmth that I feel then as I pray is indescribably wonderful."

These are not the words of a scholar or a critic or a person of elevated social standing. They are the words of an ordinary old woman, honest and unpretentious, who entrusts her life to Kannon. That is the kind of person for whom Kannon holds great attraction. And that is where faith comes from. Walking around Kiyomizudera, I remembered this poem:

> The wind blows through the pines
> And with my hands I scoop this clear water
> Falling from Mount Otowa—
> Invigorating like the wind.
> My hands are cool, my heart purified.

SECT   Hossō.

ESTABLISHMENT   Founded by Enchin in 805.

PRINCIPAL IMAGE   The Eleven-faced, thousand-armed, and thousand-eyed Kannon.

CULTURAL PROPERTIES   The Main Hall (Hondō) is a National Treasure. There are many Important Cultural Properties on the temple grounds, but the Kannon image is particularly well known.

VISITING INFORMATION   Kiyomizudera is beautiful no matter what season you visit, but spring and fall are particularly crowded periods since many school children go there on their school excursions.

OF SPECIAL INTEREST   The view from the Main Hall into

the grounds is breathtaking, as is the view of downtown Kyoto. The garden at Jōju-in, the main headquarters of Kiyomizudera, is very nice, but it is usually closed to the public. The Main Hall, Three-storied Pagoda (Sanjū no Tō), and the Amida Hall (Amidadō) are all of architectural interest. There are many statues enshrined in the Main Hall in addition to the principal Kannon image.

LOCATION AND TRANSPORTATION   Kiyomizu 1-chome, Higashiyama-ku, Kyoto. Kiyomizudera is at the base of Higashiyama, about a twenty-minute walk from the Gion district. You can also take city buses 16, 202, 206, or 207 get off at Kiyomizu Michi, and walk east for ten minutes, or city buses 1, 2, 3, 4, 5, 7, or 8 and get off at Gojōzaka.

清水寺　　京都市東山区清水一丁目

4. Rokuharamitsuji

Rokuharamitsuji is well known as a temple for the repose of the souls of those people who have no one to turn to. A statue of Kūya (903–72), its founder, can be seen in the temple's museum.

> To chant the nembutsu just once
> *Namu Amida Butsu!*
> That is all there really is.
> Chanting it, we become the Buddha
> And sit upon the lotus throne of
> enlightened mind.

Kūya is depicted barefoot and in tattered, calf-length clothes, carrying a deer-horn staff in his left hand and a bell which he strikes with a wooden hammer in his right hand. His ribs can be seen through his emaciated chest. Protruding from his mouth are six Amidas on a stick, and it looked to me as if he were glaring in anger into space. Standing in front of this somewhat frightening image, I could not help but think of him as a living Amida. What a horrifying impression he must have made on people! His hips are twisted and his cheeks are sunken, but the incredible eyes along with the animated figures of Amida coming out of his mouth caused me to feel a certain awesomeness about faith. People have always come to Rokuharamitsuji with a sense of yearning and respect for Kūya. We all have our anguish, and it was my hope on this pilgrimage to heal the wounds of suffering. Whatever healing this turns out to be, I am sure it will not make any distinctions between people of different social standing.

Fudarakuzan Rokuharamitsuji, the formal name of the temple, is the seventeenth temple on the pilgrimage to the thirty-three sacred temples in western Japan. Since, sooner or later, we all must die alone, Rokuharamitsuji is a temple for the repose of our souls as well.

Standing in front of the Main Hall (Hondō), where endless clouds of incense waft by, I realized that Rokuharamitsuji is really a temple of the people, a place where we can feel their daily suffering as well as their hopes for salvation from that suffering.

In the southeast part of Kyoto, the foot of the mountains inclines gently toward the Kamo River. Nowadays there are rows upon rows of old houses densely crowded together here, but long ago it was the location of a crematorium and a burial ground. In an almost direct diagonal line to the northwest in Saga is Adashino, another well-known burial ground. The area near Rokuharamitsuji is called the Toribeno Graveyard.

The word *rokuhara*, which means the six *paramitas,* or the six disciplines of a bodhisattva on the path to enlightenment, used to be the name of this burial ground, but it was written with different Chinese characters meaning "six fields." It appeared in various texts from the time of the Heian-period work *Tales of Glory (Eiga Monogatari)*. It was referred to as *rokuhara* and *rokusho* and still later as *dokuro* and *rokuro*. There are endless speculations we could make about these words and their origins, such as the connection between the six realms (*rokudō*) and the six paramitas. But this kind of thing is best left to the scholars. Perhaps it would better for us to consider what this area and this temple mean to people who visit them now.

The pilgrims who come to Rokuharamitsuji are looking for

六波羅蜜寺

本堂 5

収蔵庫 4

本坊 3

客殿

祥寿院 2

清盛塔 1

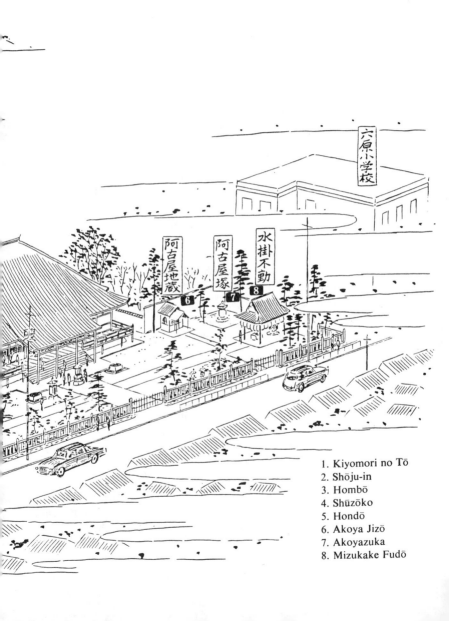

六原小学校

水掛不動

阿古屋塚

阿古屋地蔵

6 7 8

1. Kiyomori no Tō
2. Shōju-in
3. Hombō
4. Shūzōko
5. Hondō
6. Akoya Jizō
7. Akoyazuka
8. Mizukake Fudō

salvation from their everyday concerns.and anxieties. They vow to Buddha to accumulate merit in their efforts to practice the six paramitas. To see their genuineness is enough to bring tears to your eyes.

> Though I am a pilgrim
> To the Buddha's sacred temples
> Unknown to me are
> Sinners guilty of the five offenses
> Worshiping at Rokuhara's hall.

The prayers of the common people are beautiful because they are ingenuous and pure. Pilgrims do not come here because they are drawn to the splendor of the temple itself. They are looking for substantiation of their connection to the Buddha or some proof that salvation is possible. In their search, Kūya has come to life again.

Rokuharamitsuji is a treasurehouse of history. The Main Hall is an Important Cultural Property. There are also numerous images such as the Eleven-faced Kannon, Yakushi, and Jizō. A famous statue of Taira no Kiyomori (1118–81), the general who overthrew the ruling Fujiwara family at the end of the Heian period (794–1185), is also there.

The glories of the Heike clan were fleeting. The history and pathos of this era is described in *The Tale of the Heike* (*Heike Monogatari*), one of the most famous works of medieval Japanese literature. Walking around the area surrounding Rokuharamitsuji, one can almost feel the weight of Kyoto's history.

In the *Tale of the Heike* it says, "Fortune and misfortune travel the same path. Prosperity and decline follow each other in turn. The Hōgen era blossomed like the cherry trees. And now the Juei era falls like the maples in autumn." I wonder if the common people know about these theories of history, which are the same throughout time and in every part of the world? Do they know that the prosperous are doomed to perish and that all things are subject to impermanence? The neighborhood around Rokuharamitsuji is rather shabby. The old-fashioned houses, between which are sandwiched cheap candy stores and noodle shops, are built one against the other, pushing the lives of their residents one against the other as well. That is why this area has been called the "cross-roads of the six paths" (*rokudō no tsuji*).

About two or three hundred meters away and up a slope from Rokuharamitsuji is Chinkōji, where the well-known Rokudō Mairi (commonly called Rokudōhan in Kyoto) is held annually. Just before Obon, the Festival of the Dead held in August, the people of Kyoto gather here to call the spirits of their ancestors home by ringing a special bell. They go there to meet the spirits of their parents and children, wives and brothers and sisters who have died and gone to "that world."

The Lantern-lighting Festival (Mantō E) is held at Rokuharamitsuji, also in the summer, during Obon. Somehow this area impressed me as a kind of public square in which the faith of the people could be expressed and where the people of "this world" and "that world" could speak to each other. It was like a junction between our world and the world beyond.

SECT   The Chizan branch of the Shingon sect.

ESTABLISHMENT   Founded by Kūya in 951.

PRINCIPAL IMAGE   Eleven-faced Kannon.

CULTURAL PROPERTIES   The Main Hall (Hondō) and the Eleven-faced Kannon are Important Cultural Properties. There are many others, but these and the statue of Kūya are the most famous.

VISITING INFORMATION   The Main Hall and the Museum

(Hōmotsukan) are open to the public for viewing. August 8–10 and August 16 are the well-known Mantō E, or Lantern-lighting Ceremony, at which believers offer lanterns to the Buddha. Also, from December 13 to 31 the Kūya Yūyaku Nembutsu Ceremony, a kind of ecstatic dancing originating with Rokuharamitsuji's founder, is held.

OF SPECIAL INTEREST   The Main Hall is of architectural interest, and in addition to the principal image enshrined there, there are many Buddhist images in the museum.

LOCATION AND TRANSPORTATION   Nishirokuro-chō Higashi Iru, Yamato Ōji, Matsubara Dōri, Higashiyama-ku, Kyoto. Rokuharamitsuji is about a fifteen-minute walk from Kiyomizu-dera to the west. Take city buses 16, 202, 206, or 207, get off at Kiyomizu-michi, and walk to the west for five minutes.

六波羅密寺　　京都市東山区松原通大和大路東入西轆轤町

5. Chion-in

There is one childhood memory which is still fresh in my mind. At the beginning of the Shōwa period (1926–1989), I went with my elementary school class from the countryside in Gifu Prefecture to Chion-in. I still remember the famous "singing floorboards" (literally, "nightingale boards," *uguisubari*) of the temple corridors, which squeak when tread on. Perhaps it was just their unusual sound, but the mystery of Chion-in seized my imagination then and has never let it go. My pilgrimage to Chion-in began with this childhood memory.

Takeshi Umehara, the philosopher, has similar recollections: "I am certain the trip occurred when I was a fourth grader in elementary school. My adopted parents took me sightseeing in Kyoto. For someone like me, who lived in a remote part of the countryside in Aichi Prefecture, there were many unusual things to see there, but I don't remember most of them now. The two things that I do faintly remember are a trip to Kinkakuji and the singing floorboards at Chion-in. The sound was not nearly as clear as the song of the nightingale (*uguisu*). Each step along the corridor would elicit a squeaking sound which seemed to me quite ominous. It is that ominous feeling which I still remember now."

Umehara goes on to say that this squeaking sound was orig-

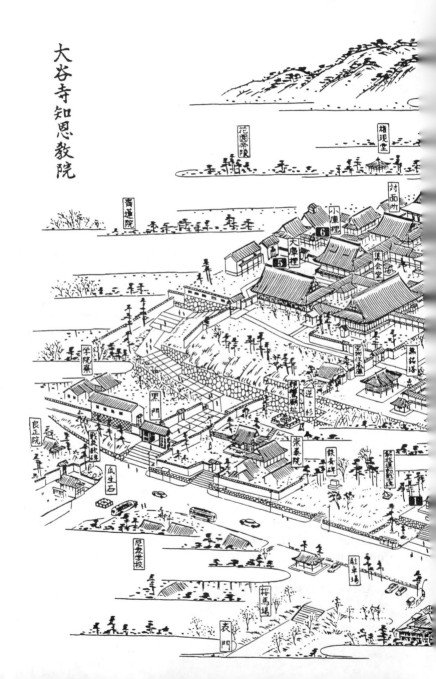

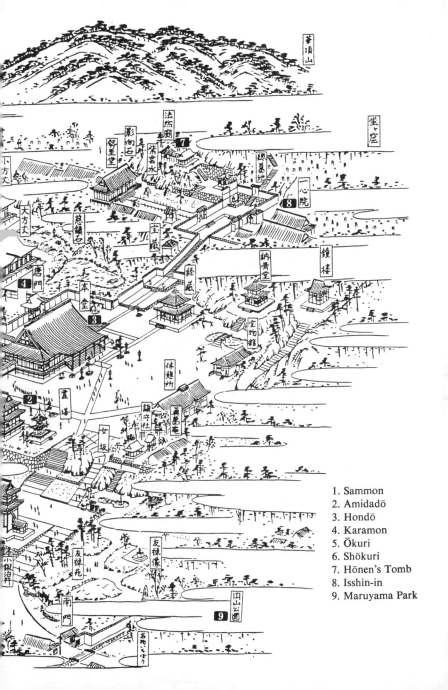

1. Sammon
2. Amidadō
3. Hondō
4. Karamon
5. Ōkuri
6. Shōkuri
7. Hōnen's Tomb
8. Isshin-in
9. Maruyama Park

inally created "not for the sake of any artistic refinement, but to prevent the intrusion of scoundrels. The Heian-period aristocrats lived in large open halls, and this is where they carried on their private discussions. The singing floorboards were designed to prevent unexpected intrusions. They were actually a sign of the apprehensions of those in power. Of course this would not be strange at a place like Nijō Castle, a center of political intrigue, but why would the priests of Chion-in, who had supposedly renounced all worldly concerns, need such a stratagem?"

There are numerous lines of historical investigation we could pursue to find an answer to that question, but the simple fact is that the priests, in spite of their professed lack of interest in worldly things, were deeply enmeshed in the political fortunes of the ruling elite, and the temples were great centers of secular power themselves until they were tamed and brought firmly under the control of the authorities in the Tokugawa period (1600–1868). From that time on, the story of the Chion-in becomes a tale of struggle against the authorities, a contest of politics and faith, the profane and the sacred.

Hōnen (1133–1212), who founded the Chion-in, rejected all of this head on. He insisted on single-minded devotion to the nembutsu, an extremely simple practice that required no special learning or esoteric training. Hōnen was the first religious reformer in Japan and, for this reason, is often called the Luther of Japan. His tradition as a reformer continued with Shinran (1173–1262), the founder of the Jōdo Shin sect, Ippen (1239–89), the founder of the Ji sect, Nichiren (1222–82), the founder of the Nichiren sect, and Dōgen (1200–1253), the founder of the Sōtō sect of Zen.

Hōnen's greatness lies in his teaching of the nembutsu, the recitation of the words *Namu Amida Butsu* ("Praise to Amida Buddha"). According to Hōnen, life in this world should be devoted to chanting the nembutsu in order to attain an eternal life, a life of truth, in the next world. He also regarded the nembutsu as an activity that would help us more truly experience the world of this life. We cannot survive if we reject the world we are living in; yet we cannot regard this world as the one and only existence. We must yearn, Hōnen taught, for another world of greater truth.

Hōnen's other world, the world of the Pure land, was the Western Paradise where Amida reigns, a beautiful and pure realm. And the only way to get there was through the chanting of the nembutsu. This is how Hōnen's ideas are described in his text *A Vow in One Page* (*Ichimai Kishōmon*), composed in 1211.

If we take a look at Buddhism and the way it prospered in Japan during the sixth through tenth centuries, we can see that it was a part of the transmission of Chinese culture in general. The assimilation of Chinese culture and Buddhism into Japan was promoted by the members of the cultural elite. Needless to say, since they were the ones in power, they were also the ones who were at the receiving end of this influx of culture. A glance at the history of the six Buddhist sects of the Nara period (646–794) provides sufficient proof of this. During the Heian period (794–1185), the relationship of Buddhism to the authorities became even more intimate. Hōnen and other Buddhist reformers, though many were themselves from the aristocracy, recognized that Buddhism had overlooked the common people and in becoming a part of court ceremonial had failed in its true purpose: the salvation of all mankind. To make the religion available to the masses, they abandoned the scholarly practices of aristocratic Buddhism and taught single-minded devotion in their stead.

Devotion ought to be pure, but the harder we try to make it pure, the more we are faced with the impurities of our ordinary world. The sacred and the profane are locked in a never-ending battle, but is this a contradiction? No, I do not think so. It is a fact and it is this fact that gives birth to and sustains our determination to experience the sacred. Standing in front of Chion-in's great gate, we ought to listen for the voice of the nembutsu, the voice of truth, which will show us the worthlessness of our worldly cravings. From where we stand now—as a devotee, practitioner, or even as a sympathizer—we will no longer be disturbed by the squeaking of the singing floorboards, warning us of the intruders and the intrusions of the world.

SECT   Headquarters of the Jōdo sect.

ESTABLISHMENT   Founded by Hōnen in 1175.

PRINCIPAL IMAGES   Amida.

CULTURAL PROPERTIES   The forty-eight-volume illustrated biography of Hōnen preserved here is a National Treasure. The Main Gate (Sammon), Main Hall (Hondō), and numerous Buddhist images are Important Cultural Properties.

VISITING INFORMATION   Chion-in might be a good place to take in along with a walk through Maruyama Park or a stroll around the Gion. The stone stairway approach to the temple is quite steep, however. The Founder's Memorial Service (Gyoki E) is held every year between April 19 and April 25.

OF SPECIAL INTEREST   The garden in front of the Chief Priest's General Quarters (Daihōjō) is worth visiting. The Main Gate is the largest in all of Japan. There is a fine view of the city from it. Most of Chion-in's temple treasures can be seen in the Museum (Hōmotsukan), which is open daily from 9:00 to 4:30. The principal image, Amida, is enshrined in the Main Hall.

LOCATION AND TRANSPORTATION   3 Hayashishita-cho, Yamato Ōji Higashi Iru, Shimbashi Dōri, Higashiyama-ku, Kyoto. Chion-in is located near the center of town and the Gion district, at the base of Mount Kachō, north of Maruyama Park. It is about a ten-minute walk from Yasaka Shrine, which is located at the corner of Shijō and Higashiyama streets.

知恩院　　京都市東山区新橋通大和大路東入林下町 3

6. Nanzenji

Anybody who hears the word Nanzenji undoubtedly recalls the lines of Ishikawa Goemon in the Kabuki play, *The Fifty-three Paulownia Trees at the Main Gate* (*Sammon Gosan no Kiri*): "How beautiful! How picturesque! The view in spring is priceless. Now, as the sun is setting in the west, how much more beautiful are the cherry blossoms at dusk. Oh! What an extraordinary sight."

This play was written by Namiki Gohei (1747–1808) near the end of the Tokugawa period (1600–1868), but it was set at the start of that long era of peace. That period comes to life for me as I look up at the gate today. It's as if I can see the people of the early Tokugawa period rushing back and forth, already driven by the influences of the incredible changes they and their country were about to go through.

Ishikawa Goemon and Toyotomi Hideyoshi (1536–98) were participants in the Tokugawa drama as well as characters in Namiki's play, but in the real-life drama to establish and stabilize the Tokugawa government, there were other actors as well: the Zen priest Sūden (1569–1633), advisor to the early Tokugawa shoguns; Tokugawa Ieyasu (1542–1616), the founder of the Tokugawa government; Tōdō Takatora (1556–1630), half-brother of Hideyoshi and later ally of Ieyasu; Honda Masazumi (1565–1637), a military and civil leader of the Tokugawa regime; and Ieyasu's faithful administrator Itakura Katsushige (1545–1624). Sūden was without a doubt the main character. In 1600, the first year of the Tokugawa rule, he was just thirty-seven years old and had been appointed Tokugawa Ieyasu's religious advisor. His position was at the crux of the complex struggle taking place at that time between the religious and political realms. By bringing the sacred and profane together, he became the great behind-the-scenes director who determined the course of history.

While most of the country stood by passively during these unsteady years of transition, Sūden shrewdly brought the country under his control by solidifying his authority over the Buddhist community, banishing Christian priests, exercising his political skill to plot the winter attack against Osaka Castle in 1614 (bringing about the downfall of Ieyasu's political rival, Toyotomi Hideyoshi, the following summer), reducing the political power of the court nobles, and consolidating Ieyasu's authority over Kyoto in general.

But the years of Sūden's influence are merely a moment in Nanzenji's long history, which began with its founding in 1264 by Emperor Kameyama (r. 1259–74). We ought to backtrack and inquire about this period as well.

At the end of the Kamakura period (1185–1333), two separate imperial lines—the Jimyō-in and the Daikakuji lines—were about to begin the infamous feuding that would eventually lead to the establishment of two imperial courts and a period in history known as the period of the Northern and Southern Courts (Nambokuchō; 1336–92). Nanzenji was created during this period, when Emperor Kameyama converted the Zenrinji Detached Palace into a Zen temple. Kameyama entered the priesthood there in 1289 as the retired emperor. Two years later, Mukan Fumon (d. 1291), third-generation abbot from Tōfukuji, was designated the official founder and Nanzenji was opened to those outside the imperial family.

Ever since Kameyama's time, Nanzenji has attracted priests

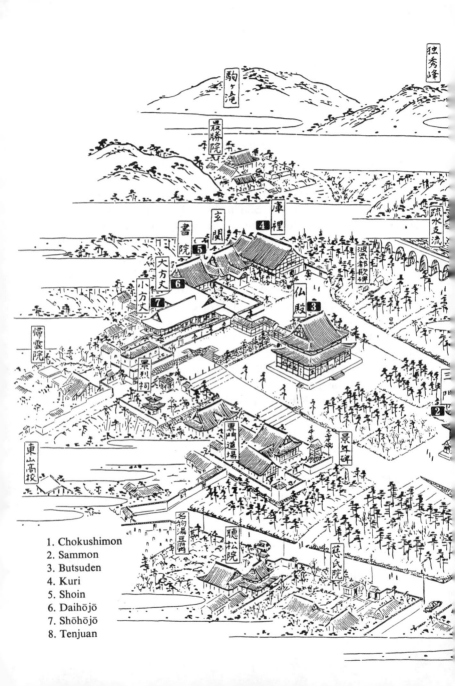

独秀峰

駒ヶ滝

最勝院

疏水支流

玄関

書院 **5**

庫裡 **4**

波浪都歌楽

大方丈 **6**

仏殿 **3**

小方丈 **7**

帰雲院

景列祠

三門 **2**

東門道場

景年碑

東山高校

名物湯豆腐

聴松院

慈氏院

1. Chokushimon
2. Sammon
3. Butsuden
4. Kuri
5. Shoin
6. Daihōjō
7. Shōhōjō
8. Tenjuan

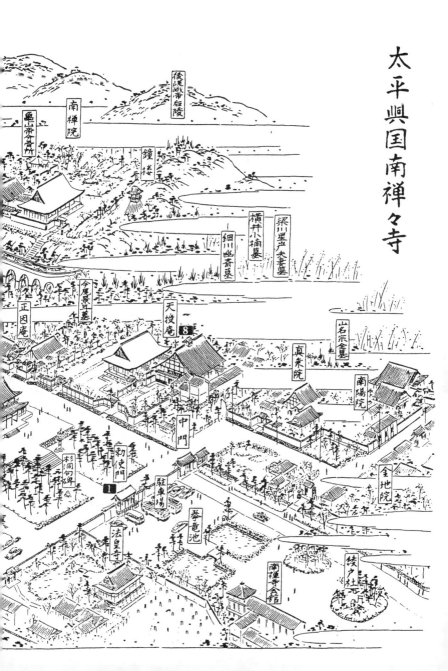

太平興国南禅々寺

後嵯峨帝后陵
亀山帝分骨所
南禅院
鐘楼
深川星戸夫妻墓
横井小楠墓
細川幽斎墓
今尾景年墓
正因庵
天授庵
山名宗全墓
真乗院
南陽院
中門
勅使門
金地院
杉同句碑
駐車場
法皇寺
蒼竜池
南禅寺会館
陵戸社

with excellent scholastic training and irreproachable ethical behavior. It has prospered and become the most prominent of Kyoto's five great Zen temples. It was also accorded a special status among the ten great Zen temples of Kyoto and Kamakura. Consequently, successive generations of abbots for Nanzenji were always chosen from these ten temples. Since 1386, when it received its special rank, Nanzenji has always been at the center of Japanese Zen history and has been a place of residence for countless eminent priests, including the Chinese monk Yishan Yining (1244–1317), the founder of Chinese learning in medieval Japanese monasteries; Musō Soseki (1275–1351), who established the Five Temples system of Zen monasteries; Qingzhuo Zhengdeng (1274–1329), a Chinese monk who was invited to take up residence in Kamakura by the Hōjō regents; the great scholar Kokan Shiren (1278–1346); the founder of the Shōkokuji subsect of Rinzai Zen, Shun'oku Myōha (1311–88); Soseki's disciple Gidō Shūshin (1325–88); and Zekkai Chūshin (1336–1405), who studied Zen for several years in China and was later a leading figure in the Five Mountains literary and cultural movement.

History as it passes sees periods of glory and prosperity as well as times of hardship and decline. Nanzenji's buildings and halls have survived numerous calamities and undergone a number of restorations over the centuries since its founding.

It is fine to recall Nanzenji's history here on its grounds, but a true pilgrimage to the old temples must not become mired in these recollections. A true pilgrimage is made for the future.

We ought to listen to the wise and principled words of the priests who have lived here and we ought to observe the daily lives of the monks practicing here. Even now the priests work solemnly with heads bowed low in the garden at the entrance to the Meditation Hall. When their work is finished, some go out into the city in search of a night's lodging as a part of their daily training. The long, arduous Zen path goes on without end.

The Chinese Zen priest Wumen (1183–1260) wrote: "In the spring there are the blossoms, and in the fall there is the bright moon. In the summer the cool breeze, and in the winter there is the snow. If one does not dwell in trivial or vain pursuits, every season is a good one." Sōtetsu Katsuhira (1922–83), previous abbot of Nanzenji, comments on this: "The Zen path is not concerned with distinguishing good from bad, love from hate, beauty from ugliness. Rather, at its heart lies the perpetual equality of all things to which we can open our eyes and hearts. Absorbed in the ordinariness of our lives, we are not enslaved by our emotions. The path is unchanging and unequivocal. If we allow ourselves to live with our hearts open to the world, we can live each day as if it is the finest."

We can't call a pilgrimage which focuses on looking at halls and gardens a living journey. We must visit the holy men who live— and have lived—there as well. We must look to those who have gone before us on the path.

SECT   Headquarters of the Nanzenji branch of the Rinzai sect of Zen.

ESTABLISHMENT   Founded in 1291 by Mukan Fumon.

PRINCIPAL IMAGE   Shakamuni.

CULTURAL PROPERTIES   The Chief Priest's General Quarters (Daihōjō) and the Chief Priest's Living Quarters (Kohōjō) are both National Treasures. The Main Gate (Sammon), the Special Gate (Chokushimon), and the Main Hall (Butsuden) are Important Cultural Properties. There are also numerous National Treasures and Important Cultural Properties on the grounds of the twelve subtemples. Unfortunately, among them only Konchi-in is open to the public.

VISITING INFORMATION   The grounds, main hall, and subtemples are open to the public throughout the year.

OF SPECIAL INTEREST   The Daihōjō Garden as well as the
gardens of several of the subtemples (Nanzen-in, Konchi-in, and
Tenju-an) are extraordinary. There is a fine view of Kyoto from
the top of the Main Gate, and the Main Hall and the Chief Priest's
General Quarters are also of great architectural interest. There
are not many images of note at Nanzenji, but there are numerous
important portraits and calligraphic works on display.

LOCATION AND TRANSPORTATION   Fukuchi-cho, Nanzenji, Sakyō-ku, Kyoto. Take city bus 5 or 27 to Eikandō Mae.
Nanzenji is a tenminute walk from the bus stop. It is also within
walking distance of the Miyako Hotel.

南禅寺　　京都市左京区南禅寺福地町

7. Zenrinji

Kitarō Nishida (1870–1945) was a well-known philosopher who would often take contemplative walks along the canal that winds its way along the base of Higashiyama. Today that trail has been made into a beautiful footpath called the Philosopher's Path (Tetsugaku no Michi). The Lake Biwa Canal beside which Nishida used to take his walks was excavated at the end of the Meiji period (1868–1912). It followed a rather meandering route into the city over the mountains from Lake Biwa and passed through the grounds of Nanzenji in the form of a viaduct, much like those of ancient Rome. It then headed north to Matsugasaki by way of Nyakuōji, Hōnen-in, and Ginkakuji.

Today many tourists walk this same route in the opposite direction, starting at Ginkakuji. Though its name is a bit presumptuous, the stroll itself is quiet and peaceful. My pilgrimage to Zenrinji took me along this path just before the cherry blossoms were to bloom, when their buds were quite full. As the trees begin to flower, many come here to walk under the boughs. As I watched people stroll through this tunnel of flowers, where petals fall like snow, I began to think about the significance of the Philosopher's Path.

Zenrinji is located at the end of the path, where it stops at

禅林寺
（永観堂）

若王子神社

古方丈

庫裡

玄関

③

浴室

魁寮

永観堂会館

中門

②

福徳弁天社

智福院

駐車場

晶子歌碑

画仙堂

図書館

①

総門

南門

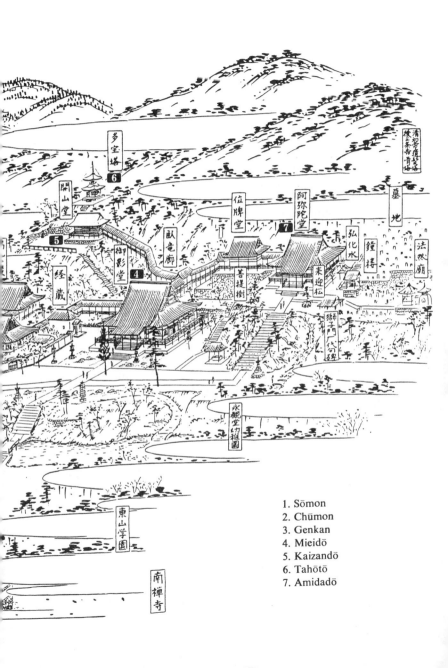

多宝塔 **6**

開山堂

5

臥竜廊

位牌堂

阿弥陀堂 **7**

弘化水

鐘楼

墓地

法然廟

御影堂 **4**

経蔵

菩提樹

来迎松

獅子ノ時雨碑

永観堂幻想園

東山学園

南禅寺

1. Sōmon
2. Chūmon
3. Genkan
4. Mieidō
5. Kaizandō
6. Tahōtō
7. Amidadō

the mountains. It is the head temple of the Jōdo Seizan Zenrinji sect and is more commonly known by the name Eikandō. The popular name comes from one of the figures of popular Pure Land belief, Eikan (1032–1111).

Eikan's father was Minamoto no Kunitsune (?–908), a scholar and teacher who served the imperial family. Eikan took the Buddhist precepts and entered the priesthood at Tōdaiji in Nara. While he was there, he studied the philosophy of the Sanron and Hossō sects of Buddhism and by the age of fourteen he was already working as a kind of examiner (*ryūgi*), testing other young priests in their knowledge of the sutras. As a lecturer on the Lotus Sutra and Vimalakirtinirdesa Sutra, Eikan's interest in study was encouraged and developed, and a devotion to scholarship became the dominating force in his life. We might even say that Eikan exhausted this path, the path of philosophy. Later, he abandoned his scholarly interests as well as the fame his achievements had brought him to devote his life to the Pure Land teaching of the nembutsu. What was it, I wonder, that led Eikan from the world of scholarship to that of faith?

Why did Eikan, who was certainly among the elite of the Buddhist community, decide to devote his life entirely to the "lowly" practice of the nembutsu? Maybe we can find a hint within the postscript to Eikan's work entitled *The Ten Superior Aspects of Rebirth in the Pure Land* (*Ōjō Jūin*), dated 1103: "Shingon *samatha-vipashyana* meditation is abstruse and can lead one astray easily. The teachings of the Sanron and Hossō schools present a logic so profound that it is difficult to attain enlightenment. Still, the court chose these teachings and encourages their practice. Students compete for recognition and only succeed in increasing their desires. The wise man, however, disavows that which is transitory. Wherever he goes, the chanting of the nembutsu does not obstruct his daily life. The Pure Land does not obstruct his daily life. The Pure Land does not distinguish between people of high and low rank. Our sins are many and terrible, but the nembutsu repeated again and again will assure us of rebirth in the Pure Land, just as Amida vowed."

It is easy to imagine the author of those words practicing sixty thousand daily repetitions of the nembutsu in an effort to sever his ties to the world by earnestly depending on Amida's saving grace.

The central object of worship at Eikandō, Amida Looking Back Over His Shoulder, seems to provide the necessary evidence for faith. This strange figure is a physical representation of Amida when he looked back at Eikan in a dream to encourage him in his practice. "Eikan, you're dawdling," he admonished. This flesh-and-blood Amida lived forever within Eikan. There is nothing strange about this vision at all if we regard it as a result of the depth of Eikan's devotion and religious inspiration. Beauty as profound as that of Eikan's Amida can only blossom from devotion which is vividly alive.

There are many temple treasures at Eikandō. Besides the Amida statue, there is also the scroll called *Amida Crossing the Mountain to Meet Us,* a National Treasure. The whole world of Pure Land beliefs seems to open up before you as you stand in front of it.

Eikan died in 1111. Shortly thereafter, in 1133, Hōnen, the founder of the Jōdo Sect, was born. Even though Hōnen is officially responsible for spreading Pure Land teachings in Japan, we ought to consider Eikan the forefather of this sect.

Everyone knows we must walk the path of life alone. Somehow, though, a pilgrimage to Eikandō eliminates the sadness of that solitude. Amida, who even today is looking over his shoulder at us, is stretching out his hand in sympathetic compassion to comfort us in our solitude. We can hear his voice calling out to us: "Come! I will accompany you on your way to the Western Paradise." Where there is faith, there is no sadness about our aloneness. In fact, there is an incredible joy in knowing that Amida is looking back over his shoulder, guiding us along the path. At Eikandō, I seem to hear that voice, the voice of Amida leading me to salvation.

SECT   Headquarters of the Seizan Zenrinji branch of the Jōdo sect.

ESTABLISHMENT   Founded by Shinshō in 863.

PRINCIPAL IMAGE   Amida Looking Back Over His Shoulder.

CULTURAL PROPERTIES   The painting in colors on silk of Amida crossing the mountains to save believers and lead them into the Pure Land is a National Treasure. Important Cultural Properties include a painting of Amida and twenty-five bodhisattvas coming to save mankind. Many other art objects at the temple have been designated Important Cultural Properties.

VISITING INFORMATION   The grounds and most of the buildings can be visited throughout the year, but the maples in autumn are particularly beautiful.

OF SPECIAL INTEREST   Though Eikandō can claim no major gardens, the walk up the side of the mountain to the Founder's Hall (Kaisandō) is quite nice. The Main Hall (Hondō) and the Amida Hall (Amidadō) are of architectural interest. In addition to the image of Amida and the other works of art mentioned above, there is a fine portrait of the Chinese Pure Land monk Shandao (Japanese, Zendō; 613–81) and other famous paintings are on view at the temple.

LOCATION AND TRANSPORTATION   Eikandō-chō, Sakyō-ku, Kyoto. Take city bus 5 or 27 and get off at Eikandō Mae. The temple is about a ten-minutes walk north of Nanzenji.

禅林寺　　京都市左京区永観堂町

NORTHERN KYOTO

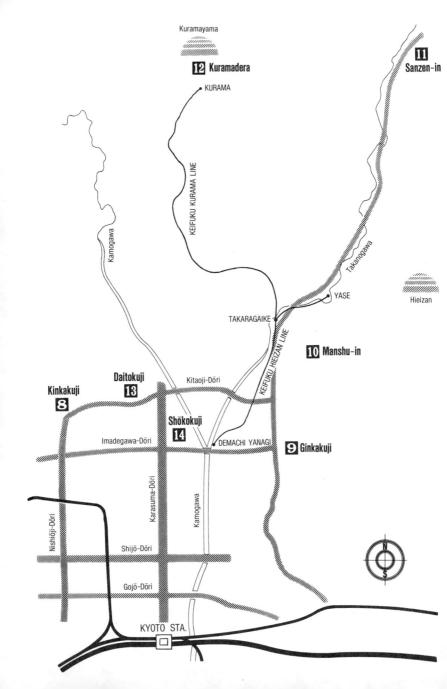

8 and 9. Kinkakuji and Ginkakuji

These two temples are so much a part of the standard tourist route through Kyoto that some tend to diminish them. But there is no room for intellectual or any other kind of snobbery here, and jaded thoughts are soon banished by the mere sight of these marvelous creations. Their architecture and gardens display a dignified beauty and purity unmatched in Japan's history. They are the jewels of Kyoto's historical legacy.

How did these temples come to be? Ashikaga Yoshimitsu (1358–1408) built Kinkakuji in the western part of Kyoto and Ashikaga Yoshimasa (1435–90) built Ginkakuji in the eastern part. They were set on opposite sides of the city with contrasting names—the Golden Pavilion and the Silver Pavilion. This is what attracts so many people to them: a quest for silver and gold. Perhaps this dream is a worldly one, but when we consider that we all work hard every day for "silver and gold," it is a dream we can all understand.

Yoshimitsu, who had Shōkokuji, the well-known Zen temple near the Imperial Palace, built in 1374, relinquished his position as political and military leader of Japan at the early age of thirty-seven and yielded to Yoshimochi (1386–1428), who was at that time barely nine years old. Shortly afterwards, he entered the priesthood under the guidance of Kūkoku Myōō (1327–1407), his

左大文字山

天神ヶ丘

夕佳亭　拱北橋

安民沢　白蛇塚

虎渓橋　滝門滝　金閣　　書院

鎮守社　銀河泉　巌下水　　　　　　　　陸舟松

漱清　　　　　　　　　　　　　　鏡湖池

出島　　　　　鶴島　葦原島　細川石

亀山石　赤松石　亀島

5

4

6

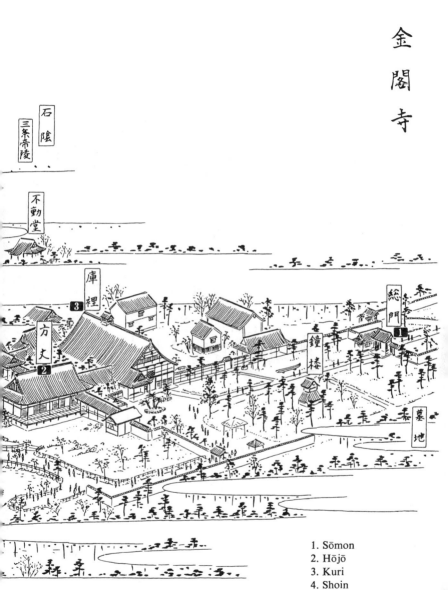

金閣寺

1. Sōmon
2. Hōjō
3. Kuri
4. Shoin
5. Kinkaku
6. Sōsei

銀閣寺

宝蔵

本堂
3

弄清亭

東求堂
4

漱蘚亭址
お茶の井

銀沙灘
5

白鶴島

座禅石

仙柚橋

大内石

仙桂橋

臥雲橋

洗月泉

月待山
11

1. Sōmon
2. Kuri
3. Hondō
4. Tōgudō
5. Silver Sand Sea
6. Chūmon
7. Ginkaku
8. Kōgetsudai
9. Sennin Islet
10. Kinkyō Pond
11. Mount Tsukimachi

personal preceptor. It was during this period that he had Kinka-kuji built.

Since Yoshimitsu had entered the priesthood and retired from the world, he had no need for a house, much less a Golden Pavilion. On the one hand, his religious commitment seemed sincere. He continued on the Zen path by visiting Musō Soseki (1275–1351), Shun'oku Myōha (1311–88), and Gidō Shūshin (1325–88), all masters in the world of Zen practice. Retirement to a grass hut would have been the logical conclusion to these years of study, but instead, after receiving the large Kitayama mansion from the Saionji family, he began the project of building Kinkakuji.

Kinkakuji was a symbol of Yoshimitsu's wealth and power. The eighty-third abbot of Shōkokuji, Keijō Shūrin (1440–1518), wrote that it was "built when Yoshimitsu was forty years old. In order to conduct the project, he gave up all of his official duties. Its beauty is incomparable. A large iron phoenix with wings spread was placed atop a great golden roof and building. A long rainbow stretched across it into the sky towards the north."

The contradictions of Zen and politics, the priesthood and wealth—in short, the struggle between the sacred and the pro-fane—unfolded upon Kinkakuji's stage. Gold symbolized wealth and power; Yoshimitsu used Zen and the priesthood as a way to display his own.

And Ginkakuji? On the other side of town is the Silver Pavilion, near the Higashiyama mountains opposite Kinkakuji, which is nestled between the Nishiyama and Kitayama mountains. Ashi-kaga Yoshimasa founded Ginkakuji about fifty years after Yoshi-mitsu died.

> From the scorched fields
> A night skylark flies off into the sky
> Over the razed capital—
> Is there anyone left to see
> My tears as they fall to the ground?

What was Yoshimasa thinking about as he went about building a beautiful mountain retreat in the midst of the Ōnin War (1467–77), which almost entirely destroyed Kyoto? Kinkakuji may have been built to display Yoshimitsu's wealth and power, but this is not what motivated Yoshimasa to build Ginkakuji. Yoshimasa was deeply disappointed in politics after the outbreak of the war; he had been shunned by his family; and he had become powerless. He was a lonely man who took refuge in dreams of solitude.

> With an untroubled heart
> I gaze at the cloudless moon
> Vexed when I recall
> This world of misery
> Here in my Silver Palace.

> Here at my hermitage
> At the base of Mount Tsukimachi
> I recall the glories of the past
> As the moon slowly descends
> Into the western sky.

Yoshimasa's sentiments were completely different from Yoshimitsu's. Though they shared some interests, such as a fascination with Chinese art, their personalities and the times they lived in were quite different. Yoshimasa was clearly more inclined towards the desolate world of the hermit's hut. It was Yoshimasa's world—what is called Higashiyama culture—that gave birth to traditional Japanese culture as we think of it now: the tea ceremony, flower arrangement, and ink painting. After Yoshimasa's death, his Silver Pavilion was turned into a temple and was called Higashiyama Jishōji.

Everybody pursues their dreams of "silver and gold," but the eras in which they are sought and the people who search for them often show extraordinary contrasts. Pondering all of this on my pilgrimages to the Golden and Silver pavilions, I was fearful and sad, while at the same time struck by thoughts of the transience of life and the mutability of history.

People will always be attracted to both the sacred and the profane. But each pilgrim must decide how he or she will get "the silver or the gold."

SECT   Both temples belong to the Shōkokuji branch of the Rinzai Zen sect.

ESTABLISHMENT   Both temples were founded by Musō Kokushi, Kinkakuji in 1408 and Ginkakuji in 1482.

PRINCIPAL IMAGE   Amida is the main image at Kinkakuji and Kannon is the main image at Ginkakuji.

CULTURAL PROPERTIES   Kinkakuji is an Important Cultural Property and Ginkakuji is a National Treasure.

VISITING INFORMATION   The grounds of both temples are open throughout the year. Kinkakuji and its garden are especially beautiful after a winter snowfall.

OF SPECIAL INTEREST   Kinkakuji and Ginkakuji can both be best enjoyed while strolling around their *chisen kaiyū*-style gardens. The Golden and Silver Pavilions are two of the most famous temple structures in Japan. There are no images of special interest at the temples.

LOCATION AND TRANSPORTATION   Kinkakuji is located in the northwest part of the city while Ginkakuji is located in the northeast part of the city. The address of Kinkakuji is Kinkakuji-chō, Kita-ku, Kyoto. City buses 12, 59, and 92 travel there. Get off at the Kinkakuji Mae bus stop. Ginkakuji is at Ginkakuji-chō,

Sakyō-ku, Kyoto. Get off at the Ginkakuji Michi bus stop on city bus lines 5, 17, 32, 203, or 204 and walk to the east towards the mountains for about ten minutes.

金閣寺　京都市北区金閣寺町
銀閣寺　京都区左京区銀閣寺町

10. Manshu-in

The ridge of the mountains which defines the eastern edge of Kyoto gently rises and then falls to the north. Mount Hiei towers above this ridge in the northeastern part of the city, the area traditionally referred to as the Devil's Gate (Kimon), where bad fortune is believed to emanate from. The scenery here is extraordinary.

Manshu-in, the next temple on our pilgrimage, is located at the base of these mountains near Mount Hiei. Shirakawa Street, which runs parallel to the mountains, has become a major thoroughfare recently, but slightly to the east is a mountain road where one can still sense the history of this area. The road snakes its way through new housing complexes and occasional farmhouses that still dot the landscape here and there.

As I was walking along this old road from North Shirakawa Street to Chayama and Ichijōji Sagarimatsu and then on to Kirara Slope, I almost felt as if I could hear the voice of history about to speak to me.

Manshu-in is situated among the red pines peculiar to this area, which are often seen in Japanese paintings. To the north is Shugaku-in Detached Palace and Sekizen Shrine. Even further north are the villages of Yase and Ōhara.

Manshu-in and its environs have an extraordinarily graceful and elegant air. The temple dates back to the Heian period (794–

1185). It was established by Saichō (766–822), the great Tendai religious leader. According to temple legend, Zesan, a Buddhist priest who was serving as superintendent at Kitano Shrine from 947 to 957, had Manshu-in built nearby. Sometime later it was moved to the vicinity of the Imperial Palace. In 1656 Manshu-in was moved to its present location in the eastern part of the city by Ryōshō (1622–93), a priest who was the son of a nephew of Emperor Gomizunoo (r. 1611–29).

At the beginning of the Tokugawa period, the third shogun, Tokugawa Iemitsu (1604–51), kept a close hold on the imperial household as well as on the nobility and their descendants through various ordinances aimed at restricting their political activity. The need for caution had been reinforced by the "Purple Robe" Incident of 1627, in which Gomizunoo bestowed the highest clerical rank of the purple robe upon several priests against the orders of the shogunate. When the shogunate revoked the awards, Emperor Gomizunoo abdicated.

As a result of the restrictions placed on the imperial family and the nobility, an imperial court culture, often called Kan'ei culture (named for the Kan'ei period, 1624–30, when it flourished) seemed to erupt in a single burst of energy. The court was obviously reacting to the restraints imposed on it as well as to the various methods used to enforce these restraints.

The imperial renaissance of the early Tokugawa period expanded and deepened Japanese culture in general: Chinese poetry, which had its origins in Confucian education, flourished; the imperial poetry anthologies were revived; refined entertainments such as linked-verse parties became popular; and the worlds of tea ceremony and flower arrangement were also systematized. Court culture expanded to influence the worlds of architecture and gardens, too, as we can see in Shugaku-in Detached Palace, a project of Retired Emperor Gomizunoo.

A thorough study of Tendai doctrines as well as education in Confucianism, Chinese poetry, poetics, calligraphy, flower ar-

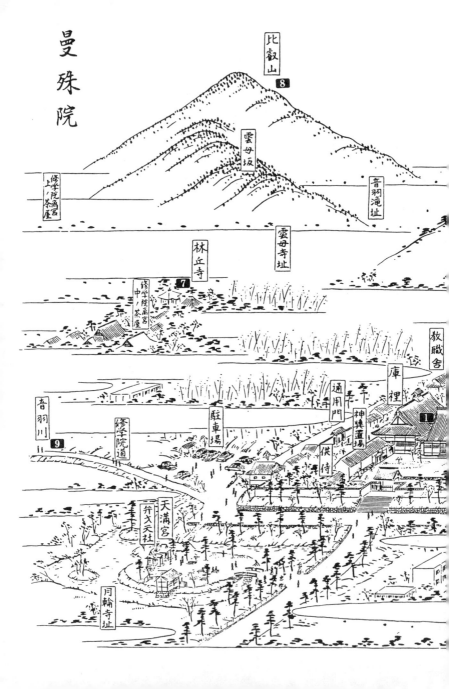

曼殊院

比叡山 **8**

雲母坂

音羽滝址

修学院離宮上ノ茶屋

雲母寺址

林丘寺 **7**

修学院離宮中ノ茶屋

教職舎

庫裡 **1**

通用門

神輿置場

音羽川 **9**

修学院道

駐車場

供侍

天満宮

弁天天社

同輪寺址

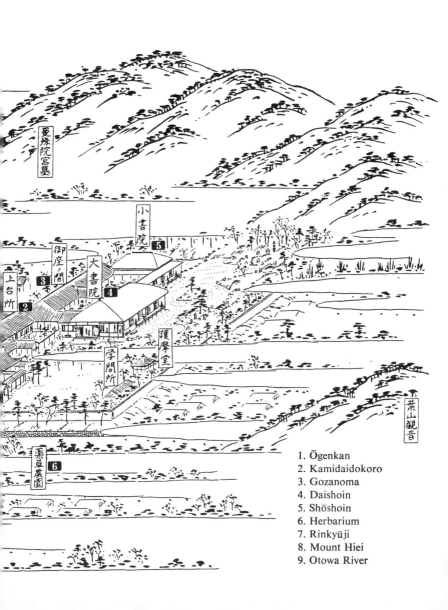

1. Ōgenkan
2. Kamidaidokoro
3. Gozanoma
4. Daishoin
5. Shōshoin
6. Herbarium
7. Rinkyūji
8. Mount Hiei
9. Otowa River

rangement, tea ceremony, incense appreciation, and painting all came together at this time to form the basis of this court culture. The blossoms of artistic taste and refinement were undeniably in full flower.

Our current ideas about traditional culture are all based on the achievements of Kan'ei culture. Even today at Manshu-in, we can see traces of refined courtly culture wherever we look, due to the steady improvements and restoration of its buildings by the present imperial chief priest, Endō Yamaguchi.

Manshu-in is beautiful all year long. We ought to feel thankful that a temple as old as this, beating with the pulse of Japanese aesthetic culture, still remains for us to appreciate.

SECT   Tendai.

ESTABLISHMENT   Founded by Zesan in 1656.

PRINCIPAL IMAGE   Amida.

CULTURAL PROPERTIES   A color rendition on silk of Fudō Myōō and a copy of the *Kokinshū* imperial poetry anthology at Manshu-in are National Treasures. The Main Hall (Hondō) and Eight-window Teahouse (Hassō Chashitsu) are Important Cultural Properties. There are many documents and written materials relating to literature and flower arrangement that have also been designated Important Cultural Properties.

VISITING INFORMATION   The grounds, Main Hall, and garden are open throughout the year.

OF SPECIAL INTEREST   The dry landscape garden in front of the Main Hall is lovely. From the beginning of May, the azaleas are in bloom and are quite beautiful. The Main Hall and the Eight-window Teahouse are architecturally interesting. There are few images of note here, but Manshu-in does have a long history of association with the world of literature. For that reason, there are many documents and manuscripts stored at the temple.

LOCATION AND TRANSPORTATION   Takenouchi-chō, Ichi-jōji, Sakyō-ku, Kyoto. Manshu-in is located south of Shugaku-in Detached Imperial Palace. Take city bus 5, 31, or 65, get off at Ichijōji Shimizu-chō Bus Stop, and then walk east towards the mountains for about two minutes.

曼殊院　京都市左京区一乗寺竹ノ内町

11. Sanzen-in

The Ōhara Highway winds to the north along the base of Mount Hiei, the large mountain which houses Enryakuji in the northeast part of Kyoto. Here, and especially in Yase and Ōhara, the winters are much colder than in the city center.

There is an anonymous poem in *Notes From Then and Now* (*Kokon Chomon Shu*; 1254) which says that Ōhara was once remote and therefore suitable as a final retreat from the world. Similar sentiments were expressed in *The Tale of the Heike* (*Heike Monogatari*), in the chapter in which Retired Emperor Goshirakawa (r. 1155–58) visits his daughter-in-law who is in retirement at Jakkō-in in "faraway Ōhara."

One day when a fine, powdery snow was swirling about Sanzen-in, the Buddhist nun Jakuchō Setouchi said, "If I had to choose just one season over all the others to spend at Sanzen-in, without hesitation I would choose the harsh, snowy days of winter. And, if I were allowed, I would like to prostrate myself and worship alone in front of Sanzen-in's Amida trinity and then read the Amida Sutra on a desolate and lonely snowy evening with only a flickering candle to keep me company."

One reason Sanzen-in is so well known among Kyoto's old temples is because of its rich historical connections to Ōhara. But there is another reason: the Amida trinity (Amida Buddha and the two bodhisattvas who accompany him, Kannon, and Seishi) which is enshrined in the Paradise Hall (Ōjō Gokuraku-in). Mankind will always be fascinated by the idea of Amida coming from paradise to welcome the spirit of a believer to the Pure Land. The paradise of the Pure Land is immeasurably far, a journey without end. When we come face to face with this immensely compassionate Amida, however, the possibility of making that journey—just as Amida vowed we could—seems a reality. Kannon and Seishi, the other two aspects of Amida which make up the trinity, corroborate this.

When the upturned eyes of the pilgrim, prostrate on the floor of this small, quiet hall where the trinity is enshrined, meet the downcast eyes of the three divinities who are almost near enough to reach out and touch, they seem to be whispering something. Indeed, one's body begins to tremble with the possibility that Amida has indeed arrived to take this devout pilgrim to the Pure Land.

One of the reasons Sanzen-in has managed to survive until now is because it enshrines an Amida Buddha of such power. But Sanzen-in has other attractions as well: the cherries in spring, the young buds in early summer, the maple leaves as they lie upon the moss-covered ground. The eternal world of Amida's paradise lies beyond this, however. The blessed joy we find there, and that we find here at Sanzen-in as well, are Amida's joy. Sanzen-in is the last stop before our journey to the Pure Land.

Many great Buddhist practitioners have lived at Sanzen-in in hopes of escaping the entanglements of the world. Genshin (942–1017), Ryōgen (912–85), and Ryōnin (1071–1132) all lived here for a time. The great teacher Hōnen (1133–12121) composed his *Ōhara Treatise* (*Ōhara Mondō*), a discussion of Pure Land doctrines in question-and-answer form, here at Shorin-in in 1186. Ōhara has played a significant role in the history of Japanese Pure Land Buddhism by providing sacred ground for the practice of the nembutsu, the invocation of Amida's name.

三千院

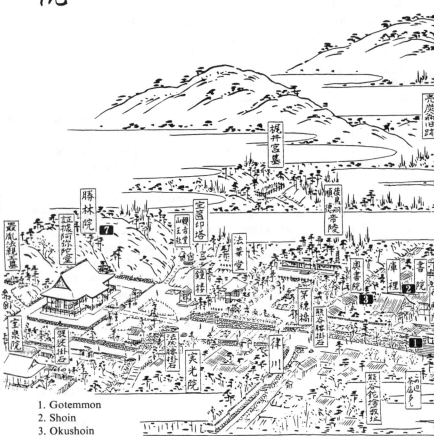

1. Gotemmon
2. Shoin
3. Okushoin
4. Kyakuden
5. Sanzen-in
6. Ōjōgokuraku-in
7. Shōrin-in
8. Gyozan Bridge

The famous monk-poet Saigyō (1118–90) also seems to have spent time in this area, as the following poems testify:

> How painful these lessons!
> My vow to abandon
> All petty concerns
> Has become a yearning for spring
> Just because of a frozen trough.

> Alone in my hut,
> Resigned to a lonesome life
> Without visitors—
> How hard it would be to live here,
> If loneliness were not my friend.

> If only there were
> One more who could bear this life
> Of loneliness with me!
> He could spend the winter nearby
> In a hut on this mountaintop.

Ōhara was also visited by a wide variety of literary and religious figures including Izumi Shikibu (late tenth–mid-eleventh century), the poetess and diarist; Jien (1225–96); the essayist Kamo no Chōmei (1155–1216); Minamoto no Toshiyori (1055–1129), a great poet; and Ōtagaki Rengetsu (1791–1875), the poet, calligrapher, potter, and painter. What did they dream about when they were here? Numerous verses and poems trace the outlines of those dreams.

Sister Setouchi continues, "The nembutsu devotee will not be able to hold back his tears as he prostrates himself here in front of Amida and realizes that because of Amida's compassionate vow to save all sentient beings the journey to the far shores of paradise can actually be realized with the help of this gentle and beautiful Buddha." These days we have turned our backs on the search for that "other world" of paradise. We affirm everyday reality and then, because of our attachments to it, we find ourselves beset by an endless circle of troubles and worries. This cannot possibly be good for us.

Sanzen-in is also noted for the Tendai-sect hymns (*shōmyō*) which were brought back from China by the monk Ennin (794–864). Since the mountain in China where these hymns originated was called Mount Yu (in Japanese, Gyozan), Ōhara is also sometimes called Gyozan and the hymns are known as Gyozan *shōmyō*. These hymns form the foundation of Buddhist music and are used in all kinds of ceremonies.

The reality which surrounds us today negates those hymns written in praise of the Buddha and chanted in the Japanized Sanskrit called *bombai*. They have been swallowed up in a maelstrom of chaos and noise. What recourse is left to us now?

Every time I head towards Sanzen-in, I cannot help but wonder about this. The winter is a cold one here in the northern part of Kyoto.

SECT Tendai.

ESTABLISHMENT Founded by Saichō in 1155.

PRINCIPAL IMAGE Amida.

CULTURAL PROPERTIES The Main Hall (Ōjō Gokuraku-in) as well as its principal image of Amida are Important Cultural Properties.

VISITING INFORMATION The area around the temple and the temple grounds are quite picturesque in each season of the year. The temple can be visited all year round, and while you are there it's a fine idea to visit Jakkō-in, which is nearby.

OF SPECIAL INTEREST   The area around Sanzen-in as well as its gardens are extremely beautiful. The best times to visit are early spring and the fall when the leaves turn. Paradise Hall is of great architectural interest and the images of the Amida trinity are moving works of sculpture.

LOCATION AND TRANSPORTATION   Raigō-in-chō, Ōhara, Sakyō-ku, Kyoto. Take the Kita 6 city bus to Ōhara and walk to the east about ten minutes.

三千院　　京都市左京区大原来迎院町

12. Kuramadera

"In this scientific age, fears and the object of those fears have been, for the most part, dispelled. My feelings here are all the more surprising since we do not often see popular temples and shrines in this sort of setting. I wonder why I felt relieved. Kurama was once a place which harbored 'dark demons' in 'dark space,' but now it has become a sacred mountain with an enshrined Buddha. Somehow it is a relief to find both the demonic and the sacred worlds side by side here on this mountain today."

Since these dark, demonic worlds of which novelist Shūsaku Endō writes above are beyond human speculation, the divine begins to evolve and that becomes our spiritual world. Perhaps, though, the demonic and the sacred are not two worlds. Perhaps they are one.

In the earliest forms of mountain worship found in Japan, people tried to alleviate their fears of what they could not understand by becoming immersed in and fused with the sacred. The deeper one goes into the mountains to the north of Kyoto along the winding road to Kurama the stealthier its demons are. There is an air of mystery here, imminent yet unseen.

The Kurama Highway heads north from Kuramaguchi, one of the seven approaches into Kyoto through the mountains. It runs

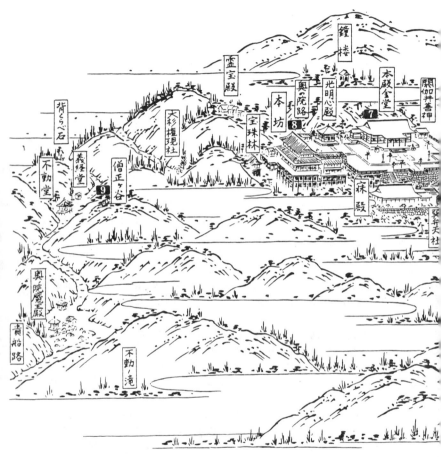

鐘楼

霊宝殿

本殿金堂

閼伽井善神

奥の院路

光明心殿

本坊

7

大杉権現社

背くらべ石

室珠林

8

不動堂

義経堂

僧正ヶ谷

床殿

9

弁天社

奥の院魔王殿

不動ノ滝

貴船路

1. Keifuku Dentetsu Kurama Station
2. Hanase Michi
3. Niōmon
4. Sammon Cablecar Station
5. Tsuzuraori Sandō
6. Tempōrindō
7. Honden Kondō
8. Hombō
9. Sōjō Valley
10. Mount Kurama

鞍馬寺

鞍馬山
10

転法輪堂
6

弥勒堂

多宝塔

ケーブル
多宝塔駅

僧正ヶ谷不動堂
東光坊址
由岐神社
川上地蔵
息つぎの水
魔王ノ滝
鬼法眼社
吉鞍稲荷
ケーブル山門駅
4

九十九折参道
5

保育園

仁王門
3

花背道
2

京福鞍馬線駅
1

parallel to the Kamo River and seems to part the mountains on either side, turning them into a kind of Japanese-style screen.

It is quite easy to get to Kurama these days, but at one time it must have much less convenient, at the very least. There is a passage in the *Sarashina Diary* (*Sarashina Nikki*), a work from the early eleventh century, which characterizes it well: "Kurama is so steep that even when you decide to make a pilgrimage there, you end up not going out of fear."

Kurama is exactly twelve kilometers north of the Kyoto Imperial Palace. It rises some 570 meters above sea level, and situated on the top of this mysterious mountain is Kuramadera.

Kuramadera is the head temple of a subsect of the Tendai sect called the Kurama Kōkyō subsect. According to its teachings, the circuitous climb up Kurama is like striving for enlightenment, while the path down is like a bodhisattva descending again to the world to help all sentient beings. This is because heaven, earth, and man are manifestations of the sutras. In fact, they are the entire Buddhist canon. As we make our way deep into these tranquil mountains, we are also on the path to the inner sanctuary (*oku no in*) where Iwakura, the demon king of the six higher realms of desire, descended to earth and is enshrined. Associated with him, as we can read in the *Origins of Kuramadera* (*Kuramadera Engi*), are innumerable good omens. These descriptions later became literature which further contributed to the mountain's sacredness.

Both the story of Kuramadera's founder, Kantei (fl. eighth century), and the man in charge of its construction, Fujiwara Isendo (759–827), are tales filled with auspicious omens and divine dreams. Old priests, white horses, auspicious clouds, women, children, the sun, Fudō Myōō, Bishamonten, giant serpents: all of these appeared together to form a kind of spirit worship, an animistic faith. Everything beyond the human realm, everything divine, dwells here.

There have been many great priests and historical figures such as Saichō (766–822), Buen (841–920), Kūya (903–72), Ryōnin

(1072–1132), and Ushiwakamaru (the childhood name of Mina-moto no Yoshitsune; 1158–85), who are strongly connected to this place. Kuramadera appears in literature and the Noh theater, where the mystery and the divinity of the place are unfolded. The religious mysteries of this mountain were probably even more colorfully elaborated by the common people as well.

The air around Kurama seems to inspire people. The location of Kurama directly north of the center of Kyoto gives it a position of authority from where Maōson, a Buddhist guardian deity, can watch over the city residents. In time, Kurama came to sym-bolize the gods and buddhas who would protect the people of the capital from evil spirits and harm.

> Oh, moon at dawn!
> Lingering in the sky
> Over this dark mountain,
> Illumine this mysterious world
> And protect us from evil.

People cannot survive without the supernormal. When they look for it in this world, it manifests itself—in the case of Kurama, as faith in the mountain itself. It is not necessary for us to discuss the doctrines and classical texts connected with Kuramadera. Just climb the mountain and you will become aware of some other presence. It is during Kuramadera's festivals—the pilgrimage to Bishamonten on the first Day of the Tiger in the New Year (Hatsu-tora Matsuri), the Bamboo-cutting Festival in June (Take Kiri Eshiki), the Flower-offering Ceremony in April (Hana Kuyō), and the Full Moon Festival in May (Mangetsu Matsuri)—that people hope to come into contact with and maybe even acquire some of these supernormal powers. If we call these powers de-monic, it sounds vulgar. It is probably more appropriate to call them the spiritual powers of Maōson.

We can better understand the respect Kurama receives as a

sacred place if we take a look at the various documents that have survived and are now stored in the temple treasurehouse. These documents also tell us that Kurama was revered as a mountain which brought beneficial rainfall to the area each year and as a temple which offered devotional prayers for good fortune on behalf of the people. Correspondence of military leaders from the twelfth through seventeenth centuries gives us vivid descriptions of life on Mount Kurama and at Kuramadera.

SECT   Headquarters of the Kurama Kōkyō subsect of the Tendai sect.

ESTABLISHMENT   Founded by Kantei in 770.

PRINCIPAL IMAGE   Bishamonten.

CULTURAL PROPERTIES   The Bishamonten, Kichijōten, and Zenzai Dōji images are National Treasures. There are also a great many temple treasures here which have been designated Important Cultural Properties.

VISITING INFORMATION   There are many celebrations and festivities at Kuramadera in which large numbers of believers gather and participate. The First Tiger Day Ceremony mentioned above is held on that day in January (it varies from year to year, depending on the old lunar calendar). This festival is held primarily for the prevention of misfortune in the New Year. The Full Moon Festival is to commemorate the Buddha's birth and is held on the evening of the full moon in May. The Bamboo-cutting Festival is held at 2 P.M. on June 20. Two groups of priests compete in cutting bamboo that represents serpents supposedly slayed by Buen more than one thousand years ago. The best-known festival at Kuramadera is the Fire Festival (Hi Matsuri) held on October 22. This festival commemorates the founding of the Kurama Kōkyō sub-sect.

OF SPECIAL INTEREST   The area surrounding Kuramadera and the temple grounds are a sacred area for mountain worship. Most of the buildings within the temple compound are of great interest, and the Bishamonten image is quite striking.

LOCATION AND TRANSPORTATION   Kurama Hommachi, Sakyō-ku, Kyoto. Take the Keifuku Railway from Demachiyanagi to Kurama, the last stop.

鞍馬寺　　京都市左京区鞍馬本町

13. Daitokuji

Daitokuji is in the Murasakino district in the northern part of Kyoto. Situated in the midst of one of Kyoto's old, densely packed neighborhoods, its physical dimensions are grand and its buildings are some of the finest in Japan.

Author and novelist Sawako Ariyoshi (1931–85) composed an essay on the temple, *Thoughts on Daitokuji,* from which I quote: "Passing through the gateway to the temple grounds, there is a large Central Gate to the right. It had recently been repaired; painted a brilliant vermilion, it seemed to soar into the sky. When I looked up at the gate, I felt as if I was looking at a great collection of mysteries. The bright vermilion must be more weathered now, I think, than when it was first painted. But still, what are we to think about a temple gate that is so resplendent that it is almost shockingly excessive. Daitokuji seems to be different from the unsullied Zen forms found here and there on its grounds, which have retained their spartan purity."

What is this "great collection of mysteries" that Ariyoshi writes of? Seven hundred years have already passed since Shūhō Myō-chō (1282–1337; later known as National Teacher Daitō, or Daitō Kokushi) built his hermitage here in Murasakino in 1315. Since that time, when the flame of the Buddhist teachings was first lit, there have been rivalries and conflicts between Daitokuji and other well-known Zen temples, as well as between Daitokuji and the political authorities. It was because of its connections to these centers of political authority that Daitokuji became the large and powerful temple center that it did. This was the cause of the temple's alternating periods of fortune and decline.

Sen no Rikyū (1522–91), the celebrated first grand master of tea, was the person responsible for turning the simple, one-story front gate into the three-storied Tower of Golden Down (Kimmōkaku), as the gate is also known. He then enshrined an image of himself there. Knowing this, one begins to wonder where the notions of *wabi* and *sabi,* so essential to the tradition of the tea ceremony, are to be found in this resplendent gate. That is one of the great mysteries of Daitokuji.

Pilgrims to Daitokuji often first recall its founder, Shūhō, and then also one of Daitokuji's most famous as well as most unconventional priests, Ikkyū Sōjun (1394–1481). A trip here also reminds us of many other great Zen thinkers, such as Takuan Sōhō (1573–1645).

From the thirteenth through the nineteenth centuries, a constant glimmering flame of the Zen spirit shone amidst the turbulent struggles for authority and wealth that took place at Daitokuji. This is keenly felt when we read the temple histories. Perhaps we ought to think of these struggles as the inevitable complications that arise out of the meeting of the sacred and the profane.

The histories of Daitokuji do not go into detail concerning those struggles, but they are eager to display the temple's magnificent traditions in the records of daily tea gatherings (*chaen*) that were, and still are, held there. Daitokuji can perhaps be regarded as the head temple for the practice of the tea ceremony. Serious students of Zen may bypass Daitokuji, but those looking to participate in *chaen* do not. Historically, there has always been a deep relationship between Zen masters and the tea ceremony. For example, three of the most famous tea masters Jukō (1422–1502), Rikyū, and Sōtan (d. 1658), studied with Ikkyū, Kokei (1532–97),

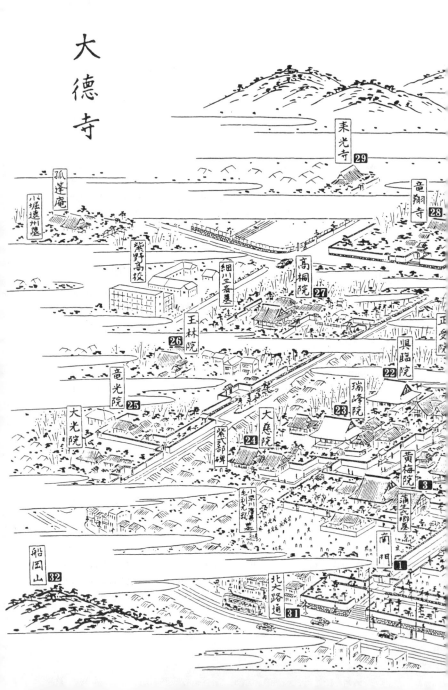

大徳寺

孤篷庵
小堀遠州墓

紫野高校

細川三斎墓

高桐院 27

竜翔寺 28

末光寺 29

正受院

玉林院 26

興臨院 22

竜光院 25

瑞峰院 23

大光院

大慈院 24

紫式部墓

黄梅院 3

小早川隆景
毛利元就墓

蒲生氏郷墓

南門 1

船岡山 32

北大路通

31

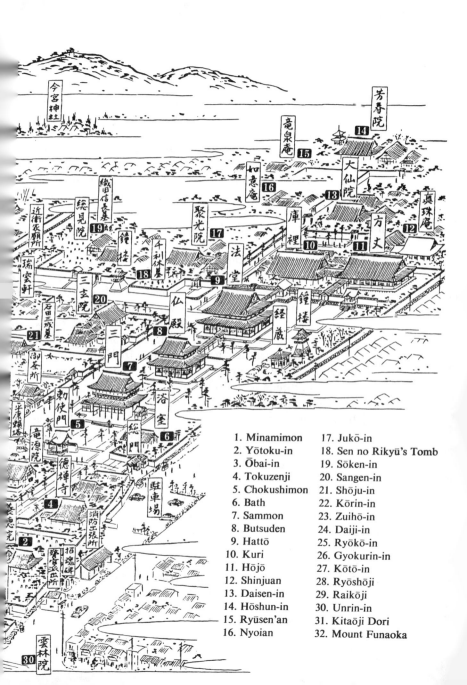

今宮神社

芳春院

竜泉庵

大仙院

織田信長墓

如意庵

近衞裏願所

総見院

鐘楼

聚光院

真珠庵

方丈

瑞雲軒

三玄院

千利休墓

法堂

庫裡

石田三成墓

仏殿

経蔵

鐘楼

御茶所

三門

勅使門

浴室

竜源院

徳禅寺

総門

駐車場

消防出張所

招魂碑

雲林院

1. Minamimon
2. Yōtoku-in
3. Ōbai-in
4. Tokuzenji
5. Chokushimon
6. Bath
7. Sammon
8. Butsuden
9. Hattō
10. Kuri
11. Hōjō
12. Shinjuan
13. Daisen-in
14. Hōshun-in
15. Ryūsen'an
16. Nyoian

17. Jukō-in
18. Sen no Rikyū's Tomb
19. Sōken-in
20. Sangen-in
21. Shōju-in
22. Kōrin-in
23. Zuihō-in
24. Daiji-in
25. Ryōkō-in
26. Gyokurin-in
27. Kōtō-in
28. Ryōshōji
29. Raikōji
30. Unrin-in
31. Kitaōji Dori
32. Mount Funaoka

and Takuan respectively, all of whom were priests from Daitokuji. But, in essence, how does the world of tea at Daitokuji relate to Zen itself? What does it mean to say that Zen and tea are "one taste" (*chazen ichimi*)? Perhaps this is what a pilgrimage should attempt to achieve—the unraveling of mysteries; in the case of Daitokuji, we endeavor to grasp the nature of tea and Zen while strolling through the temple grounds.

There are numerous teahouses at Daitokuji which have been designated National Treasures or Important Cultural Properties: Teigyokuken at Shinju-an, Kan'inseki at Jukō-in, Kō-an at San-gen-in, Sa-an at Gyokurin-in, Mittan at Ryōkō-in, and Bōsen at Kohō-an. These teahouses—more than thirty in all—are why Daitokuji is synonymous with *chanoyu*. The importance of Daitokuji as the head temple for tea ceremony is by now beyond dispute.

Any visit to Daitokuji revives the memory of Ikkyū, the unconventional priest mentioned above, who lived for only ten days at Nyoian, one of Daitokuji's subtemples. The monk Nanrei Kobori, head of Ryōkō-in, wrote the following about Ikkyū: "Ikkyū regarded obedience to organized authority as dishonest and despised those who lacked the moral courage to resist it. If this attitude is a result of his enlightenment, then his fellow Daitokuji monks Daitō, Musō, and Yōsō (?–1428), whom Ikkyū hated, were also men who had attained the same enlightenment. However, Ikkyū could not tolerate people with a spirit too weak to say no. Obedience to authority or ingratiation—even if it was passive—was intolerable to him."

It is unfortunate for the world that Daitokuji is not a center for spiritual leaders, but it is difficult for it to sever its ties with the centers of authority and wealth. These centers of authority have changed throughout history, and it is the world of tea to which Daitokuji must answer now. Gazing out upon this world of tea which unfolds itself brilliantly on Daitokuji's grounds, I recalled one of Ikkyū's verses, composed in Chinese one day after he had been reading about Daitokuji's founder:

Raise the lamp of the teachings to light
  the whole world.
Great palanquins once competed before
  the Lecture Hall to prove unsurpassable faith.
But few recall that the sky was Daitō's roof,
  water his diet;
Though he lived a pilgrim for twenty years near
  Daigo Bridge,
There were few to witness his life as
  a wandering monk.

For a pilgrim, Ikkyū's admonition that a life of practice unrec-
ognized by the world—as was Shūhō's life—holds great value
but is a bitter pill to take. Ikkyū, known also as Kyōunshi, or
Child of the Crazy Clouds, undoubtedly saw the swirling white
clouds in the sky as a metaphor for the confusion of his world.
Ikkyū once warned Yōsō with the following words: "Old man
Yōsō understands nothing of Zen. These crazy clouds swirl
about in front of his very eyes. Won't someone explain it all to
him?"

The bitter cold of winter here in Murasakino is probably fitting
for a pilgrimage to Daitokuji.

SECT   Headquarters of the Daitokuji branch of the Rinzai sect
of Zen.

ESTABLISHMENT   Founded by Shūhō Myōchō in 1325.

PRINCIPAL IMAGE   Shakamuni.

CULTURAL PROPERTIES   Among its National Treasures are
several halls, portraits, paintings, and calligraphic works. There are
also many Important Cultural Properties among the various *fusuma* paintings.

VISITING INFORMATION   In addition to the main temple grounds, there are many subtemples in the Daitokuji compound that can also be visited throughout the year. On October 10, many of the treasures at Daitokuji and its subtemples are brought out of storage for their annual airing.

OF SPECIAL INTEREST   The rock gardens at several of Daitokuji's subtemples are particularly well known, especially those of Shinju-an, Daisen-in, and Kōtō-in. The main buildings on the grounds of Daitokuji are most typical of the traditional Zen style of architecture. Temple treasures at Daitokuji are mostly Zen paintings and Zen calligraphic works.

LOCATION AND TRANSPORTATION   Daitokuji-chō, Murasakino, Kita-ku, Kyoto. Take city bus 1, 12, 61, 204, 206, or 206 to the Daitokuji Mae bus stop or take the subway to the last stop (Kitaōji) and walk west along Kitaōji Street for about fifteen minutes.

大徳寺　　京都市北区紫野大徳寺町

14. Shōkokuji

Shōkokuji was completed in 1284, ten years after Shogun Ashikaga Yoshimitsu (1358–1408) ordered the start of its construction by calling on the assistance of laborers from all over the country. Musō Soseki (1276–1351) was designated the founder of the temple and Myōha Shun'oku (1311–88) was named chief priest. Since *shōkoku* means "minister of the country" (shogun, in this case), Yoshimitsu's intentions here are reasonably clear—he intended to make Shōkokuji the "ruler" of all Zen temples in Japan. The fact that Yoshimitsu called his temple Mannensan (Mount Eternity) and entreated one of the most famous priests of that era to be its founder is a testament to the concern and deliberation he brought to the project.

There are few pilgrims here and not many tour buses either. This is one of the famous Zen temples that can rightfully be called tranquil. When I visited Shōkokuji, traditionally the second in rank among Kyoto's five great Zen temples, I was struck by the thought that this is precisely what a Zen temple should be. Its uncongested grounds and quiet peacefulness allow the pilgrim to sense a nearness to salvation.

The noise from Dōshisha University, a sprawling campus adjoining Shōkokuji, draws near. "In one hand, a banner; in your heart, Marx; between your lips, a whistle; and on your back, a

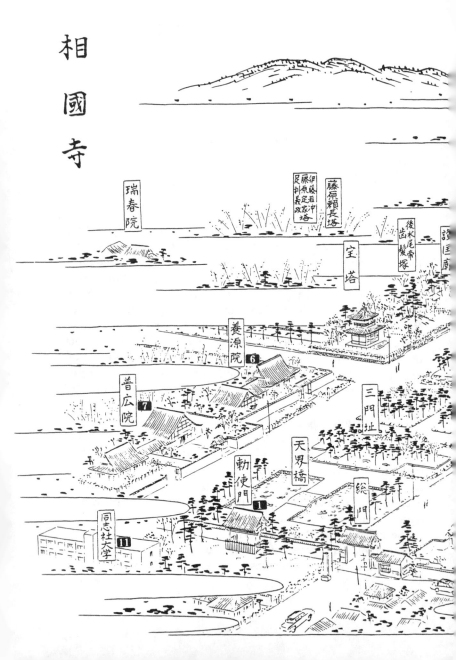

相國寺

瑞春院

伊藤若冲塚
藤原定家塚
足利義政塚

藤原頼長塚

後水尾帝歯髪塚

護正院

宝塔

養源院 **6**

普広院 **7**

三門址

天界橋

勅使門 **1**

総門

同志社大学 **11**

慈照院
慈雲院
長得院
豊光寺
大光明寺
方丈
書院
庫裡
法堂
開山堂
仏殿址
弁天社
鐘楼
宗旦稲荷
専門道場
光源院
林光院
王竜院

5
3
2
4
8
9
10

1. Chokushimon
2. Hattō
3. Hōjō
4. Kuri
5. Daikōmyōji
6. Yōgen-in
7. Fukō-in
8. Rinkō-in
9. Kōgen-in
10. Gyokuryū-in
11. Dōshisha University

knapsack." These words appeared in a university newspaper. It seems that the universities these days, no matter where they are, are great cauldrons of noise, but the ruckus quickly disappears once you enter the Shōkokuji grounds.

In 1386, Yoshimitsu made Shōkokuji one of the five great Zen temples of Kyoto, referred to as the *gozan* ("five mountains"). Until then, the *gozan* had consisted of Nanzenji, Daitokuji, Tenryūji, Kenninji, and Manjuji. Yoshimitsu elevated Nanzenji to the head of the five temples and added Shōkokuji. At that time, the *gozan* were competing among themselves for secular favor and influence. Later Yoshimitsu placed Shōkokuji in charge of all Zen temples within and without Kyoto. To help solidify this power, the Onryōken, an influential office on the temple grounds, was under the direct authority of the shogun. *The Onryōken Journal* (1435–93) is a valued document of the period, informing us of the political, economic, literary, and artistic activities of that era. In a certain sense, the Muromachi period (1392–1568) as a whole was shaped by the activities at Shōkokuji.

The history of Shōkokuji after the Muromachi period is full of calamities and subsequent recoveries. At times it was seething with political and religious disputes; at others, it was beset by natural disasters. A look at Shōkokuji's chronological tables and historical records reveals endless change, like the shifting patterns of clouds or the flowing water of a river.

In the midst of all of this one thing alone did not change: the figures of the itinerant priests seeking the truth with their begging bowls in hand. This is a religious practice that has been passed down in its original form. The steps of the itinerant priest who goes out begging with his iron bowl are light. Perhaps this is because each step brings him closer to severing all worldly desires.

It is now the season known as *u ango,* a time of heavy rains well suited to long periods of religious practice. More commonly known as *ge ango,* or "being peaceful in the summer," the custom of intensive meditation practice during the rainy season has also remained unchanged since Shōkokuji was first established.

Zen negates Buddhist forms. The various pictures and Buddhist statues of esoteric Buddhism were not recreated in the Zen tradition. Because the world of Zen emphasizes "no particular scheme," there is nothing for the tourist's eyes to feast on here. But the very same spatial disposition which denies form produces an artistic world that opens a completely different dimension. Whether it is in the portraits of the distinguished priests, or in the ink paintings and calligraphy, or in the gardens, artistic creations based on Zen enlightenment reveal a world that is ascetic and colorless.

But color, strictly speaking, can be found in the blacks and whites which form the extreme boundaries of the color spectrum. What we observe at Zen temples is the freedom derived from no color at all. The *Ten Oxherding Pictures* drawn by Shūbun (ca. mid-fifteenth century), the *Drawings of Kanzan and Juttoku* by Yishan Yining (1244–1317), the *fusuma* landscapes done in varying shades of ink by Hasegawa Tōhaku (late sixteenth century) that can be seen in the temple's library, and many other Shōkokuji treasures are all examples of art conceived by a tranquil mind, creations befitting an illustrious Zen temple.

A visit to a Zen temple as famous as Shōkokuji on a mid-summer's day in Kyoto, with the cicadas droning incessantly like falling rain, is a purifying experience. The neighboring university is on summer vacation now, and the noise of the here and now has faded for a while, letting the soft song of the eternal be heard.

SECT   Headquarters of the Shōkokuji branch of the Rinzai sect of Zen Buddhism.

ESTABLISHMENT   Founded by Musō Soseki in 1392.

PRINCIPAL IMAGE   Shakamuni.

CULTURAL PROPERTIES   There are many calligraphic works,

portraits of Zen masters, and *fusuma* paintings at Shōkokuji that have been designated Important Cultural Properties. Many of these are on display in the Shōtenkaku Museum located on the temple grounds and open throughout the year. The Lecture Hall (Hattō) is also an Important Cultural Property.

VISITING INFORMATION   Though the Shōtenkaku Museum is always open to visitors, in order to see the Main Hall (Hondō) you must make a request by sending a postcard to the address above.

OF SPECIAL INTEREST   Daikomyōji, a subtemple on the grounds of Shōkokuji, has an interesting rock garden. The arrangement of the buildings at Shōkokuji is of note because it is representative of Zen temple precincts. The Lecture Hall is especially worth seeing. Buddhist iconography is limited at Zen temples for the most part and that is true here at Shōkokuji as well. The Shakamuni image and the images of the temple founders, though, are fine works.

LOCATION AND TRANSPORTATION   Shōkokuji Monzencho, Kamigyō-ku, Kyoto. Take the subway to Imadegawa. The temple is located three minutes north of the Imperial Palace, next to Dōshisha University.

相国寺   京都市上京区相国寺門前町

WESTERN KYOTO

15. Ninnaji

Ninnaji is correctly called Ōuchiyama Ninnaji. Construction was started by imperial decree in 886 during Emperor Kōkō's reign (884–87). It was completed during the reign of the next emperor, Uda (r. 887–97).

Emperor Kōkō composed the following poem:

> For you I go out
> Into the spring fields and pick
> The young blooming greens—
> While the snow falls lightly
> Into the sleeves of my gown.

They call the range of mountains behind Ninnaj iKomatsuno, "small pine fields." The spring fields in Emperor Kōkō's poem are in this area. Emperor Kōkō was called the Ninna Sovereign.

The temple was established in a period when many prayers were being made for national peace and Buddhism was prospering. A sense of nobility can still be felt when one walks through this area now; it is a mood quite different from the vigorous bustle of the temples of the common folk, and it can be felt even when the late-blooming cherries—the common man's delight—are in full bloom here.

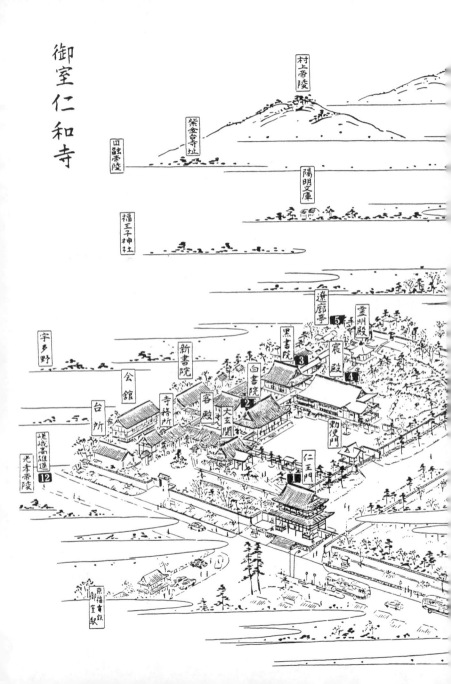

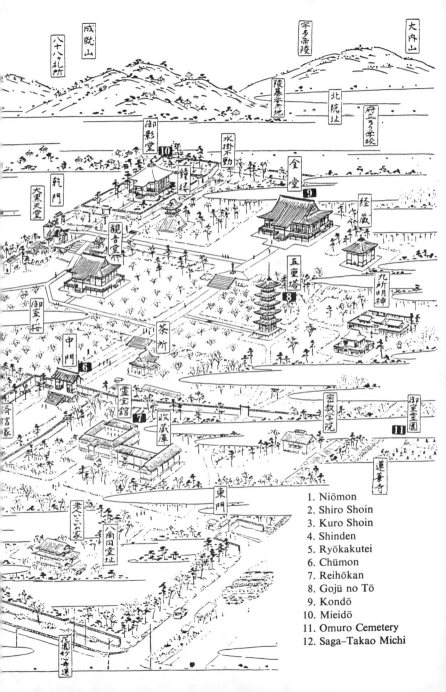

八十八ヶ所札所
成就山
宇多帝陵
大内山
陵墓参考地
北院址
府立○○学校
御影堂 **10**
水掛不動
金堂 **9**
乾門
大黒天堂
経蔵
観音堂
九所明神
御室ノ桜
五重塔 **8**
中門 **6**
茶所
霊宝館 **7**
収蔵庫
密教学院
御室霊園 **11**
蓮華寺
済宮家
東門
老いこの家
八角円堂址
花園妙心寺道

1. Niōmon
2. Shiro Shoin
3. Kuro Shoin
4. Shinden
5. Ryōkakutei
6. Chūmon
7. Reihōkan
8. Gojū no Tō
9. Kondō
10. Mieidō
11. Omuro Cemetery
12. Saga–Takao Michi

Ninnaji is known for its cherries, the last to bloom in Kyoto. They are eight-petaled and grow on the low-slung branches of the trees, which has earned them the name Otafuku cherries, after the comic folk goddess Otafuku, distinguished by her low-bridged nose. The fullness of the blossoms is the source of another name for them—*botanzakura,* or peony cherries; and they are known as Omurozakura from the name of the temple's locale, Omuro.

All sorts of songs are sung at the cherry-viewing parties held on the temple grounds in the spring. Several commemorate merry Otafuku: "We like a woman whose nose, like the blossoms, is low . . ." and "I'm an Otafuku blossom in Omuro, and people like me even though my nose, like the cherries, is low. . . ." When these songs are heard on the Ninnaji grounds, Kyoto is already deep into spring, its western mountains engulfed by the fragrance of new green.

From the time of Emperor Uda until the late nineteenth century, the lineage of the abbots of Ninnaji has remained in the imperial family. As a result of this continuity, even though there were adversities and times of prosperity depending on the period, one does not often see changes in the religious activity of the temple through the successive generations of priests.

As one example of that lack of disruption, we have many delightful depictions of Ninnaji in literature. Yoshida Kenkō (ca. 1283–1352), who built and lived in a hut at the base of Narabiga-oka, a small hill situated in front of Omuro at Ninnaji, describes various temple scenes in his *Essays in Idleness* (*Tsurezuregusa*). He describes a monk who, drunk on sake, put a three-legged kettle over his head and, while frolicking about, realized it wouldn't come off. Covering his "horned" head with a hemp kimono, he rushed to the doctor. Using all his might, the doctor pulled the kettle off, but not without considerable pain to the monk's ears and nose. Another story relates an attempt by older monks to play a trick on a sleepy temple page. In these gently humorous tales, Kenkō shows the peaceful atmosphere at Ninnaji. However, did the Ninnaji priests really live such openhearted and carefree lives?

In Kenkō's collected poetry we find: "Composed when preparing a place of intransience (a grave) at Narabigaoka and planting cherry trees on the side.

> Blossoms where I prepare
> This grave bloom side by side
> On this row of hills—
> Ah! How many more springs will
> I spend at Narabigaoka!"

These thoughts about Ninnaji reveal the religious commitment of a dedicated monk, another aspect of Yoshida that, while it is not always emphasized in his *Essays in Idleness,* cannot be overlooked.

I couldn't forget Kenkō's yearning while strolling north along the visitor's path that stretches from the Guardians' Gate and visiting the palace, which stretches from the Middle Gate to the Main Hall, on the right and the left. I couldn't but wonder what the cultured men who gathered at Ninnaji in that era—such as the potter Ninsei (?–1600); the painter Ogata Kōrin (1658–1716); his younger brother the potter Ogata Kenzan (1663–1743); and the potter Dōhachi (1783–1855)—were searching for and why they were deepening their friendships here.

In January of 1945, when the colors of defeat were deepening, the emperor is said to have held a secret meeting at this imperial temple. Probably, he, too, like many before him, wished to enter the priesthood.

On the day that Lord Fumimaro Konoe went to worship at Ninnaji, it is said that he composed a calligraphic plaque reading "Hall of the Shining Spirit." Ninnaji is the temple from which the true light of Buddhism has continued to shine since Emperor Uda's time, a temple dedicated to the peace of the nation. Written when Lord Konoe already anticipated Japan's defeat in the war, the plaque now hangs in a building of the same name, The Hall of the Shining Spirit, where prayers in the form of Buddhist mortuary tablets have been offered to the successive generations of emperors. Forty years of snowstorms have fallen since this last work of Konoe's—for he committed ritual suicide in the face of his country's defeat.

Walking around this immense area with Ōuchiyama behind you, you should listen not only to the temple legends but also to the voice of history which lives there as well. The trunks of the red mountain pines sprout up beautifully among the green of the needles. Even today, entrusting ourselves to the whisperings of the wind through the pine trees, they seem about to tell us a story.

SECT   Headquarters of the Omuro branch of the Shingon sect.

ESTABLISHMENT   Founded by Retired Emperor Uda in 888.

PRINCIPAL IMAGE   Amida.

CULTURAL PROPERTIES   The Main Hall (Kondō) and the Amida image are both National Treasures, as are many other statues and religious implements in the temple collection.

VISITING INFORMATION   The temple grounds are open to the public, as is the Museum (Reihōkan). During the middle to the last part of April, the Omuro cherry blossoms are in full bloom. Large numbers of people gather here then for cherry-viewing, which includes singing, dancing, and sake-drinking.

OF SPECIAL INTEREST   The Imperial Residence Hall (Shinden) garden and the Tea Ceremony House (Ryōkaku Tei) garden are both worth seeing. The Main Gate (Sammon), the Five-storied Pagoda (Gojū no Tō), and the Main Hall (Kondō) are each a must. Most of the art objects stored at Ninnaji can be seen in the Museum, which is open all year long. Numerous objects and documents of esoteric Buddhism are National Treasures and are on display here.

LOCATION AND TRANSPORTATION   33 Ōuchi, Omuro, Ukyō-ku, Kyoto. Ninnaji is located in the northwest part of Kyoto near Ryōanji and Kinkakuji and is accessible by city bus 8, 10, 26, or 59, Kyoto bus, or the Kitano Line of the Keifuku Railway. Whichever bus you take, the stop is the same: Ninnaji. When going by train, get off at Omuro Station and walk north about three minutes.

仁和寺　　京都市右京区御室大内33

16. Myōshinji

Retired Emperor Hanazono (r. 1308–18), who had decreed the establishment of Myōshinji, once presented the following Chinese-style poem, known as an "enlightenment verse" (*tōki no gosho*), to Shūhō Myōchō (1282–1337; also known as National Teacher Daitō, or Daitō Kokushi), the founder of Daitokuji:

> For twenty years I have struggled to find my true heart.
> At last, having found it, I can greet the coming spring.
> Invariably I just put on my clothes, eat my meals, and
>   drink my tea.
> Are there not, within this world, hindrances to satori?
>   For me, there are not.
> I dwell in a cloudless world of clarity.
> Dear teacher, how will you test me?

Shūhō replied:

> You, venerable priest, have already been tested. That's
> it!

Retired Emperor Hanazono had studied with Shūhō until his own personal experience of Zen led him to enlightenment. There was no "stamp of approval" which would have indicated the success of his spiritual journey more than Daitō Kokushi's reply. This enlightenment verse is preserved even today as a National Treasure at Daitokuji.

Shōbōzan Myōshinji (The Temple of the True Dharma and the Miraculous Heart), is the formal name for this temple which came into being when Hanazono decided to turn his own detached palace into a place where the Buddhist teachings could thrive. It is unclear why Hanazono sought refuge in the Buddhist path. Reasons are easy enough to come by, though, if we just take a look at the disruptions which occurred during the Northern and Southern Courts period (1336–92). Hanazono must have firmly believed that the detached palace could become a place where the teachings would flourish, a real "flower garden" of enlightenment.

Preserved at one of Myōshinji's subsidiary temples, Taizō-in, is the well-known National Treasure, *Catching a Catfish with a Gourd* (*Hyōnen Zu*), a painting of a man attempting to catch a catfish with a gourd. I wonder what Josetsu (ca. late fourteenth–early fifteenth century), the painter, was trying to say? Of course it's impossible to catch a fish with a bottle gourd because of its thin neck. If that is the case, why is this painting so highly valued for its insight into Zen?

Before he died, Shūhō Myōchō encouraged Hanazono to study with Kanzan Egen (1277–1360), the only teacher with whom the Zen master thought it was worthwhile to continue practicing. At that time, Kanzan was living deep in the mountains of what is now Gifu Prefecture. He came to Myōshinji to be its founder and head priest after hearing Shūhō's wishes and Hanazono's decree to establish the temple.

Kanzan's style was always marked by an elegant simplicity. His priestly robes, which are preserved at Myōshinji, were woven out of fiber made from wisteria vines. His desk had nothing religious or literary on it other than a box full of letters from Emperor Godaigo (r. 1318–39). He is said to have believed that earnest

衣笠山

西源院 大珠院 竜安寺 霊光院 多福院 仙寿院 金台寺

天球院 **25** 北門 光国寺 **20** 雲祥院 **21** 長慶院 **22**

金牛院 **26** 智勝院 随華院 幡桃院 **19** 桂春院 **23**

麟祥院 海福院 **17** 養徳院 **18** 大雄院 **24**

大雄軒 **8** 雑華院 **13** 如是院 **16**

小方丈 **7** 大心院 **12** 福寿院 **14** 東林院

玉鳳院 **11** 開山堂 **15**

涅槃堂

養源院

花園大学

1. Chokushimon
2. Sammon
3. Butsuden
4. Hattō
5. Kuri
6. Daihōjō
7. Shōhōjō
8. Taihōken
9. Tōkaian
10. Kōbai-in
11. Gyokuhō-in
12. Daishin-in
13. Zōke-in
14. Fukuju-in
15. Tōrin-in

16. Nyoze-in
17. Kaifuku-in
18. Yōtoku-in
19. Bantō-in
20. Kōkokuji
21. Unshō-in
22. Chōkei-in
23. Keishun-in
24. Daiyū-in
25. Tenkyū-in
26. Kongyū-in
27. Jushō-in
28. Tenshō-in
29. Tokuun-in
30. Dairyū-in
31. Reiun-in
32. Daihō-in
33. Gyokuryū-in
34. Tsūgen-in
35. Shōtaku-in
36. Tenju-in
37. Taizō-in
38. JR Hanazono
    Station

academic pursuits alone were not enough; if the student could not endure the master's rigorous training and be willing to step out of preconceived mental habits, then he could not really endure life's transience. Kanzan is even said to have chased his own nephew, Unzan Sōga, out of the temple twenty times for insufficient practice.

We can easily imagine the severity of Kanzan's style from these stories. Maybe this tension between teacher and student is similar to the struggle it takes to catch a catfish with a gourd. Such rigorousness rains down with the force of the Zen master's stick and resounds like thunder to awaken the student from his delusions.

It is rare to find a Zen temple laid out, as Myōshinji is, in such a typically Zen fashion, even among Kyoto's five great Zen temples. Its grounds, which cover almost seven acres, face south. When you pass through the entrance on the south side, you are facing north. After crossing the stone bridge over the pond called the Hōjō Ike, where fish are freed once a year by the priests, one can see the temple's Main Gate (Sammon), the Main Hall (Butsuden), the Lecture Hall (Hattō), the Main Reception Center (Sōuketsuke Genkan), the Chinese Gate (Karamon), and the Priests' Quarters (Daihōjō) all lined up in a neat row. The subsidiary temples are arranged systematically on the east and west sides of these structures. Walking around the grounds and stepping on the cleanly swept rocks, it almost seems as if the bell upon which the oldest inscription in Japan appears ("Twenty-third day of the Fourth Month, 698 . . .) is reverberating.

Myōshinji is quite near Narabigaoka, where Yoshida Kenkō (c. 1283–1352), a priest and the author of *Essays in Idleness* (*Tsurezuregusa*) lived. The well-known Shingon temple Ninnaji is also nearby. In section 220 of *Essays in Idleness* we find: "The sound of the bell very nearly approximates the notes of the *ōjikichō* [a Chinese scale of 12 tones]. It is a note of impermanence itself—the sound of the Temple of Transience, or Mujō-in, in Jetavana vihara."

We can't hear these notes now, but they must have reverberated with the indestructibility of the buddha-dharma, echoing the truth to the many priests who have lived on these grounds. Over 3,500 branch temples throughout the country perpetuate the stateliness of their head temple, Myōshinji. There are also many well-known subsidiary temples within Myōshinji: Taizō-in, Keishun-in, and Tōkai-an, as well as the garden at Gyokuhō-in, where visitors often stop. Perhaps they come because Zen is still practiced here in the form that it ought to be.

SECT   Headquarters of the Myōshinji branch of the Rinzai sect of Zen.

ESTABLISHMENT   Founded by Kanzan Egen in 1337.

PRINCIPAL IMAGE   Shakamuni.

CULTURAL PROPERTIES   The calligraphic works of Shūhō Myōchō are National Treasures. The Main Hall and the Lecture Hall are both Important Cultural Properties. In addition, there are many other temple treasures stored here.

VISITING INFORMATION   The entire temple grounds, including the numerous subtemples, are open to the public throughout the year.

OF SPECIAL INTEREST   One can see many beautiful gardens within the grounds of the fifty subtemples located within the Myōshinji complex. Those at Reiun-in, Keishun-in, Tōkai-an, Gyōkuhō-in, and Taizō-in are particularly noteworthy. The Main Hall and the Lecture Hall at Myōshinji are quite famous. The dragon on the ceiling of the Lecture Hall was painted by Kanō Tan'yū (1602–74) and is particularly well known in Japan. Since Myōshinji is a Zen temple, it does not have any Buddhist images of note, but there are many calligraphic works and portraits of well-known Zen priests. There are also many *fusuma* paintings done by various painters of the Kanō school. *Scenes of the Gourd and the Catfish* at Taizō-in is one of the most famous.

LOCATION AND TRANSPORTATION   Myōshinji-chō, Hana-zono, Ukyō-ku, Kyoto. Take the Kitano Line of the Keifuku Railway and get off at Myōshinji Station.

妙心寺　　京都市右京区花園妙心寺町

17. Kōryūji

It is the heart that perceives beauty which carries the pilgrim to Kōryūji in western Kyoto. The famous Miroku image that is enshrined here wears a beautiful smile. The philosopher and scholar of French literature, Isaku Yanaihara, describes that smile: "The smile is the most beautiful facial expression. However, there are many different kinds of smiles. Mona Lisa's smile is bewitchingly alluring. Hōryūji's Shakamuni triad and the Kudara Kannon are somewhat more stern and mysterious. Then there are the smiles of the images at Chūgūji, compassionate smiles to mankind from the Buddha. The Miroku at Kōryūji, though, is not smiling at mankind. Its smile seems to be an outflowing from the deepest currents of our spiritual beings. It's the innocent smile of a sleeping child. Miroku is not thinking about how he can save humanity. He is salvation. His fingers almost seem to be dancing with an innocent joy."

The joy that sweeps over you when you look at this image is proof of the fact that you are alive. This feeling surpasses all constraints of time and space. It is as if you were looking at pure form from the purest part of your being.

Kōryūji was built in what is now the Uzumasa section of Kyoto in 622, during the reign of Empress Suiko (r. 592–628). It was one of the seven great temples built on the orders of Shōtoku

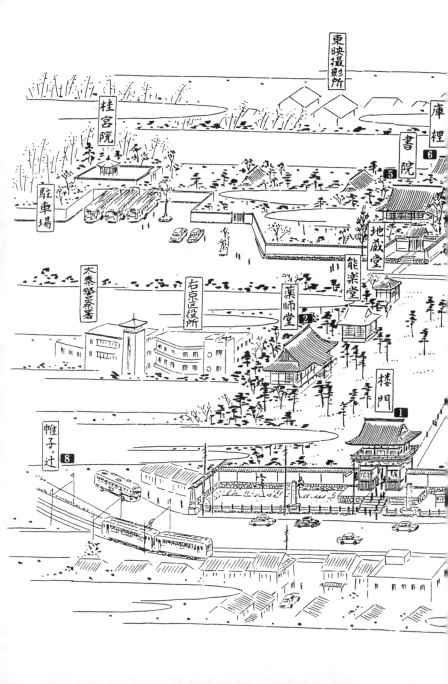

廣隆寺

霊宝館 **7**

本堂 **4**

講堂 **3**

太秦殿

鐘楼

回心峰墓

悟真寺

大酒神社

弁天池址

右京消防署

岚電太秦駅 **9**

三條街道

1. Rōmon
2. Yakushidō
3. Kōdō
4. Hondō
5. Shoin
6. Kuri
7. Reihōkan
8. Katabira no Tsuji
9. Randen Uzumasa Station

Taishi (574–622). The others were Shitennōji, Hōryūji, Chūgūji, Tachibanadera, Ikejiridera, and Katsuragidera. Since we know that Hachiokadera, the former name of Kōryūji, was moved and rebuilt by Hatano Kawakatsu, one of Shōtoku Taishi's ministers, it must be at least 1,400 years old.

A temple with this much history is indeed quite old. Miroku's robes and crown must have been beautiful when the image was first enshrined. The statue is peeling now, but it is smiling in its nakedness. According to the temple histories, Kōryūji has burned down twice since it was first built. Though Miroku has endured these great calamities, time itself has worn away the splendor of his crown and robes. Fortunately, we can take a look back at Kōryūji's history because two valuable records chronicling its existence—*An Account of Materials Used in the History of Kōryūji (Kōryūji Engi Shizai Chō)* and *A True Record of Materials Employed at the Rebuilding of Kōryūji (Kōryūji Shizai Kotai Jitsuroku Chō)*—have been preserved and are stored in the Treasure Hall. Thanks to these two works, we can easily imagine the magnificence of its buildings, which represented the finest in structural beauty of the day. Before the conflagration of 1145, there were forty-two structures on the temple grounds. Records of Kōryūji's finances confirm the temple's economic strength, which allowed it to support so many buildings.

Kōryūji was traditionally the family temple of the Hatano clan. The story of the beginning of this association can be found in the *Nihon Shoki,* the first official history of Japan. In 622, according to the history, "Shōtoku Taishi turned to his high-ranking ministers and said, 'I have a sacred image. Whoever receives it must worship it respectfully.' At that time, the head of the Hatano family, Kawakatsu, came forth and said, 'Your obedient servant will worship it.' He took the statue and then enshrined it in the halls of Hachiokadera, which he had built for that purpose." (As mentioned above, Hachiokadera is an ancient name for Kōryūji, and even today the temple is also known as Hachiokazan).

In addition to the Miroku image with a crown, which we will call the smiling bodhisattva, there is another Miroku with its hair bundled tightly above its head. This Miroku we shall call the crying bodhisattva. It is in the same cross-legged meditation posture, but its eyes are moist-looking and the lips are slightly drawn back. No matter how you look at it, it seems to be weeping. I wonder why this image—the antithesis of the smiling Miroku— is enshrined here as well? Perhaps it is weeping for all the pain and suffering in the world.

If you mention you are going to Uzumasa in Kyoto these days, it is assumed that you are going to the popular "Movie Village" which contains studios and various tourist attractions, and seems to be better known now than Kōryūji. It is an incredibly noisy area with blaring loudspeakers. The sound reaches all the way into Kōryūji's halls. I wonder if Miroku is saddened by all of this? Standing in front of Kōryūji's pair of bodhisattvas, the message I received was that both sadness and joy are part of our world, from which retreat is both foolhardy and impossible. Both must be embraced, with the effortless grace and beauty of these "beings of wisdom."

SECT   Omuro branch of the Shingon sect.

ESTABLISHMENT   Founded by Dōshō (but popularly regarded as founded by Shōtoku Taishi) in 603.

PRINCIPAL IMAGE   Amida.

CULTURAL PROPERTIES   Many buildings, including the Main Hall (Hondō), have been designated National Treasures. There are also many Buddhist statues and sculptures on display in the Museum (Reihōkan) that are National Treasures and Important Cultural Properties. The most important of these is the Miroku image, which dates from the early seventh century. In addition, Kōryuji has many documents and records that are of historical importance.

VISITING INFORMATION   The entire grounds of Kōryūji are open to the public throughout the year. The Main Hall and the Museum are the most important buildings to see here. On October 10, the Cow Festival (Ushi Matsuri) is held to ward off evil fortune.

OF SPECIAL INTEREST   Temples from this period (Kōryūji is as old as Hōryūji in Nara) placed no particular importance on gardens and therefore seem very different from later Japanese temples. The general atmosphere at Kōryūji is more evocative of Chinese than Japanese temples. The Tower Gate (Rōmon) and the Lecture Hall (Kōdō) deserve close inspection. Many of the oldest Buddhist images in Japan are to be found at Kōryūji. They tell us a lot about the origins of Japanese Buddhist art, and some regard Kōryūji as the fountainhead of all Japanese Buddhist art.

LOCATION AND TRANSPORTATION   Hachioka-chō, Uzumasa, Ukyō-ku, Kyoto. Take city bus 11 and get off at the Ukyō Kuyakusho Mae bus stop or take the Arashiyama Line of the Keifuku Railway and get off at Uzumasa Station.

広隆寺　　京都市右京区太秦蜂岡町

18. Daikakuji

Emperor Saga's temple, Daikakuji, is in the western part of Kyoto in Sagano. As a temple with former imperial connections, it has enjoyed a rather high status among Buddhist temples in Kyoto. It founder, Emperor Saga (r. 808–23), originally built the temple as a detached palace. Later it was converted into the Imperial Palace (Sentō Gosho) and eventually became known as Saga-in. Even though there are Buddhist images enshrined here, they are not the central focus of the temple. If there is a focus, it is to be found in its role as a protector of Emperor Saga's tomb in Asaharayama-chō.

Naokatsu Nakamura, the historian, wrote: "Daikakuji does not perform any religious functions. It is not a temple where esoteric Shingon teachings are transmitted from teacher to disciple in secret religious ceremonies. Nor is it a temple dedicated to relieving the world of its suffering. Rather, it is a temple where the emperor paid his respects to the gods and buddhas who blessed the country. Through proper imperial intercession, it was believed, the country would bask in the compassion of those gods and buddhas. By serving as a medium for carrying out the emperor's will to seek peace throughout the world and goodness for his people, Daikakuji became a place from which the emperor's wishes were disseminated to the whole world. This is why Daikakuji does not have

大覚寺

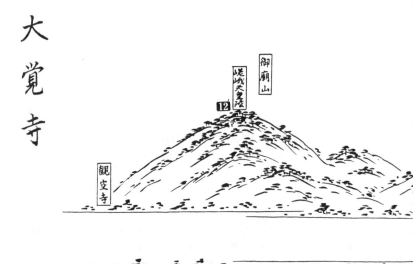

御廟山
嵯峨天皇陵 **12**
観空寺

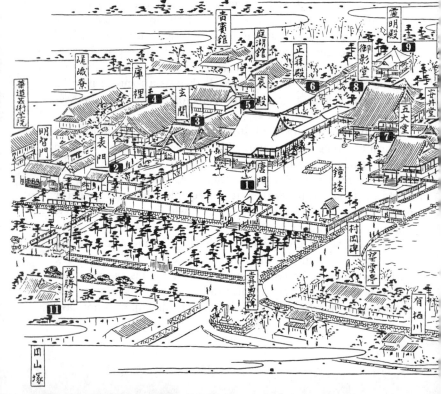

霊明殿 **9**
青賓館
庭湖館
正寝殿
御影堂
嵯峨寮
庫裡
6
8
華道芸術学院
宸殿
4
安井堂
玄関
5
五大堂
3
7
明智門
表門
2
唐門
1
鐘楼
村岡碑
望雲亭
覚勝院
有栖川
11
土井晩翠歌碑
田山塚

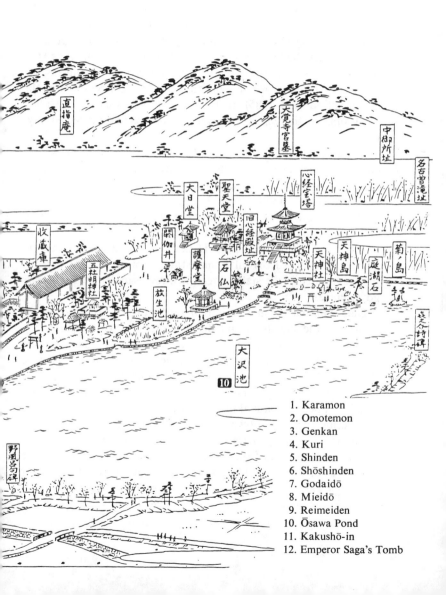

直指庵
大覚寺宮墓
中御所址
名古曽滝址
心経宝塔
大日堂
聖天堂
収蔵庫
開伽井
心経殿址
天神社
天神島
菊ノ島
五社明神社
護摩堂
石仏
庭胡石
放生池
長之介詩碑
大沢池
10

野風呂句碑

1. Karamon
2. Omotemon
3. Genkan
4. Kuri
5. Shinden
6. Shōshinden
7. Godaidō
8. Mieidō
9. Reimeiden
10. Ōsawa Pond
11. Kakushō-in
12. Emperor Saga's Tomb

the atmosphere of an ordinary temple. It is actually a detached palace with all the character of an imperial residence."

The buildings and hallways are all elegant structures—from the Front Gate (Omote Mon) to the Main Entrance (Genkan) and the Imperial Living Quarters (Shinden), the Formal Living Quarters (Shōshinden), the Go Dai Hall (Godaidō), and the Founder's Hall (Mieidō) as well as the covered passageway which connects the buildings to each other at right angles. The architecture is of the Heian-period (794–1185) aristocratic *shindenzukuri* style. Unlike most temples, there is no fragrance of incense to be detected anywhere.

There is, though, a disposition toward the refined at Daikakuji and its history as we can see, for example, in Emperor Saga's words when he relinquished the throne to Emperor Junna (r. 823–33). "Stroll among the hills and the rivers without concern for your own rank or name and take your pleasures in the harp and calligraphy without any thought for what you are to do next." So it was, then, that Daikakuji had its beginnings in prayers for the successful administration of the nation and for the tranquility of the state, a temple directly under the emperor's governance.

Daikakuji played an especially important role during the period known as the Northern and Southern Courts period (1336–92). At this time there was a dispute between two branches of the imperial line over the proper succession, and rival courts were established. The rulers of the Northern Court were known as the Jimyōin line of emperors, after the monastery of that name to which Emperor Gofukakusa (r. 1246–59) retired in 1259. The Southern Court was known as the Daikakuji line and was based at the imperial temple, where Emperor Kameyama (r. 1259–74) and his descendants lived from 1276. Since Daikakuji represented the headquarters of the leadership of the Southern court, the warrior Ashikaga Takauji (1305–58), who supported the Northern Court, ordered it destroyed. It was rebuilt almost immediately, but it was subsequently burned to the ground four more times while it was the headquarters of the Southern court.

Daikakuji survived the quagmire of the dispute, marked by endlessly shifting alignments and diplomatic trickery, but for the fifty years that the conflict raged, the flames of devastating conflagrations burned furiously. According to the *Chronicles of Daikakuji* (*Daikakuji Fu*), "There was a fire on August 28, 1338. The temple halls and priests' quarters were completely destroyed. Though they were rebuilt, the new structures never reached half the size of the previous ones."

> In spite of the fact
> I'm certain I won't forget,
> My sleeves are wet
> With the tears of my memories
> For a time of peace now gone.

This poem was composed by Emperor Gokameyama (r. 1383–92), an emperor of the Daikakuji line. It is certainly evidence of the sad history that had befallen the country during the fourteenth century, an elegy of the Southern court for the stability and grandeur of a past age.

Mitsuō Sakaguchi, a priest at Daikakuji, wrote, perhaps reflecting on his temple's fate: "People enjoy discord. We curse others for their selfishness, their conceit, or because they fall short of our expectations. Then we resent the whole world. We know that this is the basis of all discord, but our egotistic attachments will not let go of ill feelings. Because of egotism, we fight and we make others suffer, then we deprive them of their freedom, squander our resources, and destroy our precious culture. Fighting is destructive, whether we win or lose."

Time moved on since the period of fear and terror at Daikakuji. The dispute over the imperial succession was settled; Japan moved through the period of warring feudal states and on into the long age of peace known as the Edo period (1600–1868). During the reign of emperor Gomizunoo (1611–29), Daikakuji was reconstructed and revived, and now you can smell the fragrance of flowers everywhere throughout Sagano, where the temple is situated, in spring. The gentle ridges of the Kitayama Mountains cast their shadows over the area from Lake Hirosawa to Lake Osawa. Even for Kyoto it is a particularly picturesque scene. It is hard to believe that it is all the work of human hands.

The natural landscape around Daikakuji is beautiful, but the people who have lived here are sad creatures. Anybody walking the path up to the temple here would, I am sure, feel the same way. It is said that Emperor Gomizunoo had a dream of flowers as a result of his virtuous patience, and that is why Daikakuji came to be involved with the tradition of flowers and flower arrangement. In fact, this association with blossoms had been foreshadowed by the brilliant *fusuma,* ceiling, and door paintings, which depict various flowers. There are so many different kinds of flowers and plants, drawn by such famous painters as Kanō Motonobu (1476–1559), Watanabe Shiko (1683–1755), and Ogata Kōrin (1658–1716). There are poppies, bracken, aronia, Japanese allspice, narcissus, broad bellflowers, chrysanthemums, loquats, peonies, hollyhocks, tumeric, yellow roses, balsam, irises, candock, wisteria, water plantain, red starlilies, sallows, camellias, pines, cedars, cherries, and maples. Drawn to the eternity of life's cycles that these flowers represent, we pray for salvation in this transitory world. In effect, we hand over the sadness of our world to the beauty of a flower's life in hopes of finding the path to salvation.

SECT   Headquarters of the Daikakuji branch of the Shingon sect.

ESTABLISHMENT   Founded by Emperor Saga in 876. Originally, Daikakuji was Emperor Saga's private villa.

PRINCIPAL IMAGE   Godai Myōō.

CULTURAL PROPERTIES   Calligraphic works (*shinkan*) of several emperors and various ancient sutra scrolls are National Treasures. The Go Dai Myōō images, the Guest Hall (Kyakuden), and Imperial Residence Hall (Shinden) are Important Cultural Properties. There are also many beautiful *fusuma* paintings that are well worth seeing.

VISITING INFORMATION   The grounds as well as the Imperial Residencce Hall and the Guest Hall can be viewed anytime. A harvest moon-viewing is held annually on the full moon in September. Since Daikakuji is located next to Lake Osawa and there is a moon-viewing platform near the lake, it is a particularly beautiful spot from which to take part in this ancient Japanese custom.

OF SPECIAL INTEREST   The grounds are quite beautiful. The arrangement of the buildings at Daikakuji reflects the style for imperial palaces rather than temples, since this was originally Emperor Saga's villa. Daikakuji is also the headquarters of the Saga school of flower arrangement.

LOCATION AND TRANSPORTATION   Ōsawa-chō, Saga, Ukyō-ku, Kyoto. Daikakuji is located in a scenic part of western Kyoto near Arashiyama and can be included in a walking tour of the area. You can take city bus 91 or 28 to the Daikakuji bus stop or ride the Keifuku Railway from Kitano Hakubaichō or Shijō Ōmiya to Arashiyama. It is about a fifteen-minute walk from Seiryōji (also known as Shakadō).

大覚寺　　京都市右京区嵯峨大沢町

19. Seiryōji

The passage of time brings change with it. This is sad but true. It has always been this way. It is true now and it will always be true.

As the Tendai and Shingon sects of Japanese Buddhism strengthened their allegiances to the secular authorities and increased the number of adherents to their ranks during the Heian period (794–1185), Tōdaiji, which had been for a long time the most prosperous and powerful Buddhist temple in Japan, began its decline.

It is in the late Heian period that two eminent religious leaders make their appearance on the stage of history: Chōnen (938–1016) and Gizō (910–?), two priests from Tōdaiji. Determined to return their temple to its former position of power and restore its legitimacy as the orthodox Buddhist lineage in Japan, they made a pact: "It is tremendously auspicious to be born a human being among all the world's living things. Even more extraordinary than this, however, is that we were born men, took the vows of a priest, and have experienced the joy of working and practicing together." Their vow continued with a pledge to build a temple on Mount Atago in Kyoto and make it so fine that it would rival Mount Hiei, the Tendai sect headquarters. It was to be a temple where Tōdaiji's legitimacy as the only true preceptor of the teachings would again flourish. They promised that even if it took three lifetimes, they would accomplish this task, signed their names to this pact, affixed their seals to it, and included it in their possessions wherever they went. At this time, Chōnen was thirty-five and Gizō was twenty-three.

This is where the long journey to Seiryōji begins. Chōnen, meanwhile, waited ten years before he could make his trip to China to bring back orthodox teachings that would justify the founding of a new temple. Before he left, he entrusted all of his affairs to Gizō and then set out on his journey in search of the teachings.

> Donning my pilgrim's robes
> For the journey across the sea,
> I know it is far—
> Yet my mind cannot measure
> The distant path these white clouds follow.

Chōnen's trip must have been extraordinarily difficult. First he went to Hangzhou, Suzhou, and Yangzhou. Then he went from Bianjing to Da Huayansi, a temple on Mount Wutai. Finally, he made his way from Luoyang to Lungmeng—all the while pursuing the path of the teachings.

While Chōnen was on Mount Wutai, he decided to ask for a copy of the Shakamuni image that was the main object of worship at the Chinese temple Qingliangsi, Seiryōji's namesake, to take back to Japan and enshrine in his temple on Mount Atago. This is how Seiryōji's "flesh-and-blood" Shakamuni image, a copy of an image carved originally from a drawing of India's Shakamuni, came to be. It took Chōnen fifteen years in all—a particularly long and difficult journey for a priest living in the tenth century—to return to Kyoto with this statue.

Sagano is located in the western part of Kyoto. It is rather serene with Mount Ogura rising above it in the background. This is where Seiryōji is located and where Chōnen's image is still enshrined. This Shakamuni image is called a benevolent

清涼寺

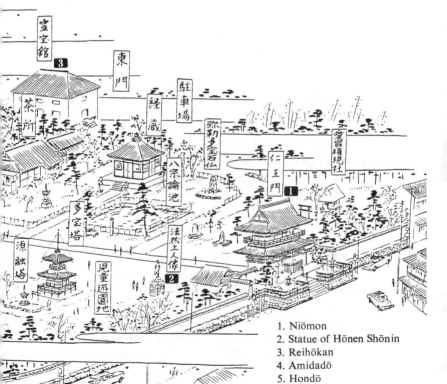

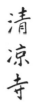

1. Niōmon
2. Statue of Hōnen Shōnin
3. Reihōkan
4. Amidadō
5. Hondō
6. Shoin
7. Shōrō
8. Yakushiji

image (*zuizō*). How much suffering has it relieved and how many hearts has it comforted, standing over the centuries in Seiryōji's Shakamuni Hall and amidst the people of Sagano?

Of the many yearly festivals at Seiryōji, one of the most famous is held in December, the Recitation of the Buddhas' Names (Butsumyō E). Occasionally, the Buddhist nun Jakuchō Setouchi and I go to this festival together. She wrote the following about Seiryōji's Shakamuni image after one of our visits: "This venerated statue, which is rarely on display, was on this day exhibited in full view for all the worshipers to see. Said to have been copied from a drawing of Shakamuni when he was thirty-seven years old, it is enshrined within a rather large room where each of us could reverently worship this extremely dignified, vigorous, and powerful figure. The simple and symmetrical lines of its robes are distinct and you can almost imagine blood coursing through the veins of its masculine body. Since I was standing next to one of the priests in the front and center, I had an unobstructed position from which to worship. Its cheeks are plump and the area beneath the eyes looks flushed, as if Shakamuni had been drinking sake. This is perhaps due to the red chinaberry wood out of which it is made. It actually looked like a human being. . . .

"I put my hands together, looked up, and prostrated myself to the floor. Suddenly, its head shook slightly and I thought I saw a smile spread across its ruddy face. I continued my prostrations while my eyes clouded up and my mind was in a haze. Was I hallucinating?"

It seems as if this Shakamuni really is a flesh-and-blood Buddha.

The streets of Sagano are crowded even today with people who cherish literature and history. It is an area which is rich with the memories of people who have visited here through the centuries and today, too, an unending stream of visitors who wish to partake of its long history continue to flock to Sagano. Seiryōji is located in the center of this area. Daikakuji and Tenryūji are also in the immediate vicinity. Other places of interest include

Nembutsuji in Adashino; Rakushisha, where the haiku poet Matsuo Bashō (1644–94) visited in 1691; and Nison-in, which houses another well-known Shakamuni statue. Seiryōji's Shakamuni seems somehow to nourish all of these with its benevolence. If this is so, then Chōnen's vision back in the tenth century is still alive today.

SECT   Jōdo.

ESTABLISHMENT   Founded by Chōnen in 986.

PRINCIPAL IMAGE   Shakamuni.

CULTURAL PROPERTIES   Seiryōji's principal Shakamuni image is a National Treasure. There are many valuable items such as sutras and other documents preserved inside the image that are also National Treasures. Among the Important Cultural Properties at Seiryōji are an Amida image, images of the Four Guardian Kings, and many other works of art.

VISITING INFORMATION   Many of Seiryōji's valuable art objects can be seen in the Museum (Reihōkan) between 9:30 and 4:30. Otaimatsu, a kind of fire festival, is one of the main celebrations here and is held March 15. Also, on a Saturday and Sunday in mid-April, a theatrical performance known as Nembutsu Kyōgen is held four times in the afternoon between 1 and 4 P.M.

OF SPECIAL INTEREST   The garden in front of the Shoin is quite beautiful. Seiryōji is a good example of a typical Jōdo-style temple.

LOCATION AND TRANSPORTATION   Fujinoki-chō, Saga Shakadō, Ukyō-ku, Kyoto. Seiryōji is located near Tenryūji and Daikakuji in the west part of the city. Take either the Arashiyama

Line or the Kitano Line of the Keifuku Railway and get off at the last stop. It is a ten-minute walk from the station.

清涼寺　　京都市右京区嵯峨釈迦堂藤ノ木町

20. Tenryūji

Tenryūji is in the Sagano district in western Kyoto. The gentle slopes of Mount Ogura, a part of the scenic area of Arashiyama, rise and fall in the background. Since it was first built, 630 years have passed, and during those years the buddha-dharma has brightened and faded depending on the whims of those in power. Walking through the grounds of Tenryūji, I couldn't help but recall the *Muchū Mondō,* a Zen treatise in the form of questions and answers by Tenryūji's founder, Musō Soseki (1275–1351; known posthumously as Musō Kokushi, or National Teacher Musō), as well as the commitment and spirit it must have taken to construct a temple this size.

> Go out to a place
> High above the clouds
> To see it clearly—
> Between yourself and the moon
> There is no obstruction.

"You are the most respected warrior in Japan now. You have gained the veneration of the whole nation. This must be the result of merit accrued in your previous lifetimes.

"But please think carefully about this. You have enemies in

天龍寺

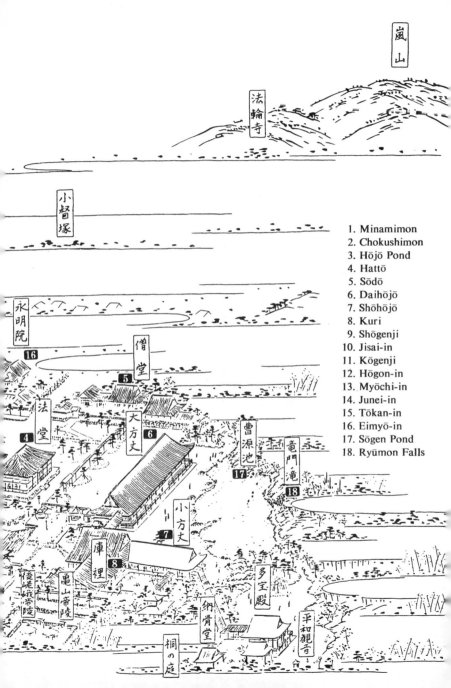

嵐山

法輪寺

小督塚

永明院

僧堂

法堂

大方丈

曹源池

竜門竜

小方丈

庫裡

後嵯峨帝陵

亀山帝陵

多宝殿

納骨堂

平和観音

桐の庭

16 **5** **4** **6** **17** **18** **7** **8**

1. Minamimon
2. Chokushimon
3. Hōjō Pond
4. Hattō
5. Sōdō
6. Daihōjō
7. Shōhōjō
8. Kuri
9. Shōgenji
10. Jisai-in
11. Kōgenji
12. Hōgon-in
13. Myōchi-in
14. Junei-in
15. Tōkan-in
16. Eimyō-in
17. Sōgen Pond
18. Ryūmon Falls

the world. It is hard to say whether you have committed more sins or devoted yourself to more good works since the Genkō Disturbance [1331].

"How many were murdered in your recent campaign? We don't know how many wives, children, and families have been made homeless—fathers left with no children, children left with no fathers, grieving people. We just don't know how many there are."

These words of Musō were presented to shogun Ashikaga Tadayoshi (1306–52) and summarized his purpose for establishing Tenryūji. Such was the dignity of Musō that he could speak so directly to the greatest warrior alive during the chaotic period of the Northern and Southern Courts. "Pray for the souls of those who died of their wounds in battle, the victims of war. And repent your sins for destroying the lives of the enemy as well as those of our friends. Fear the retribution which you have incurred during these wars. Build a pagoda to repent for these sins."

At the same time as the founding of Tenryūji, there arose a movement to erect temples and pagodas in each of the sixty-six provinces and on two islands, Iki and Tsushima. The scale of this project was comparable only to the construction of the provincial temples (*kokubunji*) that were erected across the nation during the Nara period (646–794). The temples built eight hundred years later were called *ankokuji,* or temples to pacify the nation, while the pagodas were called *rishōtō,* or pagodas to benefit sentient beings.

A group of Mount Hiei monks opposed to the opening of Tenryūji disrupted its dedication, creating an uneasy situation. What did Musō Soseki say about this? "Although three thousand monkeys are screeching, I am not startled. The dragon sleeps on Mount Kame." Sōgen Pond stretches out in front of Mount Kame, which lies behind Tenryūji. It is well known as a fine place from which to appreciate the surrounding gardens. The placement of rocks in the pond is masterful. I suddenly recalled these words while I was watching water rush down a waterfall between huge rocks, for it was then that I saw the source of the strength and power of that spirited reply to the boisterous priests from Mount Hiei: "The dragon sleeps on Mount Kame." It was the power of the very earth itself.

Unless you are one of the practicing monks inside who treads the stone walkways of the garden with frozen bare feet, head covered with a bamboo hat, you can not really perceive the extent of the winter's cold in the dragon's nest. But anyone who recalls Tenryūji's history while walking through its hallowed grounds— the story of the struggle between great warrior Ashikaga Takauji (1305–58) and his rival Emperor Godaigo (r. 1318–39), and that of the Tenryūji envoy to China, which helped shape the brilliant Momoyama-period (1568–1600) culture that followed—anyone who listens can hear every blade of grass whispering its tale, every leaf and flower soughing with the song of Musō Soseki's complete commitment to the buddha-dharma. Then the home of the heavenly dragon becomes a high place, with no obstruction between yourself and the moon.

SECT   Headquarters of the Tenryū branch of the Rinzai sect of Zen.

ESTABLISHMENT   Founded by Musō Soseki in 1339.

PRINCIPAL IMAGE   Shakamuni.

CULTURAL PROPERTIES   The Shakamuni image, an Important Cultural Property, the portraits of Musō Soseki and other Tenryūji priests, as well as many calligraphic works are well-known.

VISITING INFORMATION   Tenryūji is open to the public all

year long. Two festivals of interest are the Setsubun festivities on February 3 and the Kawa Segaki celebration on August 16. On the latter occasion, offerings are made to appease the spirits of those who have drowned.

OF SPECIAL INTEREST   The Sōgenchi garden in front of Daisho-in was built by Musō Soseki. Rocks are skillfully arranged in the garden to give the impression of a Chinese landscape. The Special Gate (Chokushimon), the Lecture Hall (Hattō), and the Priests' Quarters (Daihōjō) are noteworthy. Since Tenryūji is a Zen temple, there are not many Buddhist images enshrined here. Tenryūji's most interesting features are its garden and the arrangement of its buildings at the base of Mount Ogura.

LOCATION AND TRANSPORTATION   68 Susukinobanba-chō, Saga Tenryūji, Ukyō-ku, Kyoto. Located at the base of Mount Ogura in Sagano in the western part of Kyoto. Two minutes from Arashiyama Station on the Keifuku Railway which departs from Shijō Ōmiya or Hakubaichō.

天龍寺　京都市右京区嵯峨天龍寺芒ノ馬場町 68

21. Kōzanji

It may be a cliché to say so, but there is no temple more beautiful than Kōzanji. No matter whether it is spring, summer, fall, or winter, Kōzanji is always beautiful. It is particularly so, though, when the verdure of early spring is still new, and again in the fall during the maple-viewing season.

The Shūzan Highway winds its way northwest from Kyoto through the mountains. The cedars here point up straight to the sky looking like stripes on a piece of cloth. This area is known as Sambi, or Three Tails, and Kōzanji, which is located here, is formally known as Toganoozan Kōzanji. Jingoji, on Mount Takao, is on the other side of the mountain while Saimyōji, another well-known temple in the area, is sequestered in a valley on Mount Makinoo. The highway follows along the clear Kiyotaki River. Each step up the path to Kōzanji is an invitation to its tranquility.

Myōe (1173–1232) pursued his meditation practice here. He didn't come here to build Kōzanji, but to continue his search for the mind of Zen. Abbot Shōchō Hagami wrote the following about Myōe: "Myōe's remains are set off deep in the dense forest away from the priests's daily living quarters, where only wild boar, deer, rabbits, squirrels, and birds live. This was the spirit of Myōe's Zen: to live deep in the forest away from the world of artificiality."

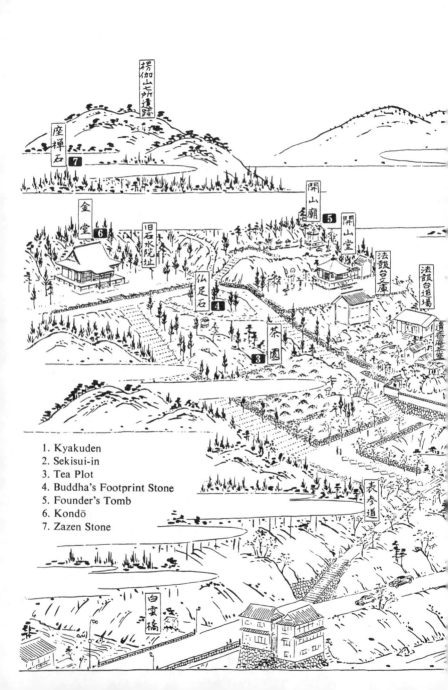

楞伽山七所遺跡

座禅石 **7**

開山廟

金堂 **6**

旧石水院址

開山堂 **5**

法鼓台文庫

法鼓台道場

遺香庵茶堂

仏足石 **4**

茶園 **3**

表参道

白雲橋

1. Kyakuden
2. Sekisui-in
3. Tea Plot
4. Buddha's Footprint Stone
5. Founder's Tomb
6. Kondō
7. Zazen Stone

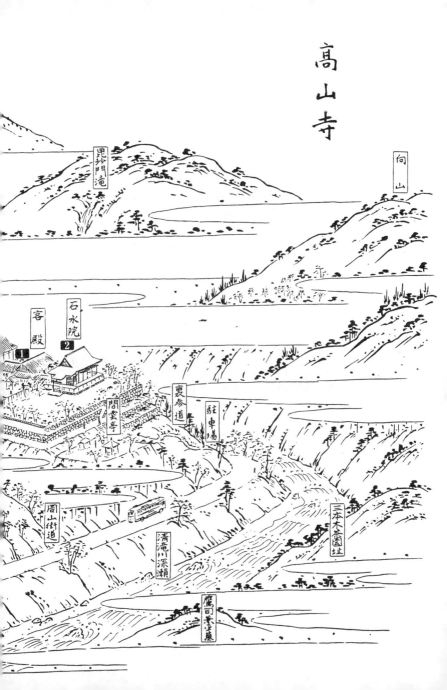

There is a well-known hanging scroll, *Jujōzenzō,* a National Treasure, that depicts Myōe on a rock under a tree persevering in his meditation practice. This scroll is evidence for us of Myōe's religious determination.

> In my robes beneath
> This pine, atop a mossy rock,
> Hail like white jewels
> Rains down upon my black robes
> And my verdant practice seat.
>
> I sit amidst the mountain ridges
> As does the moon
> Night after night
> My companion.

And with the moss-covered rock, the moon, and these poems as his companions, Myōe continued his meditation practice. Now there is a beautiful temple on this mountain, and it is this temple which comforts the pilgrim who visits here. Myōe's quest for the "proper way to live one's life" endures at Kōzanji.

I visited Kōzanji with the novelist Yasushi Inoue in the fall and the winter, in the arboreal greenery of spring, and again in the summer. I often wondered where the pine tree under which Myōe is said to have practiced is now. And where, I wondered, is the mountain ridge from behind which Myōe's autumn friend rose? Where is the stone upon which he practiced zazen? Even though I've always hoped to experience firsthand the essence of Myōe's zazen practice, I have not yet been blessed with that opportunity. I don't suppose there is any reason to expect that a simple visit to the place where Myōe practiced zazen will capture its essence for me.

Two scroll paintings are among Kōzanji's most famous treasures, *The Origins of Kegon* and *The Frolicking Birds and Beasts.*

These two scrolls—one a love story and the other a whimsical parody with animals as the main characters—are quite a contrast. The Kegon story tells of the monk Gishō, who fell in love with a beautiful woman named Zemmyō while he was in China studying the Kegon (in Chinese, Huayan) teachings. His devotion to the Buddhist path was as solid as a rock, though, so he resisted Zemmyō's enticements and persevered in his studies. When he was about to return home, Zemmyō pursued him by throwing herself into the sea and then changing into a dragon that protected Gishō's ship on its return trip.

Although the scenes of Zemmyō's suicide and her transformation into a dragon are intense and sad, as I gaze at them I feel as if I am listening to a love song reminiscent of Amida's merciful vow to save the world. This story, by the way, is based on the tale of a priest from the Korean Kingdom of Silla. The original scroll begins with the solemn warning: "This scroll is by the founder of the Kegon sect. It must not be viewed in a place of impurity or treated in any way improper to its esteemed status."

The *Frolicking Beasts* scroll presents quite a contrast to Zemmyō's tragedy. The main characters here are monkeys, frogs, and rabbits. The monkeys personify the priests on Mount Hiei while the frogs—animals who live near water—personify the priests on Miidera, which is located near Lake Biwa. In the Heian period, "mountain" referred to Mount Hiei and the great Tendai temple there, Enryakuji, while "temple" meant Miidera. The disputes between the mountain faction (*sammon*) and the temple faction (*jimon*) were terrible and often bloody.

Here in the mountains at Kōzanji I tried to reflect on the contrasting worlds these two scrolls depict. For Myōe, who devoted himself to practice and a life of simplicity, these monkeys, frogs, rabbits, deer, foxes, and owls must have been a fitting caricature of the mundane world.

SECT   Shingon.

ESTABLISHMENT   Founded by Myōe in 774.

PRINCIPAL IMAGE   Shakamuni.

CULTURAL PROPERTIES   The Main Hall (Hondō) and the scroll called *The Frolicking Birds and Beasts* are National Treasures, as is a painting depicting Myōe in meditation in the mountains. There are also numerous Important Cultural Properties.

VISITING INFORMATION   The approach to Kōzanji and its general location in the mountains makes it quite extraordinary. The grounds and the halls can be visited throughout the year.

OF SPECIAL INTEREST   There are no gardens of particular interest, but Kōzanji is surrounded by mountain greenery and is especially beautiful in the spring and in the fall when the leaves turn. The painting of Myōe doing zazen on the branch of a large tree gives the visitor some idea of the overall atmosphere of Myōe's religious practices in a mountain temple. There are no Buddhist images of note.

LOCATION AND TRANSPORTATION   Toganoo-chō, Umegahata, Ukyō-ku, Kyoto. Take the National Railways bus to the Toganoo bus stop and walk five minutes. Kōzanji is located in the northwest part of the city in the mountains.

高山寺　　京都市右京区梅ガ畑梅尾町

22. Jingoji

"There are many places to visit during each of Kyoto's four seasons. If one were to arrange them by direction, spring would lie to the east with the cherry blossoms in Gion's Maruyama district and autumn would lie to the west with the light rains at Jingoji. Summer would lie to the south with Byōdō-in and the clear river it faces in southern Uji while winter would lie to the north with the snow at Jakkō-in." Thus writes historian Naokatsu Nakamura (1900–77) on the differences between Kyoto's four seasons.

The Takao Parkway which goes to Shūzan from Ninnaji winds its way in and out of the mountains in northwest Kyoto. It was here, a place renowned for its crimson autumn leaves, that Kanō Hideyori (fl. c. 1540) painted his famous *Scenes of Mount Takao*. This area of gently rolling mountainside is known as Sambi, or Three Tails, and is made up of Takao, Makinoo, and Toganoo, each "o" referring to a "tail."

Jingoji used to be called Takaosanji, the Temple on Mount Takao. The path to the mountain temple of Jingoji begins at the refreshment stands on the Takao Pass. It is lined with maple trees that almost entirely hide the sky from view. The path then crosses over the Kiyotaki River which flows to the south. It is a rather steep incline. There is a vermilion-lacquered bridge over

神護寺

1. Rōman
2. Shoin
3. Kondō
4. Godaidō
5. Bishamondō
6. Taishidō
7. Tahōtō
8. Jizō-in
9. Kiyotaki River
10. Takao Bridge
11. Kiyotaki Michi

多宝塔
7

和気清麿墓

鐘楼

書院

庫裡
2

明王堂

和気公霊廟

宝蔵

楼門
1

防災道路

硯石

西明寺道

下乗石

高雄橋

清滝川
9

額立石

10

a clear, cold stream where the pilgrim descends before starting up another very sharp slope. The Kiyotaki River forms a natural boundary between the worlds of the profane and the sacred. Needless to say, this boundary makes it an even more suitable setting for a well-known temple.

Myōe (1173–1232), the great Kegon-sect master, and Saigyō (1118–90), the poet-monk, each wrote a poem about the area around Jingoji:

> On Mount Takao
> Where the Kiyotaki rapids
> Break high over the rocks,
> Living here storm winds
> Pass deep into the heart.
>
> From atop the peak
> The deep snow melts, sending
> White-capped currents
> Rushing down the clear
> Kiyotaki River.

The history of Jingoji begins with the history of the capital itself. Perhaps we can better grasp just how old Jingoji is when we learn that at the time of the planning of the capital by Wake no Kiyomaru (733–99), there were also plans to rebuild this temple—which already lay in ruins.

The temple histories tell us that Saichō (766–822), the leader of the Tendai sect, held discussions of the Lotus Sutra here and that Kūkai (774–834), the head of the Shingon sect, conducted the first *abhiseka*, or transmission of the secret doctrines, in Japan here in 805. Kūkai is known to have held additional esoteric ceremonies here a few years later. As a result of these ninth-century ceremonies, Jingoji had already established itself as a sacred place, and one of particular importance for the esoteric Shingon school of Buddhism.

Jingoji was subject to the vicissitudes of time and history and assailed again and again by various hardships. The fiery monk Mongaku (1120–?) appeared in Jingoji's history just as it was declining into the stormy years of the Kamakura period (1185–1333). His vow to rebuild Jingoji evolved into a dramatic conflict between faith and political ambition. Soon after Mongaku, Myōe came to Jingoji.

Temple histories are also Japanese history. Jingoji could not help but be caught up in the many uprisings and outbreaks of civil disobedience that marked the Kamakura and Northern and Southern Courts (1336–92) periods. Nor could it remain uninvolved in the political struggles that wracked Kyoto at this time. Takao was too important as a strategic center connecting the San'in and Saikoku areas to Kyoto.

The prosperity and decline of Jingoji is one of the results of history and its turmoil. Many of Jingoji's remaining treasures have been put into a storehouse, which is now second only to Tōji's in its collection of Heian art. We can get an inkling of Takaosanji's importance when we look at some of the fine works preserved there: the statues of Yakushi, the Buddha of Healing (a National Treasure), and its two attendant bodhisattvas, Nikkō ("the splendor of the sun") and Gakkō ("the splendor of the moon"), both Important Cultural Properties; several priceless literary documents; the Takao mandala (a National Treasure); and various other buddhist paintings as well as the portraits of Taira no Shigemori (1138–79) and Minamoto no Yoritomo (1147–99), both National Treasures.

It is difficult not to be aware of these treasures as we leave behind the tumultuousness of the world and take refuge here. Or to notice that the stone steps leading up the Main Hall (Kondō) are worn down. How did all the people who ever climbed them come down again? We ought to look at these as evidence of the path to faith.

SECT   Shingon.

ESTABLISHMENT   Founded by Keishun in 827 (and rebuilt by Mongaku in 1168).

PRINCIPAL IMAGE   Yakushi.

CULTURAL PROPERTIES   Many Buddhist statues, including Yakushi, iconographical representations from the esoteric tradition (in particular the Takao Mandala), and many documents and National Treasures are stored at Jingoji. The portraits of Minamoto no Yoritomo and Taira no Kiyomori are also very famous.

VISITING INFORMATION   Jingoji is open to the public throughout the year. The Treasure Hall (Shoin), however, is only open between May 1 and 5, when all of the paintings, statues, and documents are brought out for their yearly airing.

OF SPECIAL INTEREST   There are no gardens of note at Jingoji, but the path down the valley, over the Kiyotaki river, and up Mount Takao is especially beautiful. The greenery in May and the changing maples in October and November make this area one of the most extraordinary in all of Kyoto. The Main Gate (Rōmon), the Main Hall (Kondō), the Five Great Kings Hall (Godaidō), and the Pagoda of Many Treasures (Tahōtō) are especially nice. There are many remarkable statues at Jingoji, but the historical documents dating from the Heian period (794–1185) which are stored here are Jingoji's pride. The previously noted portraits of Minamoto no Yoritomo and Taira no Kiyomori also deserve particular attention.

LOCATION AND TRANSPORTATION   Takao-chō, Umegahata, Ukyō-ku, Kyoto. Jingoji is located in the mountainous
northwest section of Kyoto. Take the city bus 8 or the National
Railways bus to Takao. It is a twenty-minute walk from the bus
stop.

神護寺　　京都市右京区梅ガ畑高雄町

SOUTHERN KYOTO

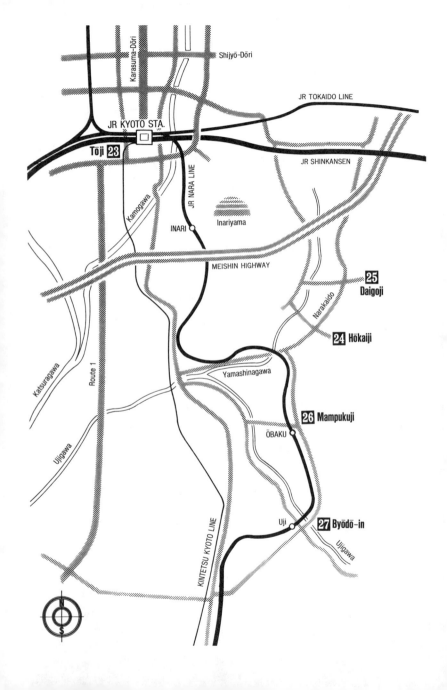

23. Tōji

The novelist Ryōtarō Shiba wrote about Tōji in his essay called "Grounds Replete with History": "Tōji is the best departure point for a pilgrimage to Kyoto's old temples, for it is here that the oldest remaining buildings from the ancient capital, Heiankyō, can be seen. Looking at the founder's Hall (Mieidō), which is much older than places like the Imperial Palace, I get the feeling that it is a kind of courtesy towards Kyoto to start here and then move on to other places. This is how one best gets acquainted. Perhaps what I feel in my heart for Kūkai (774–835; also called Kōbō Daishi) is not without some connection to this feeling of acquaintanceship with the founder's Hall."

As a symbol of the ancient capital, Tōji's huge five-storied pagoda retains its dignified air despite the recent construction of tall buildings in Kyoto. The Kōrokan, a government reception hall, was originally constructed at the entrance to the capital where Tōji now stands. Its modern equivalent might be the Akasaka Imperial Guest House in Tokyo or a reception hall in a high-class Beijing hotel. It is enjoyable to recall history of times as old as the Kōrokan while making a pilgrimage to the old temples.

The large earthen wall around Tōji is wonderful. The layers of history seem to have been plastered on one after the other. The Kōrokan was a government edifice predating Tōji, and it

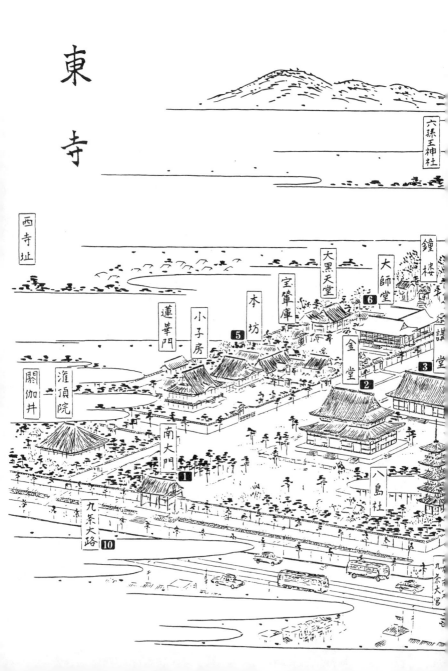

東寺

六孫王神社

西寺址

鐘楼

大黒天堂

大師堂 **6**

宝菩提堂

宝筆庫

本坊 **5**

金堂 **2**

3

蓮華門

小子房

潅頂院

閼伽井

南大門 **1**

八島社

九条大路 **10**

九条大宮

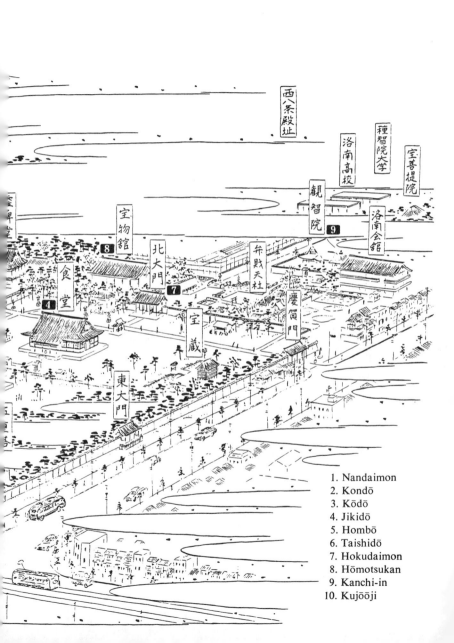

西八条殿址

種智院大学

洛南高校

宝菩提院

観智院

洛南会舘

9

宝物館

8

北大門

食堂

弁財天社

7

4

宝蔵

慶賀門

東大門

1. Nandaimon
2. Kondō
3. Kōdō
4. Jikidō
5. Hombō
6. Taishidō
7. Hokudaimon
8. Hōmotsukan
9. Kanchi-in
10. Kujōōji

reminds us of the long history of this area. The structural magnificence of the Main Gate (Nandaimon), the Main Hall (Kondō), the Lecture Hall (Kōdō), and the Dining Hall (Jikidō), which are all surrounded by the large earthen wall, did not exist until after 823 when Kūkai came here to live. This is not surprising, since nothing could have happened at this site without this great man of religion.

"Tōji was bestowed upon me by Emperor Kōnin (r. 770–81). The great joy that I feel as a result of receiving this is unsurpassable. We have brought to fruition a place of practice for the esoteric teachings. Let us exert even greater effort now." These words can be found in Kūkai's last testament. At that time, Tōji, also known as Kyōō Gokokuji, came into being as a government-supported temple.

The green of the large camphor trees rises into the midsummer sky like a gigantic column of clouds glistening beautifully. The five-storied pagoda, a National Treasure, is located to the right where one enters the grounds from the south while the main hall ahead towers into the sky. To what extent have Yakushi, the Buddha of Healing, and his two attendants, Gakkō and Nikkō, enshrined in this hall relieved the sufferings of humankind throughout time?

There have been long-endured hardships—from fires which ravaged the city during various wars and disturbances, to famines and plagues, to disasters and natural calamities. But Yakushi has kept constant guard over the southern entrance to the ancient capital in order to relieve the sufferings of its citizens.

The entire world of the esoteric teachings is on display in the Lecture Hall. In the middle are five Buddhas, with Dainichi, the Buddha who first expounded the esoteric teachings, in the center. On the right are five bodhisattvas, while on the left are the Go Dai Myōō, or Five Great Kings of Light, with Fudō Myōō, a manifestation of Dainichi, in the center. Their very presence is a manifestation of the extraordinary world view of esoteric Buddhism.

Filled with a fearful awe, I completely forgot the ordinary world the instant I stepped into this hall. To be so moved by the magnificence of the esoteric forms is fine, but fear of the world those forms represent precedes all else. Perhaps this is a fear of humanity itself and will prove to be the impetus that will force each of us to see our own humanity in those around us.

Standing in front of the Five Great Kings of Light and the Shitennō, the Four Guardian Kings, I felt the anger and resentment they must bear toward modern society. This anger appeals to the fear and trembling in each of us and inspires us to join hands in recognition of our common humanity. It leaves us no choice but to clasp our hands together in prayer and reverence.

The Great Teacher's Hall (Taishidō) where Kūkai lived lies to the northwest of the Lecture Hall. This is the same building as the previously mentioned Founder's Hall. After the intense experience of the esoteric world housed in the Main Hall, it is a great relief to see the neat, simple hip-and-gable roof of the Founder's Hall. Walking among the trails of incense smoke, one senses that this relief also comes from the fact that Kūkai actually lived here. Setting aside the origin and history of the establishment of the Founder's Hall, one can see the figure of the man whom the common people venerated so simply and forthrightly. When I first stood in front of this hall, I felt the presence of Kyōō Gokokuji as a temple built for the protection of the nation as well as its more popular status as Kūkai's temple.

Tōji really is Kūkai's temple. On the twenty-first of each month his death is commemorated there. The people of Kyoto anxiously await Kūkai's day.

Historian Naokatsu Nakamura (1900–77) writes about this day: "Ordinarily, the common people have few diversions. For these people who work diligently, exerting themselves year-round, for the citizens of Kyoto who live and die here, the northern part of the city is protected by the god Tenjin, while the southern part is taken care of by Kūkai on the twenty-first of each month. It is great fun to go there and wander around looking at the various stalls packed into the temple grounds, searching and buying, wallet in hand, ready for the next purchase."

The grounds are also filled with simple, sincere men and women who make pilgrimages to the Great Teacher's Hall, offer money and sticks of incense, and pray for recovery from illness by rubbing the incense smoke onto the part of their body that is troubling them.

Humbly they pray for tranquility during this life and favorable conditions in their future lives. I wonder if there is anything more than this for us? Watching these people make their supplications, I feel like I am looking at the true buddhas.

It is Kūkai I see standing there. The belief of the common people supported the Kōrokan as a government office, Kyōō Gokokuji as a state temple, and Tōji as Kūkai's temple. Tōji will endure, with the support of the common people, as the Temple of the Great Teacher.

SECT   Tōji is the headquarters of the Tōji subsect of the Shingon sect.

ESTABLISHMENT   Founded in 796 by Kūkai.

PRINCIPAL IMAGE   Yakushi trinity.

CULTURAL PROPERTIES   The Five-storied Pagoda and Bishamonten images are National Treasures as is Kūkai's catalogue of items brought from China and a painting of the seven patriarchs of the Shingon sect. There are many Important Cultural Properties at Tōji, including the wooden Kannon image, *The Record of Tōji* (*Tōji Monjo*), and a bronze stupa and five begging bowls.

VISITING INFORMATION   The temple grounds are open all year, and the Museum (Hōmotsukan) is open twice a year, in spring and autumn.

OF SPECIAL INTEREST   The Pagoda and the Yakushi trinity image are of special interest.

LOCATION AND TRANSPORTATION   Kujō-chō, Minami-ku, Kyoto. It is near the Tōji station on the Kintetsu railway. You can also take the city bus and get off at the Tōji bus stop.

東寺　　京都市南区九条町

24. Hōkaiji

Even the village of Hino has changed a great deal. Both Daigo and Hino are near Uji, which was once considered quite remote from Kyoto, but recently the waves of urbanization have crossed over the Higashiyama mountains that border the east side of Kyoto, pushed on into Yamashina, and have finally reached the village of Hino.

Shuō Iwaki, abbot and director of religious affairs at Hōkaiji, recalls his childhood in Hino: "During my youth, the Nara highway from Ishida to Hino was surrounded on both sides by bamboo groves, tea fields, and two graveyards. I remember feeling relieved once the car left that winding road and the thatched roof of the tranquil Amida Hall came into view."

Hōkaiji is famous for the murals on the walls of the Amida Hall (Amidadō), and today a large number of art enthusiasts make visits here to see them. Nearby is Sambō-in in Daigo, and the road in the opposite direction from Hōkaiji is particularly beautiful during the cherry blossom season.

Masakazu Yamazaki of Osaka University wrote a book entitled *Daydreams at Hōkaiji,* which includes the following description: "Hōkaiji is far from palatial and its buildings are quite different from those of other temples which are mysteriously sequestered on mountainsides. But there is a simple tranquility in the way of life here. When I gazed up at the Jōchō-style Amida image—one of the representative eleventh-century sculptures in Japan—I suddenly felt the mysterious richness of human life very keenly."

The Amida Hall, as an example of early Kamakura architecture, is certainly well known. In particular, the previously mentioned murals (all National Treasures) painted on twelve different surfaces inside the hall are executed in the same style as those at Sanzen-in in Kyoto and Fukiji in Kyushu. The hall and its murals are really a treasurehouse of art.

The original intention in building Hōkaiji, however, was not to create an art museum; it was built, rather, as a devotional offering to Yakushi to incur favor during this life. That is why even today the people who make pilgrimages here are often heard to recite the poetic hymn:

> Listen, young children!
> Divine Yakushi at Hino
> Is your staff and pillar.
> Think of him as your mother
> Kindly bestowing milk.

The "mother who bestows milk" is, of course, Hōkaiji's Yakushi Hall, and men with topknots are seen feeding children on the old votive tablet offerings (*ema*) which fill the hall. The prayers of the pilgrims to Hōkaiji are directed to Yakushi for the wonderful miracle of life.

We are already in the era of the decline of the Buddhist teachings, the era known as *mappō*. According to that teaching, we should not entertain any hopes for this world. It is better to renounce it and seek salvation in the Pure Land. Such thinking in the past led to the building of temples that would serve as earthly substitutes for the Pure Land. Once these temples were built, images of Amida, the buddha of the Pure Land, were carved and enshrined within these earthly paradises. As we can see in the Phoenix Hall

法界寺

阿弥陀堂 **3**

芭蕉句碑

庫裡 **2**

倉

表門 **1**

便所

弁天社

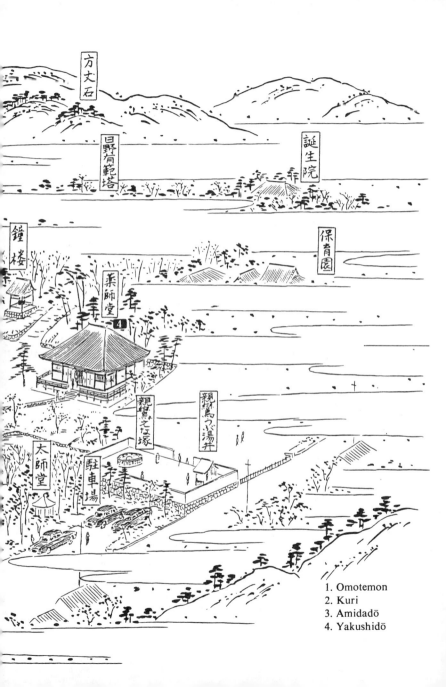

方丈石

誕生院

日野有範塔

鐘楼

保育園

薬師堂

4

親鸞えな塚

親鸞うぶ湯井

大師堂

駐車場

1. Omotemon
2. Kuri
3. Amidadō
4. Yakushidō

(Hōōdō) at Byōdōin in Uji, yearnings for the Pure Land led to a vivid path of Pure Land ideals which meant, in essence, escape from reality. Hino Sukenari (990–1070), who built Hōkaiji at a time when such thinking and ideals were widespread, enshrined Yakushi in his temple, and prayed for divine favor during his lifetime and in this world. Later, the Amida Hall shrine where one could pray for happiness in the next world and the Yakushi Hall shrine where one could pray for divine favor in this world were placed next to each other in the same building.

Perhaps it is impossible to think of anything but "that world," the world of the Pure Land, when we stop to consider the reality of *mappō*. But for Hino Sukenari, the same considerations led to a life of prayer for salvation in this world. Because this was the era of *mappō*, he was impatient to secure blessings in this life rather than wait for salvation after death. What sort of a nobleman was Hino Sukenari?

"Of course, since he was a man of that age, the concept of *mappō* was easy for him to understand. And because it was easy to understand, it was also possible to have an Amida Hall built on the temple grounds in just a few days. Sukenari was a nobleman, but he was also the perfect commoner. He had the strength of character to embrace two opposing faiths at the same time. However, even though he readily accepted the pessimistic philosophy of the Pure Land along with many other successful and accomplished noblemen of his day, it appears that whatever spiritual satisfaction he received from these beliefs was insufficient. Even if it was not for reasons of deep dissatisfaction or insinuating intent, it is still not difficult to guess why Sukenari was in a hurry to build the incredible Yakushi Hall." (from *Daydreams at Hōkaiji*)

The people who come to bathe in the beauty of the Amida Hall's architecture or its wall paintings may only be toying with a conceptual Pure Land. On the other hand, I am afraid we might also forget that there are people who come here seeking nourishment from Yakushi, the milk of a protective mother. I can't help but think how wonderful it is that prayers to Sukenari's Yakushi—also known as Chichi Yakushi, or Breast-feeding Yakushi—are still being offered today.

At the Naked Dance Festival held in January, the young men put on their white loincloths, douse themselves in cold water for purification in a ritual called *mizugori,* and push and jostle up against each other while screaming "*Chōrai, chōrai*" into the cold night wind. Theirs definitely seems to be a prayer for "this world" rather than "that world." Pregnant women take these loincloths home, use them as waistbands, and pray for an easy delivery, thus invoking the protection of Hōkaiji's Yakushi. We should not laugh at such prosaic matters. These are ingenuous and beautiful acts beyond which something greater and more profound probably lies.

The history of Hōkaiji after the Hino family followed the stormy waves of disturbances that were common to each of the succeeding periods. More important than that, though, is the fact that Hōkaiji has become a temple which continues to answer the simple prayers of the people who come here to pray. I am thankful that it still exists today for that reason more than any other.

SECT   The Daigo branch of the Shingon sect.

ESTABLISHMENT   Founded by Saichō in 1051.

PRINCIPAL IMAGE   Yakushi.

CULTURAL PROPERTIES   The Amida Hall and the wooden Amida image enshrined within it are National Treasures. The Main Hall (Hondō, also called Yakushidō), the standing Yakushi image, and the Twelve Divine Generals (Jūni Shinshō) are Important Cultural Properties.

VISITING INFORMATION   The Amida Hall and the Main

Hall are open to the public. On January 14 a Naked Dance Festival is held in front of the Amida Hall. Boys from the neighborhood gather here dressed only in loincloths. They dance and then give these cloths to pregnant women who wrap them around their stomachs in the belief that this will assure safe delivery.

OF SPECIAL INTEREST   The grounds are pleasant, but there are no gardens of note. The Amida Hall is representative of the Hogyo style of architecture in which the roof comes to a single point somewhat like the shape of a pyramid. This building was constructed in the thirteenth century. The Yakushi Hall dates from the fifteenth century. The images enshrined here and several wall paintings are all well worth seeing.

LOCATION AND TRANSPORTATION   Nishi Daido-chō, Hino, Fushimi-ku, Kyoto. Hōkaiji is located near Daigoji in the far southeastern part of the city. The most convenient way to get there is to take the Keihan train to Tambabashi and then take either a taxi or a Keihan Bus going to Hino Tanjō-in and get off at Hino Yakushi Mae.

法界寺　　京都市伏見区日野西大道町

25. Daigoji

Yasushi Inoue, the well-known author, wrote about Daigoji in an essay entitled "Pagodas and Cherry Blossoms: Mountaintop Buddhist Monasteries": "I know now that I should have seen Upper Daigo much sooner. Considering the history of Daigoji as well as the various situations surrounding its beliefs and legends, there's no doubt that it all began at Upper Daigo. Of course, this is obvious, but it can't really be understood until one actually visits here.

"The placement of the temple buildings on the mountaintop and hillside is magnificent. Buddhist mountain sects have always arranged their temple buildings in this fashion. I expected it from the various photographs and pictures I'd seen, but it is difficult to comprehend its importance unless you actually walk around to each of the halls climbing and descending the steep slopes on your own two feet."

What is this "importance" that Inoue is referring to? Daigo is at the base of a mountain where a valley extending between Higashiyama and Mount Osaka spans out connecting the area to Uji. Residential housing has proliferated into town now, but at one time the area was continuous on to the remote village of Daigo. South of here is Mimurodo where Mampukuji, the head

醍醐寺

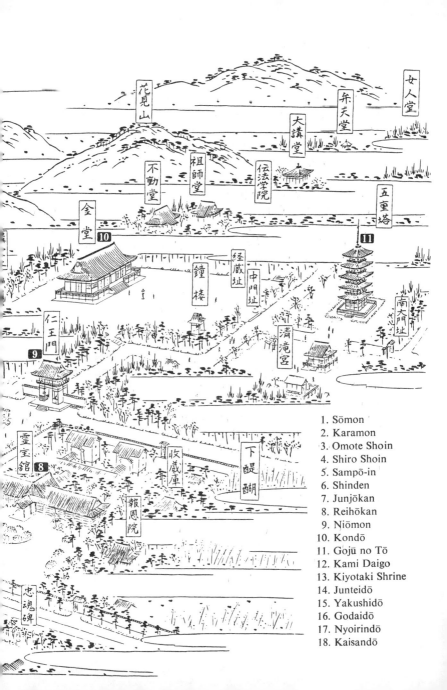

1. Sōmon
2. Karamon
3. Omote Shoin
4. Shiro Shoin
5. Sampō-in
6. Shinden
7. Junjōkan
8. Reihōkan
9. Niōmon
10. Kondō
11. Gojū no Tō
12. Kami Daigo
13. Kiyotaki Shrine
14. Junteidō
15. Yakushidō
16. Godaidō
17. Nyoirindō
18. Kaisandō

temple of the Ōbaku Zen sect, is located. The road passes by there and leads on to Uji.

Any mention of Daigo usually brings to mind Toyotomi Hideyoshi's cherry-viewing party of 1598. Since that time, Daigo's image as a well-known cherry-viewing place has replaced all others. For instance, there is also Daigoji's pagoda. The area around Daigo with its mountainside greenery is impressive, but with the pagoda amidst it all as a symbol for the temple, it looks majestic in its beauty.

But why was Inoue looking for "something important" about Daigoji at Upper Daigo?

I went with him to Upper Daigo (also known as Inner Daigo) on a humid day in late May before the rainy season began.

The slope to Upper Daigo winds its way up the hillside like a vine past the area where Hideyoshi supposedly laid out one thousand mats for his cherry-viewing party.

All kinds of people, irrespective of age or sex, climb this slope. Some walk robustly while others lag behind. Almost everybody is a pilgrim on his journey to the thirty-three sacred spots in western Japan. Maybe it was just the rays of the sun shining through the luxuriantly overgrown trees, but everyone seemed to have a look of ecstasy on his face.

After two hours of climbing slopes that were sometimes very steep and then became gentle, we reached Kōdō Pass. Here we no longer felt the air of the mundane world. Perhaps it would be better to call it "mountain air" or the "air of sacredness." In the distant hills between the trees, the tiles on the roofs of the Founder's Hall (Kaisandō), the Nyoirin Kannon Hall (Nyoirindō), and the Hall of the Five Great Deities (Godaidō) would come in and out of view. Suddenly, it was a more spacious world and one which rendered us speechless with surprise.

The feet of our guide, Priest Saitō, the head of education at Daigoji, were really light and fast. This might have been because our own feet were still ensnared by the numerous restraints of the mundane world.

The mountain air in the morning at the temple lodgings was invigorating, so we took this opportunity to worship at various halls that were located on the hillside: the Juntei Kannon Hall (Junteidō), the Yakushi Hall (Yakushidō), Kiyotaki Hall, Gongen the Worship Hall (Haiden), the Nyoirin Kannon Hall, the Founder's Hall, and the Hall of the Five Great Deities. Magnolias, which at first looked like lotus blossoms, shone through the trees and gave off a sweet fragrance.

The founding of Daigoji begins here in Upper Daigo. Inoue says, "There are stories and legends about the founding of Daigoji and it is strange that they can be comprehended quite naturally by coming to Upper Daigo and pondering them. They don't necessarily represent truth or reality, but they become a part of us here, believable in the form that they are written."

In other words, the existence of these stories and legends is inseparable from the place in which they originated. Perhaps that is their strength or mystery.

Rigen (d. 909), the founder of Daigoji, found his way to this sacred ground when looking for an auspicious place in which to propagate Kūkai's teachings. And here in a deep valley where the sky was hidden from view, Rigen encountered Yokoo Myōjin, the protector deity of the area, at a mysterious waterfall. We should regard this chance meeting as the path to those gods who protect the esoteric teachings.

It is said that this mountain is a place of extraordinary beauty from which the enlightened ones of the past can spread the teachings, a holy mountain which the gods in heaven always protect. This should not be strange since Daigoji is sacred ground manifest with spiritual power.

The history of Daigoji begins with Rigen's meeting with the sacred. According to legend, this occurred in 876. The history of the temple from that time is related in detail in the legends. Its incredible heritage of temple buildings, paintings, sculptures, and literary documents also recorded much of Daigoji's history. Six of Daigoji's remaining buildings have been designated National Treasures and five have been designated Important Cultural Properties. These, together with the roof tiles from ninety other buildings that have not survived, tell us a great deal about Daigoji's history since the Heian period (794–1185).

There are innumerable national and cultural treasures among the paintings, sculptures, sutras, and craft objects that have been preserved here. In particular, over one hundred thousand volumes of documents have helped us to chronicle the moments of Japanese history.

In the bitter February cold, great crowds of people gather for the festival of Godairiki. Gazing upon the astounding number of believers, you get dragged into the chaos of religious energy that human beings seek and that they respond to. Daigoji's buildings may have been burned to the ground during political upheavals and its valuable statues may have been lost, but the fire that ignites belief will not go out as long as there are people to keep it burning.

SECT   Headquarters of the Daigo branch of the Shingon sect.

ESTABLISHMENT   Founded by Rigen in 874.

PRINCIPAL IMAGE   Yakushi.

CULTURAL PROPERTIES   The Five-storied Pagoda (Gojū no Tō) and the Yakushi trinity are National Treasures. In addition, there are numerous Important Cultural Properties, including sutra scrolls and mandala paintings in the esoteric tradition.

VISITING INFORMATION   The cherry-blossom season in

spring and the greenery in the early months of summer are particularly beautiful. The Reihō Museum (Hōju-in) is open from the beginning of April to the end of May and from the beginning of October to the end of November. Sambō-in, a subtemple of Daigoji, is also open to the public twice a year in the spring and the autumn. The Godairiki Festival is held at Inner Daigo on February 23. Participation in this festival is thought to help prevent the intrusion of thieves and various other misfortunes. During the cherry-blossom season, a procession of people dressed in costumes of the Muromachi period reenact at Sambō-in the great cherry-viewing party held by Toyotomi Hideyoshi in 1598.

OF SPECIAL INTEREST   The garden at Sambō-in was built by Toyotomi Hideyoshi and is one of the most representative gardens in all of Japan. Unlike many Zen-influenced rock gardens which are to be observed from a fixed position outside the garden, this garden was built to be enjoyed while walking through it. The Five-storied Pagoda, the Chinese Gate (Karamon), and the Main Hall (Kondō) are all National Treasures. In general, the buildings at Daigoji are representative of Momoyama-period Buddhist architecture. The Yakushi, Thousand-armed Kannon, and Amida images are all National Treasures. There are a great many other statues, paintings, and mandalas which have been designated National Treasures and which can be seen in the Museum.

LOCATION AND TRANSPORTATION   Daigo Garan-chō, Fushimi-ku, Kyoto. Located at the base of Mount Daigo near Uji City in the southeast part of Kyoto. Take the Kyoto city bus (East 8, 9, or 21) or the Keihan bus to Samboin Mae.

醍醐寺　　京都市伏見区醍醐伽藍町

26. Mampukuji

Once you pass through Mampukuji's Main Gate (Sammon), the buildings and their environs are all Chinese in style. Having only traveled through the central and southern parts of the Chinese countryside, I cannot claim to be an expert, but I felt at Mampukuji a kind of nostalgia for that Chinese countryside. Compared to Japanese temple grounds, the grounds here seemed more clearly defined. That is to say, the temple grounds and the area outside the temple grounds seemed to have been well demarcated. Despite the fact that they have walls (without which entrance fees could not be collected) that divide the grounds from the rest of the world, it still seems that Japanese temples are more accessible, lacking a clear demarcation between the inside and the outside. It almost seems as if the quality or density of the air itself is the same inside the grounds and out.

On the other hand, you might feel that this isn't Japan at all once you've entered the grounds of Mampukuji, such is the intensity of the "Chineseness" here. The temple that we see before us today is still a reflection of its founder, Yinyuan (1592–1673; Japanese, Ingen), who was raised, entered the priesthood, and practiced *zazen* in the province of Fujing in China.

Japanese Zen begins in the Kamakura period with Eisai (1141–1215), Dōgen (1200–53), and the prosperity of the five great Zen temples of Kamakura and Kyoto. It continued to prosper through the Muromachi and Momoyama periods and survived into the Edo period. It was during the reign of the fifth Tokugawa shogun, Tsunayoshi (1646–1709), that Yinyuan came to Japan and established Mampukuji. This was during the Ming dynasty in China, in the year 1660.

Even today, all of the sutras at Mampukuji are read in a Japanized version of Chinese Tang-dynasty pronunciation:

JAPANIZED TANG PRONUNCIATION	MODERN JAPANESE PRONUNCIATION
Kimpei dachon	*Kimpaku taishū*
Sunsu jida	*Shōji jidai*
Ujiyani shinso	*Mujō jinsoku*
Koki shinsa	*Kakugi seikaku*
Shintsu fan'i	*Shimbutsu hōitsu*

I respectfully say to everyone:
Birth, old age, sickness, and death are constant;
The weak follow the strong.
Life is fleeting and death comes quickly.
Each of us should wake up from the delusions under
 which we live.
Be moderate in one's life and never self-indulgent.

The temple services and ceremonies at Mampukuji are all conducted in the Chinese style as well. These traditions were strictly observed by the monks who crossed the sea from China as Yinyuan had. The decision to have Mampukuji built on this land was intertwined with various complicated political, economic, and diplomatic concerns of the ruling Tokugawa government. In one sense, these concerns were the entanglements of political authority and religion.

These entanglements made it possible for a Chinese temple to

萬福寺

五雲峰 **10**

威徳殿

甘露殿

西方丈　法堂 **9**　東方丈

浴室

祠堂

大雄宝殿 **6**

禅堂 **5**

慰霊塔

五雲房　黄竜閣

斎堂　寺務所 **7**

庫裡 **8**

伽藍堂

聖林院

天王殿 **4**

月台

鐘楼

東林院

瑞光院

黄梅樹

鼓樓堂

法林院

元茶堂

文華殿 **3**

便所

有声軒

天真院

1. Sōmon
2. Sammon
3. Bunkaden
4. Tennōden
5. Zendō
6. Daiyūhōden
7. Jimusho
8. Kuri
9. Hattō
10. Goun Peak

be built in Japan. Among the innumerable intertwinings between political authority and religious sects after the Heian period—such as the political power of the Tendai and Shingon sects, the connections of the Rinzai and Sōtō Zen sects with the *daimyo,* and the recent rise to prominence of the Pure Land sects—there is deep historical significance to the fact that Mampukuji was built for priests who had come from China. This is also proven by the fact that most of the chief priests of the temple were Chinese from the time it was founded by Yinyuan until the late eighteenth century, when the bakufu was losing ground with the people.

There is no end to the number of eminent priests who have lived here. Muan Xingdu (1611–84), Jifei Ruyi (1616–71), Huilin Xingji (1608–81), Duzhan Xingying (1627–1706), and Gaoxuan Xing-huang (1633–96), for example, were all Ming-dynasty priests who left their mark on the distinctive combination of nembutsu and Zen practice that evolved in the Edo period (1600–1868). Recalling them, we can't help but think of the role which Obaku Zen performed.

As the center of the Obaku Zen sect and of Chinese culture in Japan, Mampukuji played a large role in the world of letters and culture.

In the art of calligraphy, the three great artists are said to have been Yin, Mu, and Ji (in Japanese, In, Moku, and Soku)—or Yinyuan, Muan, and Jifei. The numerous extant works of their calligraphy bring to mind the vigorous and generous spirit of this sect.

Calligraphy also means literature. We can't very well ignore the numerous Chinese poems that surely rival those of the Five Great Zen Temples (Gozan Bungaku) period. And then there is also the publication of the entire Buddhist canon in wood blocks by Tieyan Daoguang (Japanese, Tetsugen Dōkō; 1630–82) as well as the various carvings and paintings which serve to make Mampukuji a center of Chinese culture.

Chinese-style vegetarian cooking is still practiced at Mampukuji today, which is why some people call it the Temple of the Full Stomach, since the Chinese characters of the temple's name are homophonous with other characters that mean "full stomach." The food is extremely delicious.

From somewhere I seem to hear a voice calling out in Chinese, "Please drink some tea before you go." It is said that the Obaku priest Gekkai Gensho (1675–1763), or Baiso Ō, "the Venerable Tea Seller," as he is more commonly called, popularized green tea in this area. The taste of a cup of tea after a Chinese vegetarian meal is very special, and Mampukuji is a very special temple among Japan's many Zen monasteries.

SECT   Ōbaku Zen sect.

ESTABLISHMENT: Founded by Yinyuan, a Ming-dynasty Chinese priest, in 1654.

PRINCIPAL IMAGE   Shakamuni.

CULTURAL PROPERTIES   All of the structures at Mampukuji have been designated Important Cultural Properties.

VISITING INFORMATION   Mampukuji is a good example of a Chinese-style Zen monastery. There are many religious celebrations here each month and there are also periods of ongoing zazen practice in which laymen can take part. For further information about both, contact the main office. It is also possible to have a meal of the Chinese-style vegetarian cooking famous at Mampukuji. If you are a group of four or more contact the temple at 0774–32–3900 anytime except July, August, the end of December, or the beginning of January. There are also vegetarian-style restaurants outside but near the temple grounds.

OF SPECIAL INTEREST   There are no gardens of special

interest, but the general layout of the temple grounds is quite extraordinary. The buildings as well as the grounds are also in the Chinese style and deserve careful note.

LOCATION AND TRANSPORTATION   Sambanwari, Gokano-shō, Uji-shi. Mampukuji is located near either of two Ōbaku stations, one on the Japan National Railways and the other on the Keihan Railway. It is a short walk from either.

萬福寺　宇治市五ヶ庄三番割

27. Byōdō-in

"If you long for Paradise, then pay your respects at the noble temple in Uji." "It is said that when you look at Byōdō-in, you are looking at the majesty of Paradise. It is no wonder that it is so famous." Comments such as these are common in ancient documents. They seem to mean that it was difficult for people to grasp what the Pure Land was actually like even though they wished to be reborn there.

Byōdō-in, located in Uji in the southern part of Kyoto, has an image of Amida, the Buddha of Infinite Light, sculpted by the Heian-period artist Jōchō enshrined in the Phoenix Hall (Hōōdō). The walls that surround this image feature fifty-two figures known as *kuyōbutsu,* or bodhisattvas making offerings, who are playing musical instruments. These figures have been bequeathed to us today from the Western Paradise.

Fujiwara no Yorimichi (992–1074) thought that one's longing for the Pure Land, or paradise, grew deeper with time. We don't know whether he had the Phoenix Hall built to mourn the death of his father, Fujiwara no Michinaga (966–1027), or to display his own political power, or if he was attempting to bring paradise into this world. Whatever the case may be, the flapping of the wings of the mythical phoenix, known as the *kalavinka* in India,

最勝院

淨土院
本堂
3

養林庵書院

頼政墓
通圓墓
鳳凰堂
2

頼政碑

室物館
4

鐘樓

阿彌陀水

出口

1. Omotemon
2. Hōōdō
3. Jōdo-in
4. Hōmotsukan
5. Kannondō
6. Aji Pond
7. Uji River
8. Tachibana Island

平等院

寺務所
寺門
①

便所

受付

観音堂 ⑤
扇の芝

阿字池 ⑥

橘島 ⑧

宇治川 ⑦

along with the musical performances of the celestial *kuyōbutsu* were said to rouse one's desire for the Pure Land.

An overwhelming number of visitors come to Byōdō-in. It is estimated that as many as 1.2 million visit this temple each year. What do these visitors think about this place? What do they perceive and what remains etched in their minds when they leave?

> My humble hut lies
> Tucked away in the Uji hills—
> A simple hermit's life
> It is indeed, though they all
> Say "How sad to leave this world!"

Is present-day Uji the same one we find in this poem by Kisen, who lived during the Konin era (810–24)? Is it the same Uji after which the last chapters of *The Tale of Genji* were named? All of that is beyond my scope here, but I do hope that Byōdō-in will be proof that paradise was created on this earth.

Hiroshi Miyagi, the chief priest at Byōdō-in, remarked about Byōdō-in's historical and artistic stature: "When you enter the Phoenix Hall, you are greeted by Jōchō's Amida image and a host of endearing bodhisattvas. These sculptures, paintings, and craft products, which form the essence of Fujiwara art, surround the worshiper to form a total environment. The image of Yorimichi sitting in front of this statue and praying for rebirth in the Pure Land comes to mind along with all the splendor and majesty that must have existed in those days."

Byōdō-in's sect affiliation is not an issue. The heart of a pilgrimage lies in the discovery of spiritual roots.

The idea that *mappō*—the era of the degeneration of the Buddhist teachings—had begun reflected the uncertainties in the Heian period and formed the basis of Pure Land beliefs. The well-known Pure Land work by Genshin (942–1017), *The Essentials of Salvation* (*Ōjōyōshū*), helped to spread this sense of imminent danger to all classes of people. Since "this world" was defiled, there was nothing else to depend on but the Pure Land.

Even though the aristocratic class proclaimed their disgust for the defilements of "this world" and sought salvation in the Pure Land, they were still exhilarated by the glories of Heian society. This meant that they wished to make their connections with the Pure Land in "this world" rather than "that world."

The extravagant Amida Hall built by Fujiwara no Michinaga at Hōjōji is a sufficient reminder that paradise in "this world" was what the aristocrats sought. In that way, they hoped to extend "this world" and their influence into "that world." That's why Byōdō-in, which was built outside the capital in Uji by Yorimichi, was basically no different in conception from Hōjōji, which was built on the Kamo River in Kyoto by his father.

In the distance beyond the shallows of the Uji River lies the lush green of mounts Asahi and Buttoku to the east. When the morning sun rises from behind them, it shines beautifully on the Phoenix Hall. Sandwiching the Uji River between it and the mountains, the eastern banks of the river emerge as "this world" while the western banks and Byōdō-in emerge as "that world." Hōjōji was situated in exactly the same manner.

The first priest to be the head of Byōdō-in was Myōson (d. 1063), the former head priest of Onjōji. Many priests were undoubtedly present there at this time and numerous Buddhist services were held. One can imagine it just as it is depicted in the scrolls: processions of monks circling the lake in front of the Phoenix Hall, flowers raining down upon them, and small dragon- and bird-shaped boats floating in the water while musicians and *bugaku* dancers performed.

About this, Miyagi says, "The aristocrats and their wives who were in the procession probably felt like they were in paradise itself. Byōdō-in was, at this time, both a sacred place where one could pray for rebirth in the Pure Land and a place for grand parties. This harmonized splendidly while giving birth to an aesthetic state of rapture."

Byōdō-in seems to have transformed the reveries on my pilgrimage into excursions into the philosophy, literature, art, and music of the late Heian period.

SECT   Tendai and Jōdo.

ESTABLISHMENT   Founded by Fujiwara no Yorimichi in 1052.

PRINCIPAL IMAGE   Amida.

CULTURAL PROPERTIES   National Treasures include the Phoenix Hall, the Amida image, and the *kuyōbutsu,* or bodhisattvas playing musical instruments.

VISITING INFORMATION   Byōdō-in is open to visitors throughout the year.

OF SPECIAL INTEREST   The Āji Pond, laid out in the shape of the Sanskrit letter "Ā" (a symbol of unity), separates "this world," the world of suffering and confusion, from "that world," the world of the Pure Land, symbolized by the Phoenix Hall. Visitors here should walk around the lake taking into consideration this arrangement in order to appreciate the Heian-period idea of paradise. The Phoenix Hall is built in the shape of a phoenix with its wings spread. This shape was meant to make us think of the Western Paradise, and is an excellent example of illusionary architecture. Facing the Āji Pond, the Amida image is situated to face the suffering sentient beings of "this world."

LOCATION AND TRANSPORTATION   Uji Renge, Uji-shi. Byōdō-in is located on the Uji River in Uji City, which is southeast of Kyoto. The fastest way to get there is to take the Keihan train to Uji (the last stop) and walk about seven minutes.

平等院　　宇治市宇治蓮華

NARA

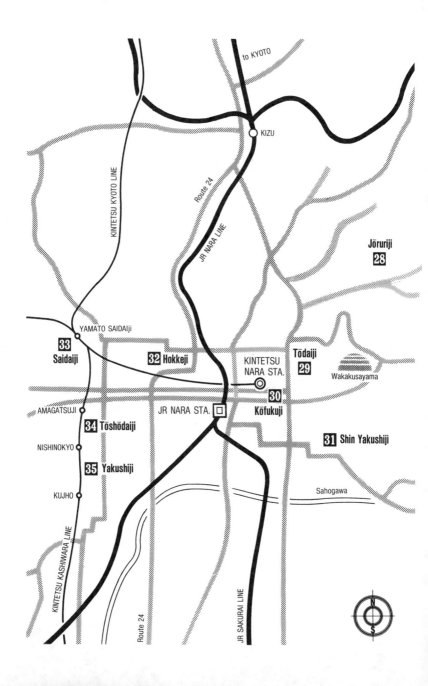

28. Jōruriji

The village of Nishio, Kamochō in the Soraku district is on the prefectural border between Kyoto and Nara. The gently sloping hills here rise and fall along a tranquil horizon. Jōruriji seems to be waiting there quietly for the next pilgrim's footsteps.

According to the current prefectural maps, Jōruriji is in Kyoto Municipal District, but the road from Nara is nearby. Maybe that's why the general environment is somewhat different from that of Kyoto's old temples.

The Kasagi Highway takes you to Jōruriji through the mountain village of Kasagi and the Yamashiro district after passing over the Nara Slope.

On my way to Jōruriji, I recalled a poem by Yaichi Aizu (1881–1956), poet, calligrapher, and artist:

> The raindrops trickle
> Off the chin of the stone Buddha
> Here on Nara Slope—
> This light drizzle signals
> The beginning of spring.

The Nara Slope is also called Utahimegoe (Song Princess' Pass) and Hannyajizaka (Wisdom Temple Slope). The road to Ya-

浄瑠璃寺

南大門址

弁才天社

三重塔
5

石灯篭

1. Sōmon
2. Shoin
3. Kuri
4. Hondō
5. Sanjū no Tō

mashiro seems to weave through the hills. This reminded me of another of Aizu's poems:

> About to ascend
> The steep Nara Slope to
> Jōruri Temple,
> Be careful not to fall
> On the slippery red clay.

The muddy clay that covered this road must have made it rather troublesome to climb in the old days. Undoubtedly pilgrims would sometimes slip and fall on the gravel and clay path. The second poem by Aizu appeared in his poetical work *The Cry of the Deer* (*Rokumeishū*).

Nobody worries about slipping and falling these days, but perhaps that sort of environment is a more suitable one for pilgrims.

The novelist Tatsuo Hori (1904–58) writes in his essay "Spring at Jōruriji": "At first we very nearly passed by there without noticing that the modest gate was a temple gate. Just at that moment, though, we were startled by something inside the gate from atop a blooming peach tree. It flew off in a flash, but its wings were of colors I had never seen before. I was stunned and stopped dead in my tracks. Directly in my line of vision was the rusted ornamental pole (*kurin*) atop Jōruriji's pagoda."

This was in the spring of 1943 and the violets and other spring flowers were in full bloom.

What a beautiful word *jōruri* (lapis lazuli) is! The eastern Pure Land is called the Jōruri Pure Land. This is where the buddha of healing, Yakushi, presides. On the opposite side, Amida, the buddha of infinite light, resides over the western Pure Land. In between, human beings carry on their worldly affairs. A lake is sandwiched between the Three-storied pagoda (Sanjū no Tō) and the Main Hall (Hondō) to the west where the Yakushi and Amida images respectively are enshrined. The roofs of both buildings are reflected clearly on the surface of the water. The four figures surrounding Amida are stretching out their hands to guide the pilgrim on his way to the Pure Land. Since there are nine Amidas enshrined here, Jōruriji is commonly referred to as the Nine-image Temple (Kutaiji).

Yakushi is situated in the east as a reminder of our past while Amida is situated in the west as encouragement for the future.

Kaishō Saeki, the chief priest at Jōruriji, has remarked: "The equinoctial days are those when Yakushi settles the karmic consequences of our past and brings us forth into the present. He serves as a kind of medicine to give us the strength to overcome the suffering in our lives. The equinox is also when Amida receives us in Paradise. Twice a year, once in the spring and once in the autumn, we are connected to them by the solar orbit. On these days we can seek salvation from our daily suffering by accepting Yakushi's healing powers. We can also turn to the west and pray for Amida's grace to lead us to Paradise."

This temple with the beautiful name was first established in 1047. At that time the world was thought to be entering the period of degeneration of the Buddhist teaching known as *mappō*. It was a time in which people were turning from their belief in this world (as represented by Yakushi) to belief in the next (as represented by Amida).

Looking at the image of Kichijōten, the goddess who gives happiness and virtue to men, is an otherworldly experience. It is enshrined on a platform as if representing female elegance itself. Since Kichijōten is generally kept from public view and is thought to control the success of the grain harvests, her presence provokes reverence in those who see her.

As a representation of female beauty from the ancient past, the image of Kichijōten is sacred, sublime, and richly suggestive. Blood actually seems to be flowing under its white surface. The small lips which seem ready to speak are vivid yet delicate. Its eyebrows are drawn in a halfmoon arc. The eyes slant upwards. It is an amalgam of all the qualities of classical beauty.

In *Miraculous Tales of Japan* (*Nihon Ryōiki*), a Nara-period collection of Buddhist tales of karma and retribution, we read the following: "Stealing a glance at this heavenly beauty brings on an ardent longing. Carrying this love deep in my heart, everyday I wish for a woman whose face I will love as much as I do the heavenly beauty's."

As the wellspring of life, Kichijōten is a deity befitting Jōruriji. She resides both in Yakushi's eastern land and in Amida's western paradise. When I woke up from this dream, drunk with Kichijōten's beauty, for the first time I was grateful for this pilgrimage to the old temples.

SECT   Shingon Ritsu.

ESTABLISHMENT   Founded by Gimei in 1047.

PRINCIPAL IMAGE   Amida.

CULTURAL PROPERTIES   The nine Amida images are all National Treasures, as is the Main Hall (Hondō). The Kichijōten image is an Important Cultural Property and is quite famous.

VISITING INFORMATION   Jōruriji is open throughout the year. Between January 1 and January 15, March 21 and May 20, and November 1 and November 30, the Kichijōten image is on view to the public.

OF SPECIAL INTEREST   The gardens here are in the *chisen kaiyū* style. The Main Hall is representative of the Heian-period-style Amida Hall. The Amida, Yakushi, Four Guardian Kings, and Kichijōten images constitute a veritable museum of Heian-period Buddhist sculpture.

LOCATION AND TRANSPORTATION   Kamo-chō, Sōraku-gun, Kyoto fu. Jōruriji is located in the southern part of Kyoto Municipal District near Nara Prefecture. For that reason, it is more convenient to take a Nara Kōtsu Bus from the Nara National Railway Station and get off at Jōruriji Mae, the last stop on the route.

浄瑠璃寺　　京都市相楽郡加茂町

29. Tōdaiji

There are many religious relics that have been passed down to us and that survive even today. From four of the world's great religions—Buddhism, Christianity, Islam, and Taoism—we have numerous legacies that are physical evidence of religious faith. However, among the religions of the world which preceded these or which have disappeared completely, there are a number of puzzling remains: for example, Borobudur, Angkor Wat, Hindu remains in India, and the relics of the pre-Inca religions in South America. There are innumerable places like these throughout the Middle and Near East and Africa. The popular excitement about the Silk Road is a prime example of how interested we are in this kind of thing. I wonder how many valuable religious relics are still buried beneath that sandy sea?

Why do people build religious monuments in the name of faith? It is difficult to prevent thoughts like these when you are standing in front of Tōdaiji's huge Indian-style South Gate (Nandaimon).

The 1,200-year anniversary of the Great Buddha at Tōdaiji was celebrated in the fall of 1952. At that time, a book entitled *Birushana,* the Japanese name for the major buddha of the Tantric tradition, Vairocana, was published in which pertinent data about the Great Buddha Hall was recorded. For example, it is 164 feet from north to south and the same length from east to west. The building is also 164 feet high and its ten columns are 98.4 feet long and 4.92 feet in diameter. There are forty thousand sets of brackets and seven hundred coffers in the ceiling, several thousands of pieces of lattice work, and 112,508 roof tiles. The Great Buddha itself weighs approximately 2,481 tons.

The Great Buddha Hall is the largest wooden structure in the world and there is really no way to express how big it is except by citing numbers.

In 1969 an enormous restoration project of the Hall was started and it eventually took eleven years to complete. In order to retile the roof, a temporary roof (which alone cost $5.76 million) was constructed. After the retiling was finished, the temporary roof then had to be disassembled, of course. The year before it was disassembled on a very cold, snowy day in March, I was taken to the top in the large, quiet elevator which the construction workers had been using. I remember how impressed I was by the swiftness of the elevator and by the overall size of the structure that was being repaired.

The Indian priest Bodhisena, in his efforts to spread the teaching of the Lotus Sutra throughout the world, traveled to Japan to attend the opening ceremony of the Great Buddha Hall. His arrival occurred at a time when Silk Road culture was migrating west through China and Korea. Kōshō Shimizu, the previous chief abbot of Tōdaiji, writes about Bodhisena: "Perhaps we can also explain the appearance of a copy of the Lotus Sutra that had been written in an oasis town along the Silk Road in the same way that we can explain all culture that was making its way east. Bodhisena had made his way to China in order to visit a flesh-and-blood Monju (Manjusri). In China he met a group from a Japanese diplomatic mission and ended up accompanying them back to Japan. I expect there were quests in both directions along the Silk Road in those days."

Proof of this transmission of culture along the Silk Road are

東大寺

1. Nandaimon
2. Chūmon
3. Daibutsuden
4. Shingon-in
5. Kaidan-in
6. Shōsō-in
7. Chisoku-in
8. Ryūshō-in
9. Ryūzō-in
10. Jihō-in
11. Hōgon-in
12. Kannon-in
13. Nigatsudō
14. Tamukeyama Shrine

建数社　二月堂　13　飯道社

良弁杉　興成社　湯屋　三昧堂

奏音所　岩渕井　仏餉屋　開山堂　三昧堂　法華堂　手向山神社　14

大湯屋　行基堂　念仏堂　鐘楼　観音院　12

辛国社　俊乗堂　七重塔相輪　東塔址

東楽門

中門　2　鏡池　春日野グラウンド

五百立山　真言院　4　北林院　東大寺塔址　東大寺本坊　収蔵庫　三　経庫

地蔵院　正観院　南大門　1

寧楽美術館　整服園　依水園　駐車場

the large number of Buddhist art treasures which date from the period when Tōdaiji was founded as well as the large number of treasures which are kept in the famous Shōsōin storehouse. How, I wonder, was this enormous structure dedicated to faith conceived and executed?

"I am the person who holds the wealth of this country. I am the person who holds authority over this country. As a demonstration of that wealth and authority, I decree that this image shall be constructed." Such was the awesome spirit of Emperor Shōmu (r. 724–49), who issued this decree for the construction of the Great Buddha and its Hall. "Use all the copper in the land; melt down all the images in the land. . . . If I die before this image is completed, it is still my wish that it be finished." Emperor Shōmu hoped to unify the country through the Buddhist religion that had just recently entered Japan. To facilitate and symbolize this, he had this huge religious monument built. The Great Buddha, or Birushana, is a fitting symbol since it occupies the center of the lotus world.

> At Tōdaiji
> The burning candles pay homage
> To the Buddha.
> How wonderful to wait here
> For Shōmu to make his visit.

This poem by Yaichi Aizu (1881–1956) comes from the eve of the dedication ceremony to the new hall when over 15,700 lanterns were ablaze in front of Birushana and over 10,000 priests were offering lotus blossoms. Similarly, in the histories from more than 1,200 years ago, there is a passage about the opening of Tōdaiji which reads: "Since the teachings came east from India and China, there has never been a ceremony as grand as this."

Restoration of the Great Buddha Hall was completed on October 15, 1980. It looked quite majestic against the blue sky that day. I wrote the following then: "The unveiling began with a hymn of praise to Birushana, with a 1,200-member chorus under the direction of Ikuma Dan chanting the beautiful words written by Daigaku Horiguchi (1892–1981). During the hymn the cover over the ridge tiles was released and lotus blossoms fluttered in the sky. In this way a connection with all the people there was created. A five-colored cloth net was also draped over the roof down to the gilt ornamental end tiles which shone brightly in the sun. Who was it that conceived such a performance? And who was responsible for the original performance in 749 when the Great Buddha was first dedicated?"

SECT   Headquarters of the Kegon sect.

ESTABLISHMENT   Founded by Rōben in 741.

PRINCIPAL IMAGE   Birushana.

CULTURAL PROPERTIES   Almost all of the halls and buildings at Tōdaiji are National Treasures, but by far the center of attraction here is the Great Buddha enshrined in the Main Hall (Kondō or Daibutsuden).

VISITING INFORMATION   The grounds and halls are open to visitors all year long. The most famous ceremony here is known as Omizutori and is held from March 1 to March 14 at the Second Month Hall (Nigatsudō). There are many different aspects to this ceremony including a spectacular Fire Festival (Dattan) which is held on the evenings of the twelfth, thirteenth, and fourteenth.

OF SPECIAL INTEREST   There are no gardens of special interest, but the general layout and location of Tōdaiji is extraordinary. The Daibutsuden in which the Great Buddha is enshrined is the largest wooden structure in the world. The Main

Gate (Nandaimon) which is located at the front of the grounds was constructed in an old Indian style known as *tenjiku yō*. Tōdaiji is a treasurehouse of Buddhist images including Fukūkensaku Kannon, Nikkō, Gakkō, the Four Guardian Kings, and Fudō Myōō.

LOCATION AND TRANSPORTATION   Zōshi-chō, Nara. Tō-daiji is a twelve-minute walk from the Kintetsu Nara station.

東大寺　　奈良市雑司町

30. Kōfukuji

If you climb up Kōfukuji's Five-storied Pagoda (Gojū no Tō) and take a look around in all four directions, you can get a feeling for Nara as the ancient capital as well as the overall layout of Kōfukuji itself. Against the background of the gentle ridges of mounts Wakakusa and Mikasa lay the magnificent beauty of various temple buildings which are now just scattered about haphazardly. If we recall the numerous subtemples and the large bathhouse which were located along the outside of an open corridor together with many other buildings like the Middle Main Hall (Chūkondō), the Sutra Storage Hall (Kyōzō), the Bell Tower (Shōrō), the Lecture Hall (Kōdō), the Priests' Living Quarters (Sōbō), the North Circular Hall (Hokuendō), the General Worship Hall (Hosodono), the Dining Hall (Jikido), and the Kitchen (Sōden), we can get some idea of the unparalleled size and magnificence of this temple, which surpassed even Tōdaiji, the most famous of all state-supported temples.

But there is nothing cohesive about Kōfukuji today. The buildings just seem to be scattered about throughout Nara Park. It is difficult to get any sense of where the Main Hall or the open corridor were located or where the outer circumference of the temple grounds met the city. The temple grounds and the park are pressed right up against the large old buildings that are scat-

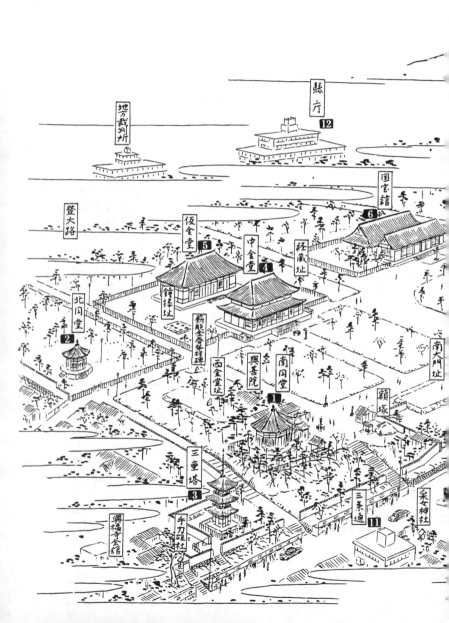

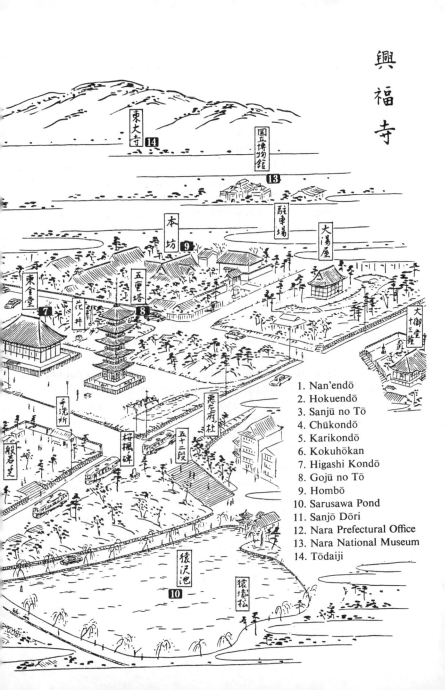

興福寺

1. Nan'endō
2. Hokuendō
3. Sanjū no Tō
4. Chūkondō
5. Karikondō
6. Kokuhōkan
7. Higashi Kondō
8. Gojū no Tō
9. Hombō
10. Sarusawa Pond
11. Sanjō Dōri
12. Nara Prefectural Office
13. Nara National Museum
14. Tōdaiji

tered about here and there. If the temple buildings were to be restored now to their original size, they would push the Nara Prefectural Office and the Cultural Hall right off the map and expand the city limits of Nara considerably.

After the Meiji-period movement to rid the country of all Buddhist influences (Haibutsu Kishaku) ended, Kōfukuji was reconstructed and the temple grounds, along with Kasuga Shrine, were opened as a park. Since the temple grounds are the park, you are visiting both when you are there. For that reason it is really questionable whether the people who come here to see the deer that roam through the park really get any feeling of being at Kōfukuji.

Reflections that one might have visiting most old temples simply do not occur at Kōfukuji. For one thing there is nothing to remind you that you are in the midst of a temple. It is not unusual to hear tape players blaring or see children playing basketball here. The only signs of tranquility that one might associate with a temple are the departing sounds of the tourist buses in the evening and the sound of the deer walking over the lawn.

So why does Kōfukuji, which is second only to Tōdaiji as one of Nara's six great temples, attract so many visitors? It is hard to imagine that the trail of history would lead pilgrims here.

Kōfukuji's history is long and rich, but it is the buddhas who are enshrined within its halls that lure pilgrims here. It is simply because the buddhas are here. The inviting hands of the buddhas are forever extended to the pilgrim.

The brows of the famous Ashura image at Kōfukuji almost appear knitted, in a subtle expression that suggests that the image bears the pain of an endless number of souls. Its eyes are completely clear and they shine. The line of its nose and the fullness of its cheeks heighten the sense of softness and calm. Its eyes and mouth are particularly fine. Whenever I look at this Ashura image, or, rather, worship in front of it, I become obsessed by its charm and power.

This unusual image, with its fearlessness and youthfulness, most certainly captures the heart of women who see it. It must be sexual attraction, since there are so many who fall in love with it. It has a pure but powerful life force that is no match for ordinary men in this world.

But it is not only women who are attracted to this image. Men, too, see here a beauty that is absolutely unparalleled in this world. Men cannot help but feel its femininity while women feel its masculinity. It seems to have a life force unrestricted by gender.

When you turn your eyes suddenly to the *ryūtōki*, and the *tentōki*, the two lantern-bearing demons, after being sexually absorbed by the Ashura image, you find yourself struck by the humor of their forms and back in the world of laughter. You can see their tongues through their gaping mouths and they are lifting votive lanterns with their muscular arms and shoulders. They are straining so much that their loin cloths have come ungirded and begun to slip down around their hips.

Off to one side are the images of Shakamuni's disciples. If you have come this far, you will certainly be captivated by this treasurehouse of Buddhist art. How should one worship the remaining images: Sharihotsu, Ragora, Mokkenren, Furuna? What sadness is Furuna hiding behind his wrinkled brows? When you are face to face with these images as well as the images of the Four Guardian Kings and the Twelve Divine Generals you begin to wonder what happened to all the worldly thoughts you had in the park. All of this made me feel as if I had become one of the people from the age of Kōfukuji's founding.

Kōfukuji has followed Japan through its periods of good and bad fortune. Its existence and its policies have always been in the mainstream of Japanese history. Today this is the only way for us to look back on the historical legacy it has left us. That is why when I visit Nara, I want to spend a little time in front of whichever image moves me and reflect on the history that has passed through this temple. The fact that Kōfukuji is the head temple of the Hossō sect of Buddhism, one of the six schools of Nara Buddhism, is a separate matter altogether.

SECT   Headquarters of the Hossō sect.

ESTABLISHMENT   Founded by Fujiwara Fuhito in about 669.

PRINCIPAL IMAGE   Shakamuni.

CULTURAL PROPERTIES   The North Circular Hall (Hoku-endō), Three-storied Pagoda (Sanjū no Tō), Five-storied Pagoda (Gojū no Tō), and the Eastern Main Hall (Higashi Kondō) are National Treasures, as are the dry-lacquered images of the eight kinds of beings who protect Buddhism and the dry-lacquer images of the Buddha's disciples. Of course, there are also many Important Cultural Properties as well.

VISITING INFORMATION   The grounds, halls, and buildings are generally open to the public. The Museum (Kokuhōkan) is also open daily from 9 to 5. Two of the most well-known events at Kōfukuji are the Onioi Ceremony and Takigi Noh. The Onioi Ceremony, in which the god Bishamonten attempts to exorcise six devils, is held during the Setsubun festivities in February. Takigi or "Firelit" Noh is performed outdoors on the evenings of May 11 and 12. It is called "firelit" because the stage area is surrounded and illuminated with bundles of burning firewood.

OF SPECIAL INTEREST   There are no gardens of special interest at Kōfukuji, but since the temple is located within Nara Park, it is ideal for a leisurely stroll. Since many of the buildings and halls are National Treasures, they deserve careful attention. The best of Kōfukuji's Buddhist images are on display in the museum. They represent the peak of the Nara-period Buddhist art.

LOCATION AND TRANSPORTATION   Nobori Ōji-chō, Nara. Kōfukuji is located a five-minute walk east from the Japan National Railways Nara Station.

興福寺　　奈良市登大路町

31. Shin Yakushiji

"The path to Kasuga Shrine leads first to the torii, or traditional Shintō gate. If you turn to the right here, the path immediately narrows and heads into a grove of trees. This whole area is covered with everything from wild azaleas that bloom at the beginning of spring to small, lovely flowers similar to the lily-of-the-valley. If the sunlight hits the leaves at just the right time, they seem to sparkle. This small path, known as "The Path of Whispers," then heads into the Kasuga Forest."

This was written by Shōkan Nataka, priest at Shin Yakushiji.

To the south and at the base of Mount Kasuga and its shrine is the highway to Yagyu. Along it, a collapsed earthen wall and other remains invite the traveler along this nostalgic path to history.

The famous Meiji novelist Naoya Shiga (1883–1971) is said to have written *A Dark Night's Passing* (*Anya Kōro*) here in a house that has now become part of the nearby university. This was at a time when many well-known writers, such as Saneatsu Mushanokōji (1885–1976), Kōsaku Takii (1894–1984), Kazuo Ozaki (1899–1983), and Kiku Amino (1900–78), had also taken up residence in this area.

What was it about the area around this temple that made it so popular among the Meiji-period writers? Perhaps it was the clear view of the mountains off to the south and the west that captured the heart of the traveler who wanted to recall Nara's rich past.

There may have been a spectacular view during the Meiji period, but today the streets around Shin Yakushiji's front gate are lined with houses.

This area also has special memories for me since it was here in December of 1943 that I was first stationed as a recruit in the 38th infantry regiment. It was bitterly cold then and the tranquility of Nara's old temples was nearly obliterated by the sound of marching soldiers in drill practice. Occasionally we were allowed to take short breaks here in front of Shin Yakushiji. Coming here as a pilgrim this time reminds me of one of Ōgai Mori's (1862–1922) poems:

> How impressive!
> These old buddhas here at
> Shin Yakushiji
> We begin and end our days together
> At the sound of the military bugle.

Standing here now under happier circumstances and looking at Shin Yakushiji's Yakushi, the Buddha of Healing, surrounded by the Twelve Divine Generals, I can recall my feelings during those more difficult times.

There are no temples more blessed with poets and their poems than Shin Yakushiji. These poems date as far back as *The Collection of Ten Thousand Leaves* (*Manyōshū*), Japan's first official poetry anthology. I wonder just how many poems about this area—from Mount Takamado to Mount Kasuga—the people of Nara have left for us.

> The bush clover blooms
> In autumn at the foot of

1. Minamimon
2. Shōrō
3. Jizōdō
4. Higashimon
5. Hondō
6. Kuri
7. Mount Kasuga

> Mount Takamado—
> Will its petals fall to the ground
> In vain for no one to see?

> Perhaps it is because
> Mount Takamado's peak towers
> So high into the sky
> That the moonlight beyond
> Has yet to reach us here.

The two poems above are typical of those about Nara that appear in this anthology. The extraordinary natural beauty they describe is particularly suitable for a temple like Shin Yakushiji. Kind Empress Kōmyō (701–60), who founded Shin Yakushiji to speed the recovery of Emperor Shōmu (r. 724–49), had the seven healing buddhas of the eastern paradise enshrined here. To pray to Yakushi was really the essence of Nara-period Buddhist beliefs. It was generally thought that a person could not go on living if he did not place his trust in Yakushi's healing powers.

The history of Shin Yakushiji is well recorded in the temple legends and is best left to them. It can be said, though, that Shin Yakushiji is representative of temples from this period of Nara Buddhism.

The poet Yaicih Aizu (1881–1956) visited here sometime after the central Yakushi image had been stolen from the Main Hall:

> With discerning eyes
> Yakushi views
> The world we've wrought—
> Yet in the distant haze he sees
> The grand Yamato past as well.

> Though I draw near and

Look up with reverence
There's just desolateness
Where once Yakushi
Buddha's gaze used to fall.

I wonder where that image of Yakushi is today.

To worship the Twelve Divine Generals surrounding the present-day Yakushi image is to feel Yakushi's compassion change into anger, indignation, and sadness. How can one worship the figure of General Mekira, with his hair standing on end with fierce anger? Aren't all of our delusions shattered when standing in front of the piercing gaze of General Basara? Can't you almost hear the roaring cry of General Indara, who seems about to leap out at you? Toward whom is all of this anger directed? Yet it is not all anger. A large tear seems about to fall from General Santera's eyes, whose expression suggests the sadness he feels for the plight of mankind. And what is this plight? Standing in front of the Twelve Divine Generals, it seems impossible to feel anything other than pathos or sadness for humanity. In fact, the Generals arouse a profound sense of uncertainty towards mankind itself. In a plea for salvation, I turn my eyes to the image of Yakushi.

We are always surrounded by the seven sufferings; as living beings, it is impossible to be alive and avoid them. Illness, enemies, uprisings, unfavorable or suspicious signs, eclipses, storms, and droughts: these were the traditional hardships by which humanity was constantly assailed. Furthermore, if one adds to these the nine unexpected causes of death, it becomes obvious that ordinary human life is nothing more than a path of constant suffering. Faith in Yakushi is aroused by our wish to rely on a spiritual power that will eliminate the threat of the seven sufferings and the nine unexpected causes of death. This faith is made possible by our sad, humble prayers which beseech Yakushi to bestow his compassion upon us.

Whenever I think about the missing Yakushi image here at Shin Yakushiji, I cannot help but grieve at the same time for this world where suffering and death are always imminent.

SECT   Kegon sect.

ESTABLISHMENT   Uncertain, but it is said that Empress Kōmyō founded Shin Yakushiji in 747.

PRINCIPAL IMAGE   Yakushi.

CULTURAL PROPERTIES   The Main Hall (Hondō), the Yakushi image enshrined there, and the Twelve Divine Generals are National Treasures. The Tower Gate (Rōmon) and numerous Buddhist images have been designated Important Cultural Properties.

VISITING INFORMATION   The halls and the grounds are open to the public daily from 8:30 to 5:30. On April 8, a Fire Festival (Otaimatsu) is held, starting at 7 P.M. This particular Fire Festival is a one-thousand-year-old tradition at Shin Yakushiji.

OF SPECIAL INTEREST   The visitor here should pay close attention to the Main Hall, since it closely approximates the Nara-period architectural style. Shin Yakushiji's principal image is surrounded by the Twelve Divine Generals and all are enshrined in the Main Hall.

LOCATION AND TRANSPORTATION   Fukui-chō, Takabatake, Nara. Take the city loop bus and get off at Wariishi-chō Bus Stop and then walk about ten minutes.

新薬師寺　　奈良市高畑福井町

32. Hokkeji

Once when Yukio Mishima (1925–70) was working out the plot for *The Sea of Fertility,* the tetralogy which became his final work, he told me that he wished the setting of the last novel to be a Nara or Kyoto nunnery with imperial connections. With such a goal in mind we set out together to make a tour of some of these nunneries.

Premising his novel on theories gleaned from the *Shōdaijōron,* a commentary on the *Vijnaptimatrata* by the Indian Buddhist philosopher Asanga (fourth century), Mishima had long admired the idea of human transmigration. In the end, as it turned out, he severed his own ties with this life and realized his own dream of transmigration.

I recall that we visited both Hokkeji and Enshōji in Obitoke in the southern part of Nara that day. Sometime later I received the following letter from Mishima: "I would like to express my most sincere gratitude for your generous assistance in guiding me to various temples. In particular, your introduction to Professor Susumu Yamaguchi has been immeasurably beneficial and has paved the way for further direction in the future. Because of your help, I have been able to solve, for the most part, the thorny problem of the theme of my novel. I could not have dreamed of a more ideal temple than Enshōji in Nara. It brings to mind the

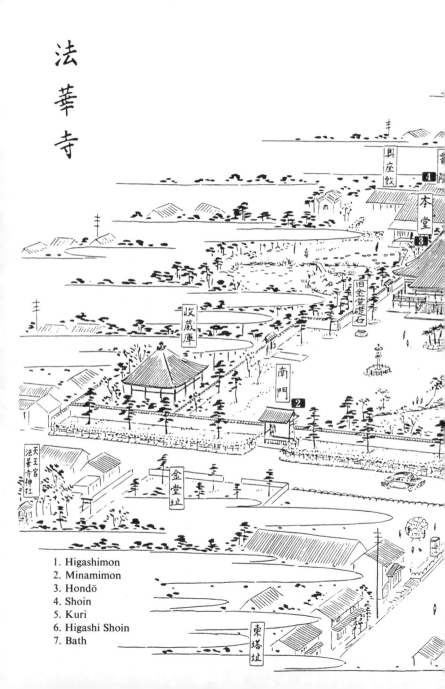

法華寺

1. Higashimon
2. Minamimon
3. Hondō
4. Shoin
5. Kuri
6. Higashi Shoin
7. Bath

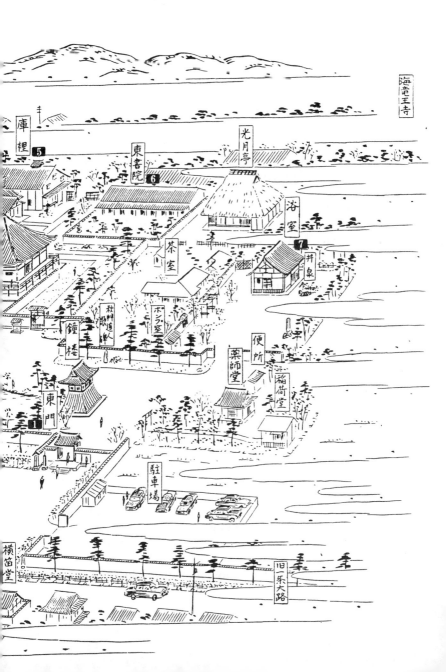

final chapter of *The Tale of Genji,* "The Bridge of Dreams." Because of your help, I have been able to develop, for the first time, a concrete image of the structure of my novel.

"I cannot thank you enough for your help. I am looking forward to meeting with you again in the future."

This letter was postmarked March 1, 1965. That means that Mishima and I walked around the temples of Nara on a cold day near the end of February sometime before the annual event at Tōdaiji called Omizutori.

The head nun at Hokkeji is Kōshō Kuga. The temple itself is so neat and refined as to suggest that there is not a speck of dust anywhere. It seems to inspire prayer while it absolves us from sin.

Hokkeji's Main Hall (Hondō), with its gently sloping, single-layered hipped roofs, is an Important Cultural Property. The gentleness of the sloping roof lines befits a building that houses the graceful yet masculine Eleven-faced Kannon, a National Treasure. Yaichi Aizu wrote a poem about this image:

> As if I had seen
> The Emperor's consort herself,
> A Fujiwara daughter—
> Kannon's lips are
> As red and full as a woman's.

According to temple legend, the Kannon image was sculpted using either Empress Kōmyō (701–60), the wife of Emperor Shōmu (r. 724–49) or Empress Danrin (876–850), the wife of Emperor Saga (r. 809–23) as a model. Whoever it was, both empresses were leading figures during the eras their husbands ruled, eras marked by raging political conflicts. As human beings we do not seem to be able to avoid these murky conflicts. That is why we have to live by our prayers in order to dispel our sins through Kannon's good graces.

Emperess Kōmyō is said to have bathed with a thousand lepers and sucked out the pus from their infected skin with her red lips. Empress Danrin, on the other hand, is said to have shown the world the transience and fragility of human life by having her own decaying corpse exposed to public view.

From deep within Kannon's compassionate gaze comes an almost terrifying, unmovable strength. That strength is the Buddha himself and not just something that is found in the beauty of a statue. Kannon's red lips, with their sheen, are drawn tightly in order to enable them to suck the pus from the leper's skin. Her body seems like it is about to move—her hip is turned to the left and her right foot is extended. The image is so realistic it refuses our inquiries into who the real model was. In fact, it supersedes thought altogether and leaves us with nothing to do but clasp our hands together in prayer.

These days many people stop to stare at the stone pillars erected in front of Nara's temples that warn visitors about the eating of meat, the drinking of alcohol, and the consumption of any of the five bitter foods (garlic, leek, shallot, onion, and *hiru*). In the old days, the abstention from these foods was strictly regulated and people who did not obey those restrictions were not permitted on the temple grounds.

Temples throughout Japan have become tourist spots. The management of their images and buildings has created what we see today. The consumption of alcohol, meat, and the five bitter foods is probably quite common as well. Even though Buddhism remains intact in terms of its form, where, I wonder, has its heart gone? At Hokkeji I felt relieved when I realized that this stone pillar with its warning was still standing. Hokkeji is a nunnery where the strict, everyday observances of practice are still being closely followed.

Sonoko Sugimoto, the author, visited here and was treated to a vegetarian meal, of which she wrote: "When I left the temple completely stuffed from all the food I had eaten, my mouth felt almost purified, as it might after sipping water from a clear spring.

It was strange to feel so rejuvenated. Even though I felt as completely full as I might after eating meat or having my fill of fish, it was the kind of satisfaction that made me realize my blood had been purified. Essentially, this kind of spiritual satisfaction is what I expect of temple food."

Certainly, the fact that those who live at Hokkeji and look after its Kannon observe the precepts at all times is also what allows Hokkeji's history to endure.

SECT   Shingon Ritsu.

ESTABLISHMENT   Founded by Empress Kōmyō in 745.

PRINCIPAL IMAGE   Eleven-faced Kannon.

CULTURAL PROPERTIES   The Eleven-faced Kannon enshrined in the Main Hall and a painting of the Amida trinity on silk are National Treasures. The Main Hall is an Important Cultural Property.

VISITING INFORMATION   Hokkeji is a nunnery and a *monzeki* temple, or one which was originally headed by a member of the imperial family. There are many ceremonies and religious celebrations here, but for the most part they are not open to the public. The Main Hall and the grounds, however, are open for public viewing. The nuns at Hokkeji make small dog amulets which are said to bring divine favor.

OF SPECIAL INTEREST   The Hombō Garden, an imitation of the Sentō Villa Garden in Kyoto, is quite famous and is open for viewing from May 1 to 15 and from October 25 to November 8. The Main Hall, dating from the sixteenth century, is worth seeing. Hokkeji's principal image, the Eleven-faced Kannon, is said to have been carved using Empress Kōmyō as a model.

LOCATION AND TRANSPORTATION   Hokkeji-chō, Nara. From the Japan National Railways Nara Station, take the Nara Kōtsu bus for Saidaiji Eki Kitaguchi and get off at Jieitai Mae. From there it is a five-minute walk. Or take a Nara city bus and get off at Hokkeji Mae.

法華寺　　奈良市法華寺町

33. Saidaiji

The writer Takeshi Umehara described Nara's Tōdaiji and Saidaiji: "It seems that whenever we talk about east and west, east is
always first while west is secondary. Nara and Kyoto both prided
themselves long ago on their pairs of 'east' and 'west' temples that
played important roles as large government-supported temples:
In Nara there were Tōdaiji and Saidaiji and in Kyoto, Tōji and
Saiji. As time passed, however, the eastern temples (Tōdaiji and
Tōji) remained as they were while the western temples (Saidaiji
and Saiji) fell into decline. Tōji in Kyoto is much the same today
as it was in the past, but nothing remains of Saiji. Likewise, Tōdaiji
in Nara contains the largest Buddha in all of Japan and has main-
tained its overall magnificence, while Saidaiji, having lost much of
its past grandeur, has managed only to preserve its buildings. Is
there some tradition, then, that the east should always win and the
West lose?"

Compared to the incredible impressiveness of Tōdaiji, Saidaiji
is living evidence of the world's sorrowful history and the severity
of change. East versus West: the sun that rises in the east symbolizes the future while the sun that sets in the west represents death.
There seems to be no choice but to accept these inescapable laws
of the universe while retaining as pure a heart as possible.

So what is there in the chasm between east and west? Nothing, I think, but human beings. The east prospers and the west falls into ruin. But even if this proves to be a fundamental law of the universe, there is nothing we can do about it.

The Kintetsu Railway express train goes from Kyoto to Nara along the Yamato Road taking barely thirty minutes to arrive at Saidaiji Station. At this point, the line branches off towards Nara in the east, Asuka in the south, and Osaka in the west. As an Osaka suburb, this well-situated area has developed rather quickly, until it has quietly begun to encroach on Saidaiji itself.

There is a diagram at Saidaiji of the temple complex as it used to exist. It was drawn according to records from the seventeenth century and shows just how large Saidaiji used to be. The complex measured almost three quarters of a mile east to west and almost half a mile north to south. It was bounded on the east by the Saki Road, on the west and north by the Kyōgoku Road, and on the south by the Ichijō Minami Road. Overall it surpassed Tōdaiji in size. This became clear in 1956 when the ruins of one pagoda were excavated. The remnants of this pagoda measured almost 88.5 feet in diameter, indicating that the structure was originally planned as a seven-storied octagonal pagoda. It is similar in size and shape to the present-day Taigan Pagoda in Xian, China.

Saidaiji's pagoda is an example of the fervent dreams people had in this chasm between east and west. Perhaps this was the dream Empress Kōken (r. 749–58) and her lover, Dōkyō (d. 770), had for another world. Whenever I come to Saidaiji I remember their story.

One interesting thing about Saidaiji is that two Golden Halls (Kondō) were built there, a Yakushi Golden Hall and a Miroku Golden Hall. Perhaps these were meant to be places where statues of Kōken and Dōkyō would be enshrined. Or perhaps they were meant to commemorate their love in this world and the next. According to *A Private Record of a Pilgrimage to the Seven Great*

西大寺

奥の院

西塔址

護摩堂

愛染堂

大師堂

子育地蔵

本坊 ③

菩提樹

大黒天堂

北通用門

本堂 ④

一之室院 ⑤

東塔址

増長院

鐘楼 ②

護国院

南門

①

駐車場

四王堂南門

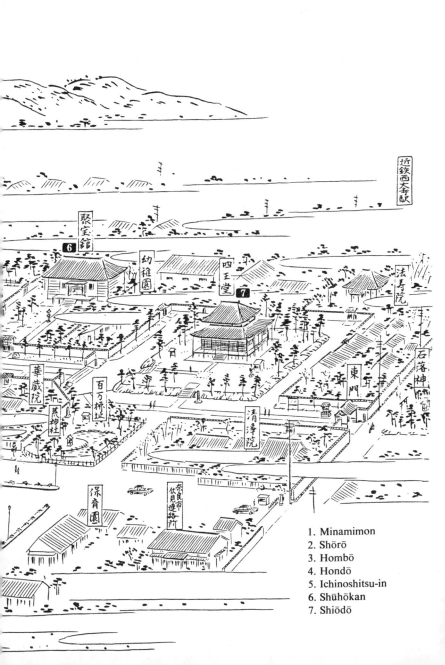

近鉄西大寺駅

聚宝館 **6**

幼稚園

四王堂 **7**

法寿院

華蔵院

茗神社

百万枅址

清浄院

石落神

東門

保育園

奈良市
飲具連絡所

1. Minamimon
2. Shōrō
3. Hombō
4. Hondō
5. Ichinoshitsu-in
6. Shūhōkan
7. Shiōdō

Temples (*Shichidaiji Junrei Shi Ki*), these two halls once contained a great number of unusual Buddhist images. It is thought that these might have been scenes of the Pure Land.

Human fate, incredible in its sacredness and its profanity, is here at Saidaiji for everyone to see. Perhaps it is the complex struggle between our world and the next which is the inescapable path we must all follow.

Empress Kōken died before she could see either of her Golden Halls completed. I wonder how her spirit has reacted to the decline of her beautiful temple after her demise. Dōkyō, on the other hand, lived on only to be exiled to Shimotsuke (modern Gumma Prefecture), where he eventually died. In the meantime, the capital was moved from Nara to Kyoto, and Saidaiji fell victim to the fires, storms, typhoons, and other natural disasters which came its way through time. The path of decay, which all things of form must take, was particularly severe and pathetic in the case of Saidaiji, which had been inaugurated and planned with great fanfare.

Until the appearance of Eison (1201–90) in the thirteenth century, Saidaiji was subject to the tricks of fate which time had dealt it. When Eison came to Saidaiji, though, he set about to restore it as a worthy center of practice for the observance of the Buddhist precepts, feeling that "For many years Saidaiji has been in a state of desolation and has lay in ruins. This is terrible beyond words."

Saidaiji did not prosper within the traditional framework of Japanese Buddhism until the thirteenth century. The very fact that Dōkyō's mere structure of a temple could become a place where the precepts were properly observed is proof of the indestructibility of mainstream Buddhism.

According to the idea of *kōbō rishō* (encourage the teachings and make all people happy), everything begins with and depends upon observing the Buddhist precepts. If the precepts are not honored, there is no Buddhism. Most of Eison's ninety years were devoted to the bodhisattva act of restoring the precepts in order to propagate the dharma and bring benefit to all sentient beings.

Saidaiji's most famous yearly ceremony is the Ōchamori Shiki. During that time all discrimination of social position and sex are discarded and everyone drinks tea from the same enormous cup. At last, during this friendly and warmhearted ceremony, I felt that I was looking at the new and revived Saidaiji.

SECT   Headquarters of the Shingon Ritsu sect.

ESTABLISHMENT   Founded by Jōtō and Empress Kōken in 764.

PRINCIPAL IMAGE   Shakamuni.

CULTURAL PROPERTIES   The Twelve Heavenly Deities painted in color on silk are a National Treasure. The images of Amida, Shakamuni, and Ashuku are Important Cultural Properties.

VISITING INFORMATION   The Main Hall (Hondō) and the Museum (Shūhōkan) are particularly important to visit. The entire grounds are open to the public, however. The most well-known ceremony at Saidaiji is the Ōchamori held on the second Saturday and Sunday in April and the second Sunday in October. Tea is prepared in an oversized tea bowl (measuring approximately 11.7 inches in diameter) and passed around to each guest. Drinking from this bowl is thought to prevent illness and misfortune during the next year. This ceremony is said to have originated with Eison, who rebuilt Saidaiji in 1239.

OF SPECIAL INTEREST   There are no particularly important gardens here, and all of the old buildings at Saidaiji were burned down in various conflagrations, so the remaining buildings are relatively new. The statues worth seeing here are on display in the museum.

LOCATION AND TRANSPORTATION   Shiba-machi, Saidaiji-chō, Nara. From Kyoto, the quickest way to Saidaiji is to take the super express Kintetsu Railway train to Saidaiji Station.

西大寺　　奈良市西大寺町芝町

34. Tōshōdaiji

The Kintetsu train runs from Kyoto to Nara. At Saidaiji station it branches off, stretching on to Yoshino from Asuka, where Kashihara Shrine is located. The next station after Saidaiji is Amagatsuji. If you get off at the following stop, Nishinokyō, you will be at Tōshōdaiji.

They say that the earth here is called *amai tsuchi,* or "sweet earth." Jianzhen (Japanese, Ganjin) the founder of Tōshōdaiji, retired from his position at the office of the ordination platform and went looking for land on which to build a new temple. When he tasted the earth here, he chose it as the site for Tōshōdaiji for the similar sweetness of the earth at the Qinggong ordination platform in his native Tang-dynasty China.

Even if this is just legend, it seems plausible, for Jianzhen was blind at this time. This sacred land is linked to Daimingsi in the province of Yang in China, the temple where Jianzhen resided until deciding to come to Japan.

Standing on the spotless grounds of this temple, one feels Jianzhen's unswerving strictness. Yaichi Aizu (1881–1956) composed this poem about Tōshōdaiji:

> The rays of the moon
> Strike the round pillars of

唐招提寺

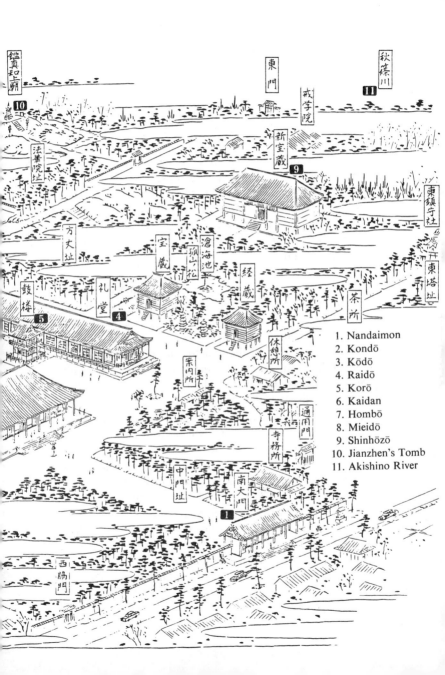

鑑真和上廟 **10**

法華院址

東門

戒学院

新宝蔵 **9**

秋篠川 **11**

東鎮守社

東塔址

方丈址

宝蔵

滄海池

孤山松

経蔵

茶所

鼓楼 **5**

礼堂

4

休憩所

案内所

通用門

寺務所

中門址

南大門 **1**

西脇門

1. Nandaimon
2. Kondō
3. Kōdō
4. Raidō
5. Korō
6. Kaidan
7. Hombō
8. Mieidō
9. Shinhōzō
10. Jianzhen's Tomb
11. Akishino River

> This noble temple—
> Treading this sweet earth and
> Deeply pondering all this.

It is that very earth which is the foundation of this temple. Determined to come to Japan, Jianzhen planned five trips and failed as many times. It must have been the fragrance of the earth that Jianzhen, who finally accomplished his goal, dreamed about while undergoing his twelve years of hardships.

In April 1980, a Nara-period statue of Jianzhen was returned to his home village in China after a lapse of 1,200 years. At the same time, a joint Japanese-Chinese movie relating the story of Jianzhen's life, in which the Chinese scenery is splendidly filmed, was playing in Japan.

And yet, one wonders what has happened to the precepts in present-day Buddhism. Others besides Yaichi Aizu must wonder the same thing as well. Nowadays one never hears the three precepts: obey all the commandments; do virtuous deeds; be merciful to all sentient beings.

The significance of Tōshōdaiji for the present age, as the head temple of the Ritsu sect, is entering a period of reevaluation.

Perhaps there is no sense in discussing the precepts these days. Rather than discuss them, wouldn't it be better to walk along the stone path which extends serenely from the large southern gate to the Main Hall and prostrate oneself in front of the various statues of buddhas? They will surely be witnesses there.

The sitting Birushana, a National Treasure, accompanied by a thousand buddhas with halos, is enshrined magnificently. To its right is another national treasure, a standing Yakushi, and to its left is a thousand-armed Kannon, also a National Treasure, accompanied by Bonten, a revered Hindu god; Taishakuten, a Buddhist tutelary god; and the Four Heavenly Guardians. These will indeed stir the heart of the pilgrim.

The halls are filled with various other images. Of course, the pilgrim cannot leave without paying reverence to the statue of Jianzhen himself, which is in the Founder's Hall.

> The young summer leaves!
> How I'd like to wipe
> The tears from his eyes.
> —Matsuo Bashō (1644–94)

While I was quietly paying reverence to the statue of Jianzhen, the words of writer Yasushi Inoue came to mind: "Isn't the living memory of his home province in Yang, which he abandoned, tucked away behind the slightly swollen eyelids of Jianzhen? I expect he had no idea what kind of a place Nara or Japan was, since he came here after he went blind."

Still, one cannot but feel the tough and tenacious spirit hidden behind the calm smile of this statue with the blind eyes. If one looks at Jianzhen's life through the description given in the *Tōseiden* (Jianzhen's Japanese biography), one can only imagine how long and arduous Jianzhen's trials were. I wonder if it isn't this that lies at the heart of Bashō's verse.

The hardships which Jianzhen endured after he was entreated to come to Japan by the Japanese monks Fushō and Eiei and after the subsequent decision to make the journey were all for the sake of the dharma. The travel time between China and Japan these days is extremely short. The physical distance, however, hasn't changed in the last 1,200 years. How would Jianzhen, who crossed the rough seas of hardships, deal with today's students of Buddhism?

Indeed, it was by the statue of Jianzhen that my heart was moved even when I stood in front of all these Buddhist images.

These days, Kōjun Morimoto, an elder priest at Tōshōdaiji, is busily running about preparing for the restoration of the modern-day ordination platform. The treasure pagoda of the ordination platform is already completed.

But just what is a modern-day ordination platform?

The peacefulness in my heart when I was making my pilgrimage to the old Nara temples and finally found my way to Tōshōdaiji seemed to change into a wordless sermon about the correct form of the dharma.

Isn't the modern-day ordination platform a restoration of the precepts, which are themselves the fundamental principles of Buddhism? No matter whether it's the season of the budding summer grasses or the blossoming bush clover, this is a temple whose grounds hold the highest position among old temples. It is all the more for this reason that I am carried away by the feeling that, as a practice center which will spread the true spirit of Japanese Buddhism to the world of tomorrow, I don't want Toshodaiji to become a temple for tourists' amusement. I want it to be a temple where only those who are believers can live, as they did when the temple was first built.

SECT   Headquarters of the Ritsu sect.

ESTABLISHMENT   Founded by Jianzhen in 759.

PRINCIPAL IMAGE   Birushana.

CULTURAL PROPERTIES   The Main Hall (Kondō), Lecture Hall (Kōdō), and most of the other halls and buildings are National Treasures, as are the statues of Birushana, Jianzhen, Thousand-armed Kannon, and Yakushi. Shakamuni and many of the statues enshrined in the Main Hall are Important Cultural Properties.

VISITING INFORMATION   Many of the Buddhist statues here can be seen in the Museum (Shinhōzō). Tōshōdaiji is the most beautiful of Nara's temples. The loveliest of the many festivals held here each year is the Fan Festival (Uchiwamaki) on May 19. Jianzhen's Memorial Celebration day on June 6 and the Moon-

Viewing Ceremony in praise of the Buddha which is held in mid-autumn are also impressive.

OF SPECIAL INTEREST   The entire grounds of Tōshōdaiji are quite extraordinary. The halls and buildings are the most beautiful in all of Nara. The most representative Buddhist statues of the Nara period are almost all at Tōshōdaiji.

LOCATION AND TRANSPORTATION   Gojō-chō, Nara. At the Yamato Saidaiji Station of the Kintetsu railway, take the Kashihara Line to Nishinokyō. From there it is about a ten-minute walk.

唐招提寺　　奈良市五条町

35. Yakushiji

A single cloud floats
Above the pagoda
At Yakushiji
Here in ancient Yamato
In the waning days of autumn.
　　　　—Nobutsuna Sasaki (1872–1963)

This famous poem about the pagoda at Yakushiji, a temple in the western part of Nara, is partly responsible for its becoming so well known. It is easy to imagine the celestial nymphs playing music as they fly about the ornamental flames that decorate the top of the pagoda. The single cloud floating above the pagoda further enhances this vision. One can hardly miss this beautiful world visible from almost any road in the Nara area. It is so extraordinary that it was once described as a "moment in music frozen in time."

Such deep feelings about Yakushiji date from long ago.

For a long time there was no Main Hall at Yakushiji and the hall where the images were enshrined was just a temporary building which leaked when it rained. These images were exposed to all kinds of weather. For the most part, the grounds too had been abandoned and left to decay. The pilgrims who came to visit

Nara's old temples heard about Yakushiji's fate and came to verify it for themselves.

Many men of letters such as the Nobutsuna Sasaki, Tatsuo Hori (1904–53), Katsuichirō Kamei (1907–66), and Yaichi Aizu (1881–1956) were drawn here to see the famous temple in its waning days. And here they chanced upon and understood the meaning of a journey into the past; here they felt sorrow for all of those things which pass into decay.

But Yakushiji is different now. The Main Hall (Kondō) is quite dignified and towers above the grounds. The red paint on the Western Pagoda shines brightly in the sky. The Western and Eastern Priests' Quarters (Nishi Sōbō and Higashi Sōbō) as well as many other temple buildings have either been built recently or are being restored. The sound of construction work here never ceases as workers attempt to build a temple as grand as the original.

These days it is not possible to think only of a single cloud the way Sasaki did in his poem. That's because there is now a Western Pagoda to complement the Eastern Pagoda: a dramatic coexistence of the ancient and the modern. In fact, Yakushiji is no longer just an old temple left over from the Hakuhō period (646–710); it has a certain energy which seems to be pointing it into the future.

It is of little use to visit Yakushiji as did the men of letters of the past that I previously mentioned hoping to arouse the sentiments of a journey to a past age. Just like the single cloud, no such sentiments exist here anymore. That "moment in music frozen in time" has vanished and has been replaced by more modern pieces in praise of its present stature. All that remain now are our fantasies about the ancient world of Nara when it was the capital.

Yakushiji is still being reconstructed. Perhaps we can even say this is its era of creation. Japan's incredible economic growth has even affected the building of temples—all in the name of faith. It is too facile to say that this transformation is just a matter of our changing times. We also ought to consider, within our faith, the

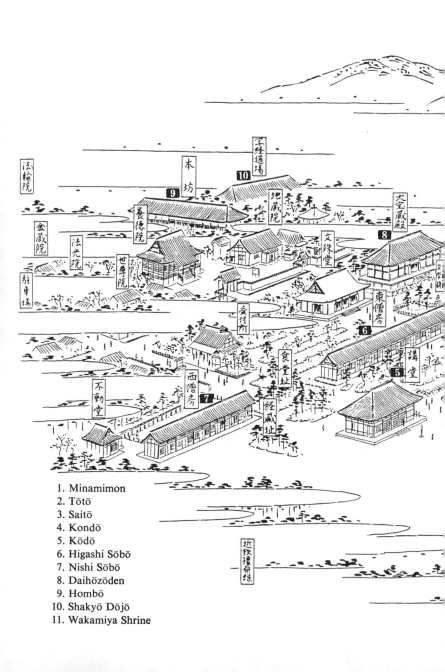

法輪院

金蔵院
法光院
駐車場

世尊院

本坊 **9**

養徳院

地蔵院

写経道場 **10**

文殊堂

大室殿殿 **8**

東僧房

講堂

食堂址

受付所

不動堂

西僧房 **7**

経蔵址

近鉄橿原線

1. Minamimon
2. Tōtō
3. Saitō
4. Kondō
5. Kōdō
6. Higashi Sōbō
7. Nishi Sōbō
8. Daihōzōden
9. Hombō
10. Shakyō Dōjō
11. Wakamiya Shrine

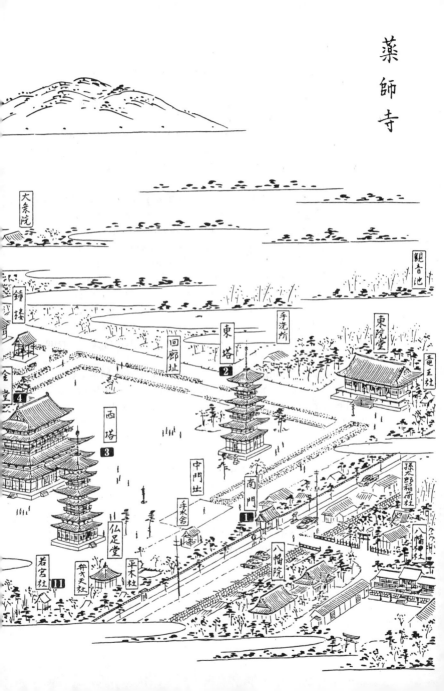

meaning of those things which have form, the tangible, and the material. All the old temples in Nara have undergone transformations of some kind, but the changes at Yakushiji are probably the most dramatic. Yakushiji's greatest period of transformation occurred twenty years ago. Before that, when Gyōin Hashimoto (1897–1978), was the chief abbot of the temple, the main quarters consisted of only a simple kitchen. That past is now beyond recognition.

One after the other large buildings have gone up here: the Main Quarters (Hombō), the Sutra Copying Hall (Shakyō Dōjō), the Great Treasure Hall (Hōzōden). The person in charge of continuing the collection of funds on behalf of Yakushiji is the present abbot, Kōin Takada. He undertook the enormous task of obtaining donations from one million people in exchange for copying a sutra. Takada remembers the days when he was criticized for undertaking something so improbable. People told him it would be like trying to cross the Pacific Ocean without a boat. But now he has attained his goal by going around the country and preaching the virtues of sutra copying.

"I had a consuming desire to reconstruct the Main Hall ever since I first came to Yakushiji as acolyte in the fifth grade. Ever since the temple was burned down in 1528, the temporary Main Hall had leaked water and the inside of the building had been exposed to the rays of the sun, bathing the Buddha in sunlight. On rainy days, un umbrella had to be held over its head to protect it from the rain. The wind would also blow in and in the evenings, the moonlight would shine through. It was really a weatherbeaten Yakushi trinity."

Of course, there are no traces of this now. Today it is housed in a hall glowing with color. All worries about the wind and the rain have long been forgotten.

Yakushiji was originally built by Emperor Temmu (r. 673–86) as a part of his prayers for the recovery of his sick wife. Along with Daikantaiji (later called Daianji), it was one of two large representative temples of Nara.

Can Yakushiji cure our modern society of its incurable ills? Ours is no longer an imperial era; illness affects everyone all over the globe. Inside the large Main Hall and standing in front of the Yakushi trinity, our prayers for good health become a cry of the spirit.

I do not know of any modern poems about this new Yakushiji. Now that it has at last met the dawn of its new existence, though, poems dedicated to its long life are necessary. Some 1.5 million visitors come to Yakushiji every year. How, I wonder, are their hearts reflected in the merciful eyes of Yakushi, and how will our prayers for good health, safety, and long life be fulfilled in the present age?

SECT   Headquarters of the Hossō sect.

ESTABLISHMENT   Founded by Emperor Temmu in 680.

PRINCIPAL IMAGE   Yakushi.

CULTURAL PROPERTIES   The Eastern Pagoda and the Yakushi trinity enshrined in the Main Hall (Kondō) are National Treasures, as is the portrait of Kichijōten on hemp cloth. This painting is most famous and is available for public viewing once a year between October 20 and November 10. There are, of course, many well-known Important Cultural Properties as well.

VISITING INFORMATION   The grounds and halls are open to the public. Some of the buildings, including the Western Pagoda and the Main Hall, were rebuilt as recently as 1981 and 1976 respectively. The liveliest ceremony here each year is held between March 30 and April 5 and is known as the Flower Festival. It originated as a kind of penitential ceremony. Flowers made of Japanese paper are placed in front of the principal image in the Main Hall.

OF SPECIAL INTEREST   The grounds in general are worth seeing at one's leisure. The Eastern Pagoda and the Eastern Hall (Tōindō) are National Treasures which of course reflect Nara architectural styles, but the newer buildings as well have been constructed in the same style so that the visitor there even today can get a good sense of what the temple styles were like in the Nara period. In addition to the Yakushi trinity, which is in the Main Hall, many other images can be seen in the Hōzōden.

LOCATION AND TRANSPORTATION   Nishinokyō-machi, Nara. Take the Kashihara Line of the Kintetsu Railway to Nishinokyō. The temple is a five-minute walk from the station.

薬師寺　　奈良市西ノ京町

THE OUTSKIRTS OF NARA

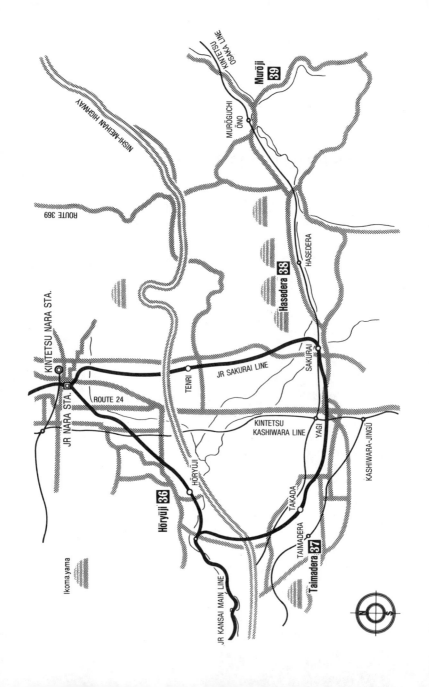

36. Hōryūji

One should begin one's pilgrimage to the old temples of Nara at Hōryūji in the village of Ikaruga.

In Ikaruga, where that which we do not want to change exists side by side with that which ought to change, we are made aware, willingly or not, of the transitoriness of life and the awesomeness of humanity. At the same time, regardless of any changes within humanity, those things which are better off as they are exist solemnly beside the unchanged past. This, in truth, makes us aware of the joy and redemption of life. Hōryūji is a place where the joy and suffering of life complement and respond to each other.

The poet Yaichi Aizu (1881–1956) wrote the following poem entitled *Staying at the Village near Hōryūji*:

> Autumn is surely near.
> The young women living in
> Ikaruga
> Work their looms all night long
> Weaving silk for the winter.

It is impossible to see such a thing now in Ikaruga. And it is almost impossible to recall the early part of the century, when Tetsurō Watsuji (1889–1960) and Yaichi Aizu came here on their

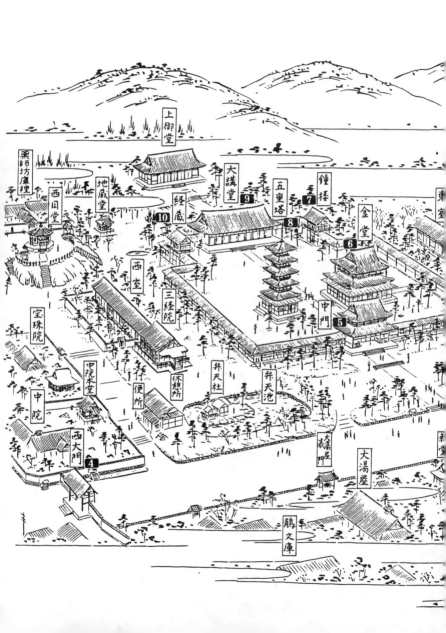

上御堂

薬師坊庵裡　西円堂　地蔵堂

大講堂　9

経蔵　10　五重塔　8　鐘楼　7

金堂　6

東室

西室　三経院

中門　5

宝珠院　中院本堂　便所　休顔所　弁天社　弁天池

中院

西大門　4　大湯屋　表門　大湯屋

鵤文庫

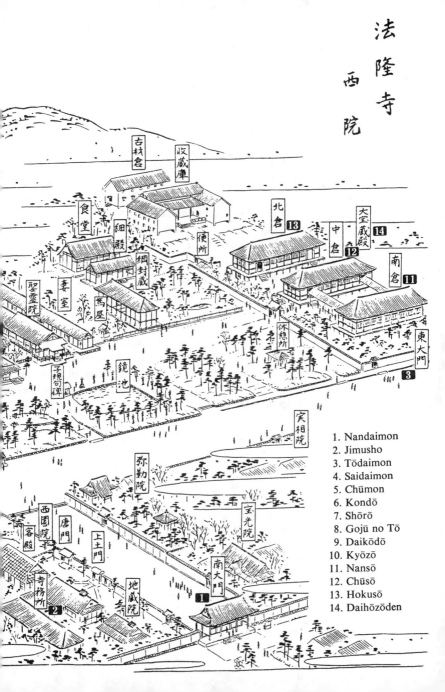

法隆寺 西院

古材倉　収蔵庫
食堂　細殿
聖霊院　妻室　綱封蔵　萬屋
子規句碑
鏡池
北倉 **13**
便所
中倉 **12**　大宝蔵殿 **14**
南倉 **11**
休想所
香
東大門 **3**
実相院
弥勒院
西園院　唐門　宝光院
客殿　上土門
寺務所 **2**　地蔵院
南大門 **1**

1. Nandaimon
2. Jimusho
3. Tōdaimon
4. Saidaimon
5. Chūmon
6. Kondō
7. Shōrō
8. Gojū no Tō
9. Daikōdō
10. Kyōzō
11. Nansō
12. Chūsō
13. Hokusō
14. Daihōzōden

pilgrimages to see the old temples. These days automobiles crowd against each other on the superhighway leading to Nara and the buses carry noisy young children here on their school excursions, weaving in and out between the cars.

The age of the masses is an amazing thing. The advent of this age completely changed the village of Ikaruga. It has now been transformed into a temple-gate town with restaurants and souvenir shops with their welcome signs lined up in a long row, just as one might see at a tourist spot anywhere. Well-known Japanese-style inns such as the Daikokuya, where many writers and artists once stayed, have fallen into ruin and look like haunted houses.

Both that which we feel should and should not change will, in the end, be transformed. It is the intermingling of emotions about the inescapable passage of time and the human condition which awakens me to this when I stand here before Hōryūji's front gate.

It is best to avoid the hustle and bustle outside Hōryūji as much as possible. One step inside the Main Gate (Nandaimon) and you are inside the grounds. Once inside I felt as if history at last had extended the hand of salvation to me. The immaculate white sand on the path and the serenity of the subsidiary temples and buildings lined up on either side of it and enclosed by their roofed mud walls made it clear to me that the path to the Main Hall (Kondō) is a path towards something unchangeable.

The white of the visitors' path and the green of the pine trees seem to quicken the pace of my steps to the Middle Gate (Chūmon). Perhaps they are also the incentive for wanting to hasten the time I can spend in dialogue with that which has not changed.

Aizu wrote the following poem about this dialogue when he went to see the Kannon image at Chūgūji, a temple founded by Shōtoku Taishi (574–622) for his mother in 607.

> Facing Kannon,
> I felt completely alone

> In the universe
> Until this gentle bodhisattva
> Smiled upon my solitude.

I expect similar sentiments would be felt by anyone who had a chance to see the images that are enshrined in the Main Hall.

Probably the joy that Aizu felt in his fortuitous meeting with history unchanged—the Kudara Kannon, the Yumetagai Kannon, the Shakamuni Trinity, and the Four Guardian King images—became inseparable from the sorrow he felt about his own transitory life. "I felt completely alone / In the universe." But when he experienced the bodhisattva's profound compassion in that gentle smile, the pathos and loneliness he felt for the transitory world completely disappeared.

Time is mysterious. The mundane, which exists within an ordinary time framework, completely blots out the passage of time here at Hōryūji.

What were the circumstances involved in the founding of Hōryūji and how can we interpret the political situations that surrounded Shōtoku Taishi in the seventh century? And the sculptors who gathered here—in particular, Tori Busshi, the first known sculptor of Buddhist images in Japan—how did they acquire their skills? We might like to spend our time in such inquiries, but the urgency of our encounter with the past does not permit it. Because there are so many tourists who come here now, the doors of the Main Hall are always open. And as Aizu observed,

> From between the cracks
> In these heavy doors—just slightly
> Ajar—already
> I can see the face of the
> Old buddhas waiting inside.

In the old days when pilgrims came here, they could only enter

Hōryūji's halls on fixed days. Surely their encounters must have seemed like sacred blessings from heaven.

Controversies about Hōryūji abound. Various opinions are still being tossed about as to by whom and why Hōryūji was built. Be that as it may, however, it is probably best to think of these opinions and theories, as Shōtoku Taishi himself lamented, as the ramblings of a world without truth. It is so much more germane to make a pilgrimage to Hōryūji, to look for the truth by oneself, even though the sense of salvation you experience on such a journey may just be a temporary escape from the world.

The vicissitudes of life are merciless. And it is we who are not easily comprehensible in this world of half-truths. Yet it is also we who wish to realize the truth of buddhahood.

I expect there are things among us which will not change. The ordinary world, however, will continue its journey of transitions. Yet, it is our desire for the unchanging that makes a pilgrimage possible. Among those young people who burst forth from their tour buses, there must be some within whom the truth continues to live.

The world may or may not be steeped in half-truths even while the various buddhas and bodhisattvas are safely enshrined at Hōryūji, but each and every one of them continues to bestow their smiles of buddhahood upon us.

SECT   Shōtoku sect.

ESTABLISHMENT   Founded by Shōtoku Taishi in 607.

PRINCIPAL IMAGES   Shōtoku Taishi and Shakamuni trinity.

CULTURAL PROPERTIES   The entire temple complex is a National Treasure, as are the Shakamuni trinity and the various Buddhist statues in each of the halls.

VISITING INFORMATION   The orderly arrangement of the buildings at Hōryūji has prompted scholars to refer to temples like this as in the Hōryūji style. This is the most ideal architectural style in Japanese Buddhism. There are, of course, various Buddhist ceremonies and celebrations held here each year, but since the temple was founded by Shōtoku Taishi, faith in this extremely famous historical figure is predominant. Hōryūji is probably the most popular temple for sightseeing in all of Japan.

OF SPECIAL INTEREST   The entire grounds of Hōryūji are of interest. The Middle Gate (Chūmon), Five-storied Pagoda, the Main Hall (Kondō), and the Great Lecture Hall (Daikōdō) will give you some idea of the enormity of Japan's ancient temples. Also, you should visit Chūgūji, which is located just to the east of Hōryūji. The images enshrined in the Main Hall reflect the styles prevalent within the Buddhist tradition when it was first transmitted to Japan.

LOCATION AND TRANSPORTATION   Ikaruga-chō, Ikoma-gun, Nara Prefecture. From Nara City, take the Kansai Honsen Line to Hōryūji Station.

法隆寺　　奈良県生駒郡斑鳩町

37. Taimadera

Taimadera is situated on a quiet hillside near the base of Mount Nijō. To get there you take the Abeno Line of the Kintetsu Railway from Kashihara Jingū Station in the direction of Osaka and get off at Taima Station.

At one time the Takenouchi Road ran between Asuka, the Imperial capital of Japan between 552 and 645, and Naniwa, the old name for Osaka. Undoubtedly, many people traveled back and forth along that road and, as they did, they probably paid reverence in the evenings to the beautiful setting sun over Mount Nijō.

Traditionally, mountains are considered to be places of mystery since it is there that the sun was thought to set. In the case of Mount Nijō, the sun sets right between its two peaks, Odake (the male peak) and Medake (the female peak). Certainly, to people during the sixth and seventh centuries, this was a place for something or someone beyond the scope of human imagination to dwell. This idea eventually became the basis for a mandala as well.

Zemmyō Nakata, a priest at Taimadera, wrote the following about its most famous mandala, the Chūjōhime Mandala: "The sun, as it approaches the saddle from between the clouds and heads towards Mount Nijō's two peaks, is a golden color. Its dazzling light forms a halo. Whenever I get absorbed in the natural mystery or magnificence of this picture, I am convinced that Chūjōhime was in fact greeted by twenty-five bodhisattvas from the Pure Land and thus found her way to paradise."

Whenever I look at the setting sun over Mount Nijō I get carried away by fantasies concerning the Pure Land, a final resting place, peaceful and calm, for all of humanity. The unusual shape of the mountain reminds me of a woman's soft skin, while the setting sun evokes a kind of sexual tranquility. Such simple reflections have, in the past, added to Mount Nijō's sacredness.

The people of Asuka traveled this road as if it were the road to salvation, worshiping the setting sun over Mount Nijō along the way. Even Genshin (942–1017), the author of *The Essentials of Salvation* (*Ōjō Yōshū*) and a noted Buddhist scholar-priest, was known to have been captivated by this scene as a child.

Gazing at Mount Nijō, I noticed that sexual thoughts quickly change into yearnings for the other world. We might even think of this as the mysterious struggle between life and death. It requires tremendous exertion on our part, however, to substitute for sexual pleasure the eternalism of life after death.

The imperial funeral processions made their way to Mount Nijō year after year in those days. Emperors Bidatsu (r. 572–85), Yōmei (r. 585–87), and Kōtoku (r. 645–54), Empress Suiko (r. 592–628), Shōtoku Taishi (574–622), and Ono no Imoko (early seventh century) are all buried here. The proper Pure Land lies beyond Mount Nijō and the mandala is proof that Chūjōhime made her way there with the accompaniment of twenty-five bodhisattvas.

Taimadera is now well known for its peonies. In spring people come here in droves to see them. Though we do not know when they were first planted, they appear in the legends surrounding Chūjōhime as well.

The story of Chūjōhime also reminds us of the young prince, Ōtsu no Miko, emperor Temmu's son, who is also buried on Odake. According to an explanation in *Descriptions of the Dead*

當麻寺

西塔 9

念仏院

東塔 4

中之坊 3

松室院

鐘楼

安波堂 2

末坰松

駐車場

東門 1

公民館

紫雲院

薬師堂

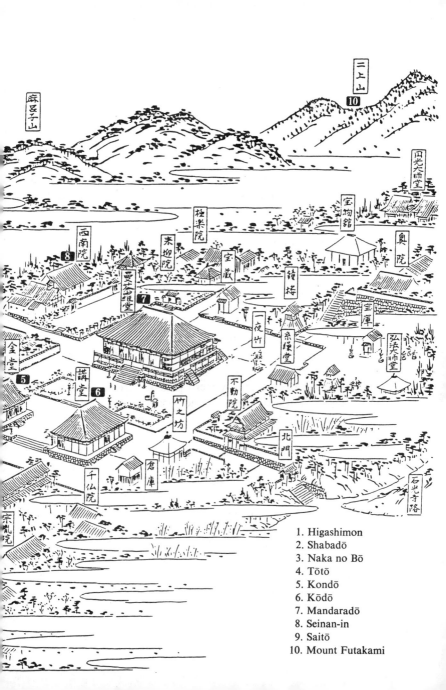

1. Higashimon
2. Shabadō
3. Naka no Bō
4. Tōtō
5. Kondō
6. Kōdō
7. Mandaradō
8. Seinan-in
9. Saitō
10. Mount Futakami

(*Shisha no Sho*) by the ethnologist Shinobu Origuchi, (1887–1953), Chūjōhime fell painfully in love with the young prince who had died long before. The sounds she made on her weaving machine while she dreamed of her impossible love were quite erotic.

The world of the mandala at Taimadera is depicted as one of great joy. Numerous Buddhist tales originated from this world. These tales probably provided a way for people to indulge in reveries about the Pure Land. There is nothing less interesting than historical speculation about the existence of a character like Chūjōhime. And likewise, it does not much matter whether the experts tell us if the Taimadera Mandala was made with lotus-fiber thread or silk, or was painted, embroidered, or woven.

What might be interesting, however, would be to speculate about the tales of the mandala world that were created by the noblewomen who longed for the Western Paradise as a crystallization of their prayers and wishes. Noh plays such as *Taima* and *Hibariyama* give us some idea of the tremendous beauty of Buddhist Pure Land faith and devotion to mandala representations, as well as the tales that occur within these, focusing on Chūjōhime as the heroine.

Taimadera's eastern and western pagodas are surrounded by a veritable ocean of green trees. In the distance are the softly curving ridges of Mount Nijō. On each side of the temple grounds from the Eastern Gate (Higashimon) to the Mandala Hall (Mandaradō) are subtemples lined up along the sloping path that guides visitors on their pilgrimages here. It is this very path that connects paradise to the ordinary world of suffering, or *shaba*. As might be expected, then, the area around the Shaba Hall seems to be somewhat in disarray, an inevitability within our ordinary world. But since the Mandala Hall is a kind of Paradise Hall (Gokurakudō), it is fine for the Shaba Hall to be as it is.

The sloping path through Taimadera is the same path the twenty-five bodhisattvas traveled on their journey from the Pure Land to take Chūjōhime back to paradise. And it is the path which eventually returns to the Paradise Hall too. Finally, it is the same path where the Oneri Ceremony, a ceremony in which priests and lay people circumambulate the halls and sculptures of the temple, is held every May 14.

The people described in the *Taimadera Engi* and the *Chūjōhime Engi,* valuable temple legends, are, because they are human, suffering. Human beings are the battlefields upon which the horrors of malice, jealousy, desire, and murder are carried out, and these must be borne as our destiny. That is why belief in Chūjōhime becomes salvation itself and shines forth. In this tale we see the salvation of a beautiful woman who humbly submitted herself to the Pure Land depicted in the mandala.

> Climbing the stone steps
> At Taimadera
> Near Mount Nijō
> No one escapes the mountain dew
> As it falls, drip, drip,
> > from the autumn trees.
> > > —Yaichi Aizu

At Taimadera we can touch the evidence of Chūjōhime's salvation.

SECT   Shingon and Jodo.

ESTABLISHMENT   Founded by the Taima family in the seventh century.

PRINCIPAL IMAGE   Miroku.

CULTURAL PROPERTIES   The Main Hall (Hondō or Mandaradō), image of Miroku, and Taima Mandala are National Treasures. The Eleven-faced Kannon is an Important Cultural Property.

VISITING INFORMATION   The Mandala Hall, the Lecture Hall (Kondō), and the Museum (Hōmotsuden) are all open to the public. On May 14, a Nerikuyō Ceremony is held in which a procession of twenty-five people dressed as bodhisattvas enact their coming from the Pure Land to save Chūjōhime, the main character in the Taima Mandala. This ceremony is usually attended by many people.

OF SPECIAL INTEREST   The garden at Nakanobō, a subtemple of Taimadera, is scenic as well as historically important. The peonies at Okuno-in, another subtemple, are also quite well known. The Mandala Hall, where the Taima Mandala is enshrined, the Main Hall, and the Lecture Hall, are all worth viewing, as are the images of Miroku, the Four Guardian Kings, and Amida. There are numerous other Buddhist images as well. Probably the most important treasure here is the Taima Mandala, supposedly woven with lotus thread and telling the story of Chūjōhime. The visitor here should not fail to take a careful look at this beautiful work.

LOCATION AND TRANSPORTATION   Taima-chō, Kitakatsuragi-gun, Nara Prefecture. Take the Kintetsu Minami Osaka Line to the Taimadera Station. From there, it is a 15-minute walk.

当麻寺　　奈良県北葛城郡当麻町

38. Hasedera

Hasedera, in the old Yamato region near Nara, is well known for its peonies. It is a gentle climb up the 399 stone steps—which traverse almost 215 yards—to the Main Hall (Hondō) from the Deva Gate (Niōmon). On both sides of the stone stairway, seven thousand bushes of more than 150 varieties of peonies bloom in profusion. According to temple legend, Hasedera became famous for its peonies during the eighteenth century. The entire area is fragrant with the smell of Hasedera's flowering attire.

> How terrible!
> I passed right by the temple
> Where the peonies bloom.
> —Buson (1716–83)

It is said that the eighteenth emperor of Tang China, Xizong (r. 874–89), had a wife whose name was Ma Tou, or Horse Face. After she prayed to Guanyin (Kannon) at Changgu (Hase) in China and became a beautiful woman without peer, the emperor professed his love for her by presenting her with peony bushes. This is the legendary origin of the peony bushes at Hasedera in Japan. Kyoshi Takahama (1874–1959), the poet, wrote the following at a banquet at the temple of flowers:

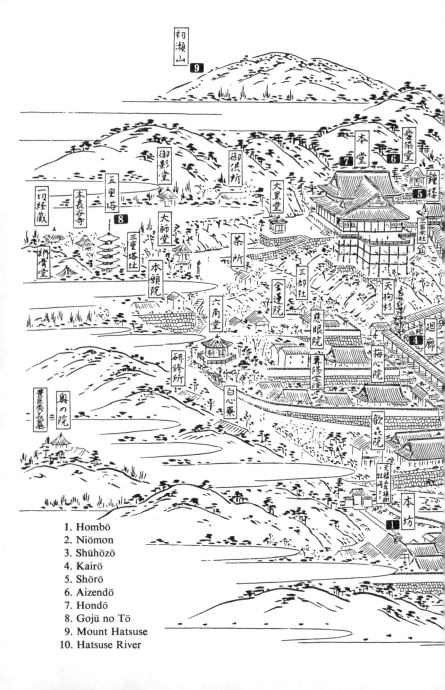

1. Hombō
2. Niōmon
3. Shūhōzō
4. Kairō
5. Shōrō
6. Aizendō
7. Hondō
8. Gojū no Tō
9. Mount Hatsuse
10. Hatsuse River

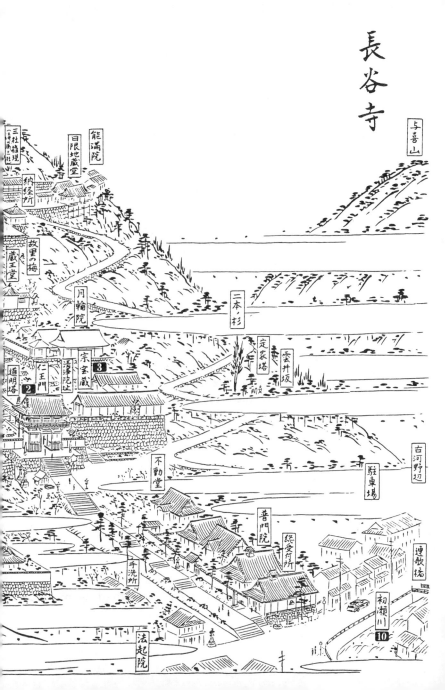

長谷寺

与喜山

能満院
日限地蔵堂
三柱権現
（三尊蔵王権現）
納経所

故里の梅
蔵王堂

月輪院

二本杉

定家塔
雲井坂

宗宝蔵 **3**
仁王門
浄院辺
道明塔 **2**

古河野辺

不動堂
駐車場

普門院
総受付所

手洗所

連歌橋

初瀬川 **10**

法起院

> If the peony
> Blossoms bloomed here today,
> The halls would all vanish.

Of course, there are not only peonies here. The Edo-period poet Masaaki Asukai (1611–79) wrote the following about the cherry blossoms:

> I journeyed here to see
> The famous peonies but instead
> I found the famed cherries
> Of Yoshino living in
> The village of Hase too.

Akiko Yosano (1878–1942), the renowned poetess, also visited Hasedera:

> In the late spring
> Of my twentieth year
> I tread the stone steps
> Of the great temple at Hase
> Rapt in my own thoughts.

If we look back even further to the literature of *The Collection of Ten Thousand Leaves* (*Man'yōshū*), there are a number of poems inspired by this area:

> Despite the trouble
> Of treading each small stone
> Across the river
> I came to my beloved wife
> Here in the land of Hase.
> —Kakinomoto no Hitomaro (fl. ca. 685–705)

There is also the well-known poem offered to Prince Toneri (677–735):

> At the close of day
> Crossing the Hase River
> I made my way
> To the golden gate of the house
> Where my beloved lives.
> —Kakinomoto no Hitomaro

Even as far back as *The Chronicles of Japan* (*Nihon Shoki*), completed in 720, there is mention of Hase:

> The mountain at Hase
> Stands tall against the sky . . .
> Such a fine mountain!

Hase's fame, often read about in works by women such as *The Gossamer Years* (*Kagerō Nikki*) and *The Tale of Genji* (*Genji Monogatari*), has always been a lure to console the weary heart of the female traveler, prompting her to seek refuge within Hasedera itself. The Hasedera which appeared in Japanese literature was a temple where a woman's feelings could linger unresolved.

There are many old legends about the origins of Hasedera. One is that during the time of Emperor Temmu (r. 673–86), a priest by the name of Dōmyō founded a temple on the western hill of Mount Hase while a priest by the name of Tokudō founded a temple on the eastern hill. Eventually, these united to become Hasedera.

As the Nara period (646–794) gave way to the aristocratic age of the Heian period (794–1185), women of the nobility came here seeking Kannon's compassion. To them this compassion took the form of worldly benefits such as wealth, glory, good fortune, and children. Their attachments are all shut away within the confines of this mountain. But their devoted prayers to Kannon have been recorded in some detail in various works such as *Miraculous Tales of Japan* (*Nihon Ryōiki*), *The Pillow Book of Sei Shōnagon* (*Makura no Sōshi*), *The Gossamer Years,* and *The Sarashina Diary* (*Sarashina Nikki*). What is it about this place, about Hasedera, that has captured women's faith?

During the Muromachi period (1333–1573) faith in Hase Kannon became associated with the common people and their pilgrimage to the Ise Shrine. In this way the pilgrimage to Hase entered the mainstream of people's beliefs.

Hasedera has met with several conflagrations, but still its buildings are unusually beautiful and dignified. The building where the Kannon image is enshrined could even be described as a castle. Each of the stones on the stairway I mentioned before have been rubbed down to a dull shine due to the continual stream of pilgrims visiting here.

I wonder how many men and women have climbed this stairway to the Main Hall? The 215-yard distance there is 108 *ken,* a unit of traditional Japanese measure. Perhaps this particular distance was arrived at on purpose to correspond to the 108 worldly desires human beings are supposed to have. Determined with all of my heart to absolve myself of my sins, I continue up the stairway step by step in hopes of entrusting my fate to Kannon's compassion.

The front of the Main Hall is almost 98.5 feet wide and the building is 88.5 feet deep. It towers over the village of Hase on the slope of the mountain. This is where the Eleven-faced Kannon is enshrined. The Kannon image is a little less than ten yards high and it is carved by the *yosegi zukuri* method, which means that the head and the body were carved separately and then assembled after they were completed. How was a statue this large built? It almost seems impossible to worship something of this size when you are standing in front of it. I fear the only thing to do is put one's hands together in prayer in front of this bodhisattva who seems to have appeared on earth from someplace deep below the planet's surface.

> Who is it, I wonder,
> That's ensconced in prayer here
> On this spring evening?
> —Matsuo Bashō (1644–94)

Bashō's poem comes from his own feelings. Someone has been able to come here to worship, and Bashō is curious but thankful for that. But are people really able to feel how transitory and insignificant they are in this world? It all becomes a kind of dream in one corner of this strange world within Kannon's hall.

To get to Hasedera, you take the Kintetsu Railway from Kyoto Station and change at Yagi for Nagoya. About twenty minutes into the mountains, there is a station called Hasedera. The train to Hasedera Station runs along the ridge of the mountains, so the scenery is particularly beautiful. When you get off the train, there is a temple town there. At one time, this town, which straddles both sides of the Hase River, was quite prosperous. In *The Japanese Family Storehouse* (*Nihon Eitaigura*), by Ihara Saikaku (1642–93), this prosperity and the popular devotion that was accorded this Kannon were described as "the eyes of Kannon, which had been snatched away by the world."

But it seems all of this has changed now. Still, as the eighth temple on the pilgrimage of thirty-three temples in western Japan, pilgrims with their characteristic bells and packs never stop coming:

> No matter how often
> I come to Hasedera
> It's always like new—
> So strong are the vows I make
> Here in this river valley.

SECT   Headquarters of the Buzan branch of the Shingon sect.

ESTABLISHMENT   Founded by Dōmyō in 686.

PRINCIPAL IMAGE   Eleven-faced Kannon.

CULTURAL PROPERTIES   Sutra scrolls in the temple collection have been designated National Treasures and the Main Hall and the Eleven-faced Kannon image are Important Cultural Properties.

VISITING INFORMATION   The grounds and buildings are open to the public from April to September, 8:30 to 5:00, and from October to March, 9:00 to 4:30. There are many annual events here, but Hasedera is best known for its peonies, which are in full bloom in May. There are some 150 varieties of peony and almost 7,000 bushes and trees.

OF SPECIAL INTEREST   The outdoor corridor which goes from the Deva Gate (Niōmon) to the Main Hall is 108 *ken* in length, and to walk along it will help to extinguish the 108 illusions under which we live and which are the source of all suffering. The view from the Main Hall is particularly nice. Just like Kiyomizudera in Kyoto, the Main Hall has a kind of stage-like veranda built onto it that dates from the seventeenth to eighteenth centuries. The Eleven-faced Kannon image, which is the principal image at Hasedera, is approximately 26 feet high and dates from the sixteenth century.

LOCATION AND TRANSPORTATION   Hatsuse, Sakurai-shi, Nara Prefecture. Take the Osaka Line of the Kintetsu Railway to Hasedera Station. From there it is a twenty-minute walk.

長谷寺　　奈良県桜井市初瀬

39. Murōji

Physically
I am still here at Mount Kōya
But my heart lingers on
At Murō where I watched
The morning moon in the sky.
　　　　　—Kūkai (774–834)

Murōji is a temple we should be thankful for. The reason we
should be thankful is that Murōji has essentially remained unchanged from ancient times in a form that is so ideal it is hard to
imagine. I feel especially grateful for this on a pilgrimage to the
old temples. Murōji is comforting to visit during every season of
the year. It is a temple to be thankful for because it reminds us of
the preciousness of being alive.

It is not certain when Murōji first came to be called Kōya for
Women. However, from ancient times women were looked down
upon as beings who were homeless in the three worlds of past,
present, future. Mountains like Mount Kōya were closed to women
in the name of faith. These were the sad conditions under which
women had to live. Their sufferings ran even deeper than those
of men. Ever since they were designated as the guilty ones, the
fervor of their prayers for salvation intensified well beyond that

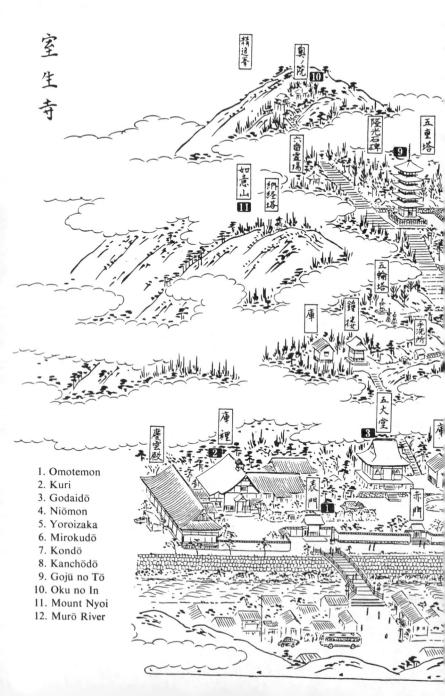

室生寺

精進峯　奥ノ院 **10**

隆光石碑　五重塔 **9**

六番霊場

如意山 **11**　納経堺

五輪塔　鐘楼　手洗所

庫

庫裡 **2**　五大堂 **3**　庫

慶雲殿

表門 **1**　赤門

1. Omotemon
2. Kuri
3. Godaidō
4. Niōmon
5. Yoroizaka
6. Mirokudō
7. Kondō
8. Kanchōdō
9. Gojū no Tō
10. Oku no In
11. Mount Nyoi
12. Murō River

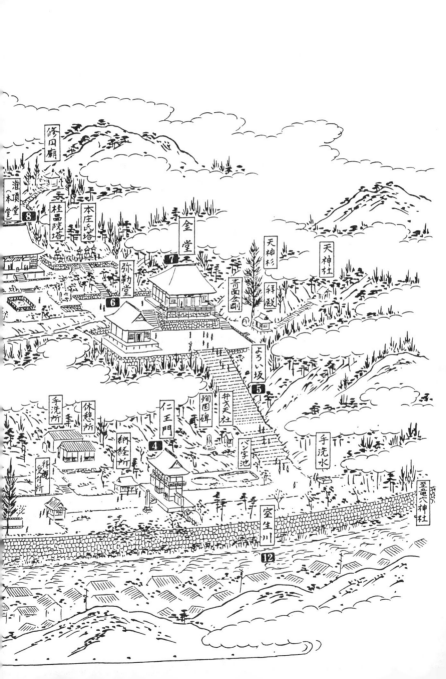

of men. Their love, their jealousies, their children, and their husbands all became the source of anguish. For women to just resign themselves to this as fate was too cruel.

> Soft-skinned with
> Plump, rounded elbows,
> A buddha image sits
> In the lush green of the mountains
> So summer warm, it almost sweats.
> —Yaichi Aizu (1881–1956)

Many women have made pilgrimages here and many have found solace.

There is an old Japanese-style inn in front of Murōji called Hashimotoya that has been there for many generations. Visitors who stay there are encouraged to write their impressions of their travels in notebooks which, over the years, have accumulated and can be pursued. In these we can find a kind of record of the human soul. It tells us that life is painful and tiring. And it tells us that because of that pain and exhaustion, people seek salvation or, at least, some comfort. These notebooks are not just a record of women's anguish; they record the suffering of all people.

One of the mysteries of Murōji is what we might call the belief in the dragon god. This belief is a kind of animistic mountain worship in which the area is regarded as the sacred dwelling of the dragon god. It is the mystery of the natural environment around Murōji that has awakened the belief in the sacred here. Mount Murō is said to resemble a lotus flower on the verge of blossoming, the surrounding peaks corresponding to the eight petals of the flower. Geographically speaking, these peaks form the outer crater of the Murō volcano. Such a topography must have seemed like an appropriate dwelling place for a dragon god. Murō-ji is located in the dragon god's cellar (*murō*), where caves and seas surround it. Murōji's roots go back to the belief that this area was an auspicious place to pray for rain, which is equivalent to a prayer for life.

The clear water of the Murō River comes from the dragon's cave. You immediately enter Murōji's grounds once you cross the river over the vermilion-painted Taiko Bridge. Climbing the armor-patterned stone steps from the Deva Gate (Niōmon), the pilgrim passes many different buildings on his or her way to the Inner Shrine (Oku no In): the Miroku Hall (Mirokudō), the Main Hall (Kondō), the Abhiseka Hall (Kanjōdō), and the Five-storied Pagoda (Gojū no Tō). In particular, this Five-storied Pagoda is a symbol of Kōya for Women because it gives the impression of softness and femininity. It is especially nice if you look back at it over your shoulder as you are walking away from it rather than looking up at it directly from the front. The path up to the Inner Shrine is lined with very old cedars which point directly up into the sky, making the pilgrim's journey to the other world even more enjoyable.

This area is sacred. Even though it is the home of the dragon god, it is not a strange mountain. People of ancient times who saw gods in nature must have seen the Murō dragon god lurking around within its valleys.

At times one sees here the exposed trunks of cypress trees, where the bark has been stripped off and the insides are dyed the color of blood. It looks much like our bodies would if our skin had been peeled off—almost painful in its exposure to the wind and the rain. That bark is used to rethatch the roofs of the temple buildings on Murōji's grounds and to protect the images enshrined inside.

All of the images inside the Main Hall—Shakamuni, the Eleven-faced Kannon, and the Twelve Divine Generals—have been designated National Treasures and are befitting a building like the Main Hall, also a National Treasure.

Hatsuyo Okumoto, the proprietress of Hashimotoya, across from Murōji, comforts the pilgrim even today with her smiling face.

It almost seems as if the beauty of the buddhas across the road has become manifest in her. Her benevolent and dignified manner lead us to believe that there are indeed living buddhas in this world. Her presence is fitting for a village like Murō, where she continues to protect one of Kōya for Women's lodgings.

I hope you will stay here just once, as you surely will feel the joy of salvation and be thankful for a person like Hatsuyo Okumoto. All of the villagers of Murō seem like living buddhas to me.

SECT   Murō branch of the Shingon sect.

ESTABLISHMENT   Founded by Kenkei at the end of the eighth century.

PRINCIPAL IMAGE   Shakamuni.

CULTURAL PROPERTIES   The main halls (Hondō and Kondō) and Five-storied Pagoda (Gojū no Tō) are National Treasures, as are both the seated and standing Shakamuni images and the Eleven-faced Kannon image.

VISITING INFORMATION   The entire grounds all the way up to the Oku no In, or Inner Hall, are open to visitors. Winter here is cold and snowy. For that reason, Murōji is perhaps best visited in the spring, summer, and fall. The two biggest celebrations here are on October 15, the Dragon Festival (Ryūketsu Sai), and Kūkai's Memorial Ceremony (Shōmeiku Nerikuyō) on April 21.

OF SPECIAL INTEREST   There are no gardens of special interest here, but Murōji's location in the mountains and the long pathway up to the Inner Hall (Oku no In) are quite beautiful. In May the alpine rose blooms here and fills the area with various shades of red and white. The various halls and buildings of Murōji are beautifully placed on the side of the mountain.

LOCATION AND TRANSPORTATION   Murō-mura, Uda-gun, Nara Prefecture. Take the Osaka Line of the Kintetsu Railway to Murōguchi Ōno Station. From there, board a Nara Kōtsu Bus for Tatsuobashi or Chiharabashi and get off at Murōji Mae Bus Stop.

室生寺　　奈良県宇陀郡室生村

OTHER AREAS

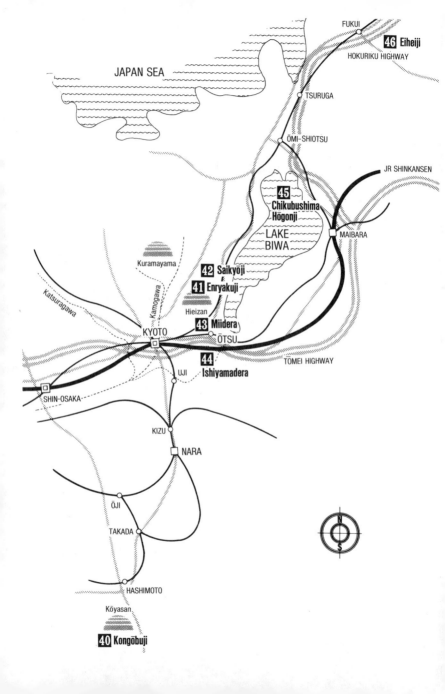

40. Kongōbuji

I have been to Mount Kōya very many times. I have been there both in the summer and in the winter. In the summer it is nice because it is cool, but still people bring with them the noise and confusion of their own worlds. As I look at the children playing in their summer school camps, which dot the countryside on the way up to Mount Kōya, I cannot help but feel that they do not fit in here very well.

But Mount Kōya is splendid during the summer and the winter. I particularly like it in midwinter. To look out from the Main Gate (Daimon) at the incessant snowfall is one of the special sights here. The intensity of the winter here can also be a source of joy. Like an ink painting of a sea of clouds on a scroll, the landscape here at Mount Kōya changes moment to moment.

"Beyond the Main Gate is heaven. The mountain ridge extends out to the wide open sky. When you look out at that sky from the Main Gate, this religious city does not actually seem real anymore. It seems like an illusion reaching out to the sky. Mount Kōya is really one of the most unique places in all of Japan," writes the novelist Ryōtarō Shiba.

This gate is nothing less than the departure point of the great path to the esoteric teachings. Numerous times I have walked along the frozen, snow-covered visitors' path here. And whenever

高野山
壇上伽藍図

大塔

2

愛染堂　大会堂　三昧堂　東塔

1

智泉廟

不動堂

8

手水舎

至奥之院

10

勧学院

常喜院

増福院

1. Tōtō
2. Daitō
3. Saitō
4. Shōrō
5. Sannō-in Haiden
6. Sannō-in Honden
7. Shōrō
8. Fudōdō
9. toward Daimon
10. toward Oku no In

I do, I cannot help but wonder why Kūkai came here in the first place. Shiba reflects upon this same question when he says that Kōya might be "an illusion reaching to the sky." But if it is not—if it is a manifestation of truth—why do I feel so transitory when I am here, if my existence itself is an illusion?

Inevitably, questions about Mount Kōya become questions about humanity itself. There is no room here to tremble in the cold. Is there hot and cold, I wonder, in Tushita Heaven, where Miroku lives?

Kūkai left behind these words before his death: "When I die, I will go to Tushita Heaven and serve Miroku. And when Miroku appears in this world in 5.67 billion years, as it is prophesied in the scriptures, I too will come back and visit Mount Kōya."

If that is the case, then Mount Kōya must be the departure point for Tushita Heaven as well. As "an illusion reaching to the sky," its significance lies in the fact that it is a bridge to Miroku's heaven.

When surrounded by the mysterious, ethereal environment of Mount Kōya, we tend to become somewhat naive. In particular, when we walk up to the Inner Sanctuary (Oku no In), where it is believed Kūkai still dwells, we leave our doubts behind and bow to his presence.

> How grateful I feel!
> In the shadow of a rock
> Deep in the heart
> Of Mount Kōya,
> Our great teacher lives on.

It is not only the world at the bottom of the mountain, though. Even in the city of Kōya here on the mountain, we can feel the presence of the worldly. But that does not present any problems in particular. It is enough to be able to feel the cry of our own soul which shakes the root of our being.

Mount Kōya experienced few moments of Pure Land tranquility

in the years after it was established. In that sense, it was no different at all from the rest of the world. Periods of gloom and tragedy were filled with the cries of those whose blood was spilled here. Paradoxically, it was the grief and sadness of the secular world which blanketed Mount Kōya and helped to make it holy. It was the suffering of humanity's self-made hell which would transform it into a sacred place.

A look at the chronological history of Mount Kōya's Kongōbuji reveals periods of both prosperity and decline. Buildings were burned to the ground and rebuilt; feuds, riots, and massacres occurred within the context of a struggle for secular authority. This was the destiny that Mount Kōya had to follow to survive. And that is why Mount Kōya, a mountain that people climb to pray for divine favor, has come to be considered one of the major holy places of the Orient. Pilgrims do not come here in pursuit of the deep ideals elucidated in Shingon philosophy. They pray simply and with purity that their great teacher Kūkai will continue to dwell here and teach them.

We must come into this world alone and we must die alone. This is a law which treats everyone equally. Dying alone, of course, is terrible—it is sad and it is lonely. We all want to be with somebody. We want to live in this world and know that we can rely upon someone. Faith does not exist in the comparison and contrast of the exoteric and esoteric doctrines of Saichō (the founder of Tendai in Japan; 766–822) and Kūkai. The esoteric doctrine of "becoming a Buddha in this lifetime" (*sokushin jōbutsu*) or the theories of the diamond-scepter (*kongō*) and womb-store (*taizō*) mandalas are extremely difficult to understand and may be beyond the comprehension of people. One cannot deny that esoteric Buddhism since the Heian period did degenerate into a system of religious ceremonies to invoke the blessings of the Buddha or dispel misfortune. But this was far from Kūkai's original intention in spreading the teachings in Japan.

Human beings want to be cured quickly from sufferings caused by illness and released from the grief of their own or others' deaths. That is the extent of their prayers. The means of invoking good fortune and blessings is a prayer to induce benefits or favor. Because of this, we must make our journey with Kūkai. On the train down from Mount Kōya, I saw the shining and peaceful faces of many men and women as the train rushed on callously into the noisy and confused world of Osaka.

SECT   Headquarters of the Kōya Shingon sect.

ESTABLISHMENT   Founded by Kūkai in 816.

PRINCIPAL IMAGE   Kūkai.

CULTURAL PROPERTIES   Mount Kōya is a storehouse of National Treasures and Important Cultural Properties. The mountain and its temples are by far the most representative example—along with Mount Hiei in Kyoto—of the combination of mountain worship and Buddhism in Japan. There are numerous architectural National Treasures and numerous other artifacts, images, and documents which are stored in the Museum (Reihō-kan). The Fudō Hall is a National Treasure, as are the Eight Great Children (Hachi Dai Dōji) image, the Lotus Sutra scrolls, and the painting of the Buddha's nirvana on silk. The two Dainichi Buddha images are Important Cultural Properties.

VISITING INFORMATION   Because Mount Kōya is some three thousand feet high, the winter here is hard. Spring, summer, and fall are perhaps better times to visit than winter. In particular, there are large numbers of tourists and pilgrims as well as children here in the summer. Mount Kōya really surpasses any other temple complex in Japan. It is a holy place. Because of its sacredness, many historically famous people are buried here.

OF SPECIAL INTEREST   There are of course gardens at the various subtemples on Mount Kōya, but more important is the general location of the monastery on the mountain, which seems to impose itself upon the whole monastery complex.

LOCATION AND TRANSPORTATION   Kōya-chō, Ito-gun, Wakayama Prefecture. Mount Kōya is in Wakayama Prefecture, but it is still within the general vicinity of Osaka. From Namba in Osaka, take the special express train of the Nankai Railway to Hashimoto where you will board a cable car to the top of Mount Kōya. From the cable car, board a bus to get to the city of Kōya.

金剛峯寺   和歌山県伊都郡高野町

41. Enryakuji

I continued my pilgrimage to the old temples up to Mount Hiei, the center of the Tendai sect in Japan, whose head temple, Enryakuji, seems almost too big in both a historical and a physical sense for the task of pilgrimage, a word which conjures up serious religious purpose. I get the feeling somehow that the two are just not compatible. I guess that is to be expected with a temple like Enryakuji. It is something like comparing a dignified university such as Tokyo University with a two-year junior college. But it is not just the visual aspect—the physical space and the buildings—which strikes visitors as large. The spatial aspect of Enryakuji is not particularly surprising. But in a temporal sense as well, Enryakuji is huge.

From the point of view of Japanese Buddhism, Enryakuji seems like a Buddhist university with its attending Zen, Jōdo, and Nichiren colleges, since each of these sects got their start here in some way. On the other hand, Kyoto looks like a small temple-gate town from the point of view of its own and Japanese history— a town that was manipulated by the concealed power of the temples. Since Enryakuji controlled much of the country's political and economic situation, it is often seen as a kind of central government office scowling down upon the rest of the world with an air of authority.

Historically speaking, Enryakuji solidified its power over the country regardless of problems concerning the sacred and the profane. There were plenty of reasons for this and they become clear when we consider the intentions with which Enryakuji was founded. As long as Enryakuji existed as a kind of large university for the education of priests who would assume control of powerful temples all over the country, then its position of authority was assured.

The sentiments which took me on my pilgrimage to the old temples also accompanied me to the small temple buildings which dot the mountainside on Mount Hiei. There are different ways to get up to the vast world of Enryakuji: the Mount Hiei Parkway and the cable car are two of them. On the way up, various buildings from this "campus"—buildings with long, secret histories—come in and out of view. At one time, Enryakuji extended 20 miles east to west, 20 miles north to south, and had a circumference of 244 miles. Within that area there were three pagodas, sixteen valleys, and more than three thousand buildings.

Saichō (767–822), the founder of Enryakuji, wrote the following in the opening section to *The Annual Student Ceremony of the Tendai Lotus Sect* (*Tendai Hokkeshū Nembun Gakusei Shiki*), in a description of three different ranks of Tendai monks, *kokuho, kokushi,* and *kokuyū:* "What kind of a person is the *kokuhō*? The *hō,* or jewel, is the heart that practices the dharma. Thus, one who has such a heart is named "the jewel of the country" (*koku*). A wise man of old once said, 'Even if one gathered ten jewels each one inch in diameter, they would not equal a *kokuhō*. Only that which shines into every corner of the realm is a national jewel.' "

In other words, real jewels are no match for the national jewel (*kokuhō*) trained in the practices of the dharma at Enryakuji. Saichō defined a national jewel as someone who had secluded himself for twelve years, continually engaged in Buddhist practices, excelled in scholarship, and became a teacher to other students on the path. A *kokushi,* or national teacher, was one who excelled at

延暦寺

大比叡 10

智証大師廟
霊牌殿
阿弥陀堂 4
千手がん
延暦寺木二阪車駅
比叡山ドライブウェイ 9
無動寺谷
坂本ケーブル 8
戒壇院
前唐院
大講堂 3
鐘楼
根本中堂 2
和労堂
大黒天堂
文殊楼
事務所
書院
蓮如堂
坂本道
延暦寺会館
庄堂大師廟
東　塔 1

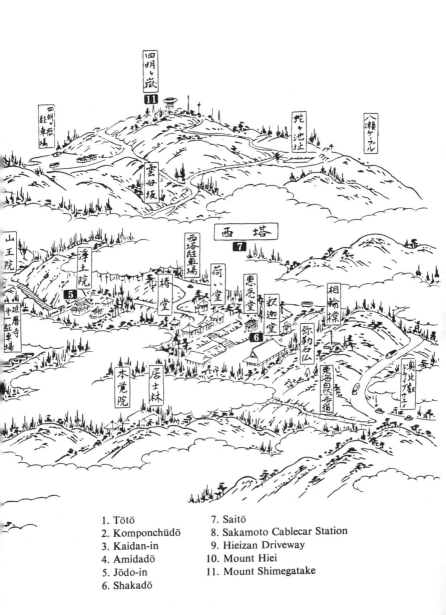

四明ヶ嶽
11

四明ヶ嶽駐車場

蛇ヶ池址

八瀬ケーブル

雲母坂

山王院

西塔駐車場

西　塔
7

浄土院
5

延暦寺本坂駐車場

椿堂

荷ヒ堂

恵亮堂

釈迦堂
6

相輪樘

弥勒石仏

本覚院

居士林

東海自然歩道

奥比叡ドライブウェイ

1. Tōtō
2. Komponchūdō
3. Kaidan-in
4. Amidadō
5. Jōdo-in
6. Shakadō
7. Saitō
8. Sakamoto Cablecar Station
9. Hieizan Driveway
10. Mount Hiei
11. Mount Shimegatake

scholarship. While a *kokuyū,* or national servant, exercised his leadership in the practical matters of the world. The *kokushi* and *kokuyū* were dispatched to provinces throughout the country and instructed to lead its officials and citizens. In this way religion, and particularly Tendai religious ethics, became the basis of Japanese statecraft. In other words, the spreading of Tendai doctrines led to the establishment of Buddhism as a protector of the state.

To continue with Saichō's words: "Propagate the dharma for eternity. Since the dharma is for the benefit of the state, it is also for the benefit of all beings. Repay your indebtedness to the country by prospering the dharma.

"As students of *sammon* (the teachings of the Enryakuji Tendai lineage), even if we were beggars on the street, we could still become the emperor's teachers. In the temples, we must not abandon our pride as teachers to those in the three worlds. Truly, there is no path more worthy for us to follow and no obstacle too great for us to overcome. About this we have no doubts."

Men of brilliance and talent who had the will to practice the dharma gathered here on Mount Hiei. Except for Kukai, the great teacher of the Shingon tradition, the teachers and the teachings of the other great sects emanated from this one source. This includes Hōnen (1133–1212), Shinran (1173–1262), and Nichiren (1222–82), as well as a number of Zen priests. The religious and intellectual world that sprang up around these men had its roots in the traditions of Enryakuji.

The history of Mount Hiei is, in one sense, the history of Japanese Buddhism. The problem is that the volume of that history is so great there is no way to put it in perspective and consider its various aspects on a pilgrimage. Over and over, the images of the devoted scholars and scholar-priests who once gathered here keep coming to mind.

It is nice to walk around alone on Mount Hiei recalling the various feuds that beset Nara-period Buddhism. Stretching out below the mountain is Kyoto, which was besieged with periodic wars and revolts during the Heian (794–1185) and Kamakura (1185–1333) periods. Here and there we can there we can still find traces of the misfortunes which befell the city and this mountain during the Warring States period (1482–1558) as well as traces of the rivalry between the *sammon* and *jimon* factions of Tendai Buddhism. If we listen hard enough, we might even be able to hear the hammers rebuilding the temple structures as ordered by Abbot Tenkai (1536–1643) in the seventeenth century.

But we cannot spend our time in historical recollections alone. We would be better off considering Saichō's incredible energy, which was the major force behind making Mount Hiei one of the most powerful religious centers in Japan and is still the source of Hiei's vitality today. His final instructions to his disciples before his death consisted of the following: "Do not make Buddhist images for me and do not copy the sutras for me. Transmit what I have taught you to everyone. Buddhist practice is not divorced from our everyday lives, but if we are drawn only to the most trivial aspects of our lives, we will not be able to practice. Let us live properly between the world of practice and our everyday world. Let us study the "three learnings"—wisdom, meditation, and the precepts—and spread the Buddha's teachings by means of our one-pointed minds of enlightenment. If there are any who think as I do, adhere to the teachings and practice. And then wait for the time to spread the teachings so that they will be useful to all."

I wonder how many have heard the soft yet uncompromising voice of Saichō here as they made their pilgrimage to Mount Hiei: "Wait for the time to spread the teachings so that they will be useful to all."

SECT   Headquarters of the Tendai sect.

ESTABLISHMENT   Founded by Saichō in 785.

PRINCIPAL IMAGE   Yakushi.

CULTURAL PROPERTIES   The Main Hall (Hondō) is a National Treasure, as is the Central Hall (Komponchūdō). The Ordination Platform Hall (Kaidan'indō), Shakamuni Hall (Shakadō), the Turning the Wheel of the Dharma Hall (Tempōrindō), and the Thousand-armed Kannon are Important Cultural Properties. There are many other Important Cultural Properties dating from the Heian period and later.

VISITING INFORMATION   Spring, summer, and fall are the best seasons to visit Mount Hiei. Winter is extremely cold and the mountain is often covered with snow. The temple grounds are divided into three sectors: the Eastern Precinct, the Western Precinct, and the Northern Precinct. The arrangement of the grounds provides a good example of how mountain monasteries were traditionally laid out.

OF SPECIAL INTEREST   The Central Hall, the Ordination Platform Hall, Shakamuni Hall, and the Turning of the Wheel of the Dharma Hall are worth seeing. The location of the buildings on the mountainside is quite extraordinary.

LOCATION AND TRANSPORTATION   Sakamoto Hommachi, Ōtsu-shi, Shiga Prefecture. Enryakuji is located at the top of Mount Hiei in the northeastern part of Kyoto. Take the Keihan Railway to Sakamoto from Sanjō Keihan. At Sakamoto take the cable car to the top and you will be near the temple grounds. Another way is to take the Keifuku Railway from Demachiyanagi to Yase and from there to take the cable car and ropeway to the top. Once you arrive from this direction, however, there is a considerable walk to the grounds. There are also buses that will take you right to the temple. One of these leaves from the corner of Imadegawa and Shirakawa streets.

延暦寺　滋賀県大津市坂本本町

42. Saikyōji

The Kosei Line, which splits off from Kyoto in Yamashina, heads towards Sakamoto along the foot of Mount Hiei after cutting through the hillside grounds of Miidera. In the morning, Lake Biwa glistens beautifully as the rays of the rising sun reflect off of it. To get to Saikyōji, you get off the train at Eizan. From here, when you look to the west, you can see old houses stretching all the way from Sakamoto to Hiyoshi Shrine along a gently sloping ridge. Just before you come to the second torii at Hiyoshi Shrine, there is an old sign posted which reads "The road to Seimon Honzan Saikyōji is to the right."

The road to the right, as well as the road to the left, continues up a slope to the northwest. The thing which strikes your eyes first here is the stone wall built in the haphazard style common to this area. All of the surrounding houses are old and the wall is moss covered. The area is blanketed in white flowers that seem to make a kind of striped pattern shining in the autumn sun. In the spring, the green grasses are soft, giving the area an even more peaceful feeling.

Saikyōji has been the site of many battles. During the Warring States period (1482–1558) in particular, conflicts between monks living on Mount Hiei and in Sakamoto were unusually bad. Much of this has been recorded in *The Tales of Nobunaga* (*No-*

1. Sōmon
2. Chokushimon
3. Shūso Taishiden
4. Hombō
5. Hondō
6. Shoin
7. Kyakuden
8. Shinzei's Tomb
9. Mount Hiei

西教寺

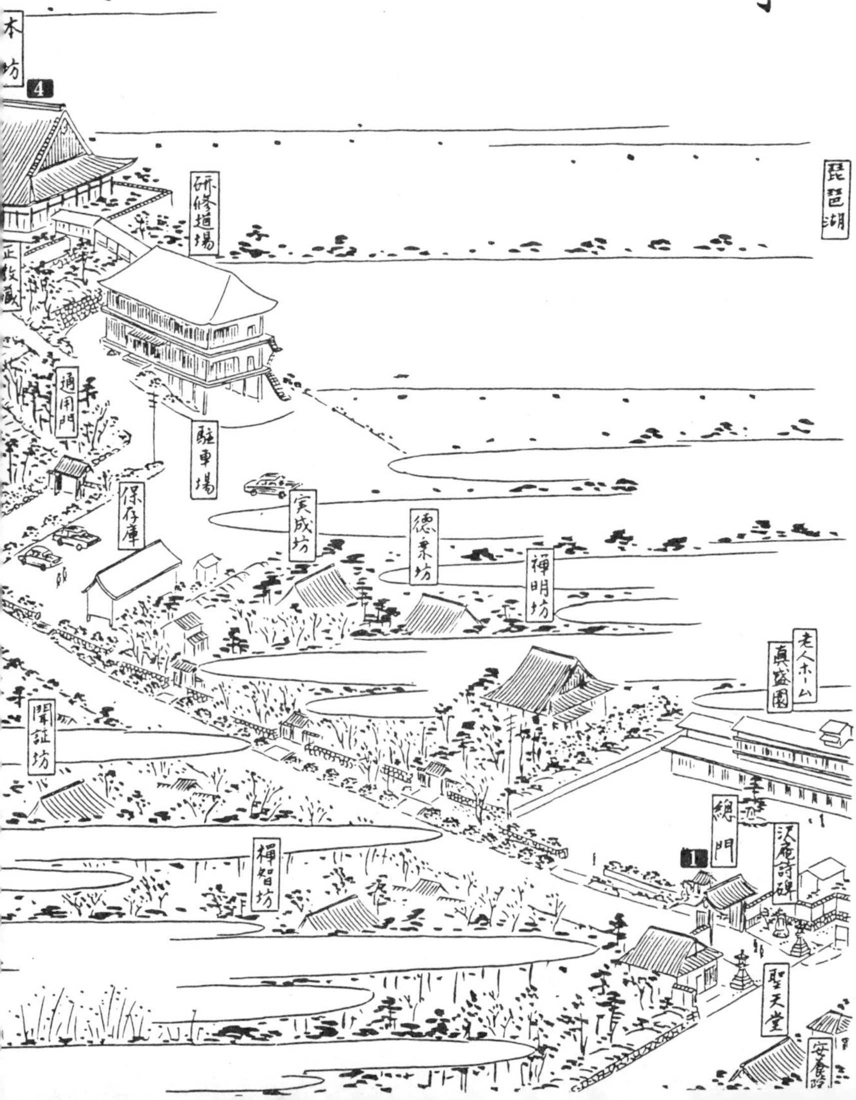

琵琶湖

木坊
4

研修道場

正教蔵

琵琶湖

通用門

駐車場

保存庫

実成坊

徳乗坊

禅明坊

老人ホーム
真盛園

証坊

聖天堂

総門

天台詩碑

禅智坊

1

聖天堂

安養院

bunaga Ki), but during one such conflict some three thousand priests from Mount Hiei as well as a large number of innocent citizens and lay practitioners were massacred here.

This area has a long history of periods of decline followed by periods of restoration. Sakamoto, which was completely destroyed in a hellish fire, was brought back to life by Akechi Mitsuhide (1526–82) and Toyotomi Hideyoshi (1536–98). And Saikyōji, which purportedly dates back to the time of and has connections with Shōtoku Taishi (574–622), was reconstructed by Shinzei (1443–95) in 1486, burnt down by Nobunaga, and once again rebuilt by Mitsuhide and Hideyoshi. Thanks to the efforts of Shinzei, Saikyōji became a center for the practice of the *fudan,* or unceasing, nembutsu, a unique combination of nembutsu practice and the observance of strict discipline.

Statues and portraits of Shinzei that exist today depict a truly handsome man. Common people pursued their thirst for the teachings by pursuing the handsome priest himself. According to *The Biography of Rebirth (Ōjō Denki)*, young women who had lost the will to live followed Shinzei in death by drowning themselves. They did this in the hopes of being blessed with the teachings of the nembutsu by the "nembutsu saint who practices, by nature, without any desire or ambition."

Shinzei was nineteen when he went to Mount Hiei to study and for the next twenty years he stayed there training himself well in Tendai doctrines. When he was forty years old, his mother died, and he decided to seclude himself at Seiryūji in the Kurodani section of Mount Hiei. This was an auspicious place to practice since it was where Hōnen, the great nembutsu practitioner and founder of the Jōdo Sect, had achieved enlightenment after a long period of devoted nembutsu practice. For Shinzei this period of seclusion was devoted to reading the basic writings of Pure Land Sect leaders Hōnen (1133–1212) and Genshin (942–1017) and thereby gaining a thorough understanding of the nembutsu teachings.

Shinzei's conception of the nembutsu was different from Hōnen's and from that of Hōnen's disciple Shinran (1173–1262) as well. Shinzei's *fudan* nembutsu was based on a daily observance of the Buddhist precepts, the fundamental regulations governing a practitioner's life. The following, for example, was meant to encourage thoughtfulness before taking refuge in the priesthood: "It is difficult to repay one's kindness for a bowl of rice or a drop of water. Therefore, we must be careful not to eat that which is given to us thoughtlessly or to accept a place to sleep without gratitude. Each of us must be our own teacher and avoid the temptation of looking only for that which is pleasurable." The *fudan* nembutsu tradition is still very much alive at Saikyōji today.

The monkey gods, in the form of the Migawari no Saru, or "substitute monkeys," who used to ring the bell at the Main Hall (Hondo) are still at Saikyōji, too. It is said that these monkey gods would ring the main bell of the temple to warn the priests of imminent attacks by rampaging warrior-priests from Mount Hiei who were jealous of Saikyōji's prosperity.

Shinzei's efforts to spread the teachings of the nembutsu unfortunately coincided with the Ōnin and Bummei Disturbances of the fifteenth century, when hardly a day went by that it was safe to walk through the capital. Despite the warfare and danger, though, he would walk through the streets of Kyoto which, for the most part, had been completely leveled by fire, and preach to the people about the certainty of salvation through the practice of the *fudan* nembutsu.

The handsome priest Shinzei died at Sairenji in present-day Mie Prefecture, the final stop in his pilgrimage. His last instructions to his disciples were: "With a ready heart, you must practice the nembutsu often, purely and without desire."

There is a stone monument on the grounds of Saikyōji that was erected to commemorate the completion of the first 170,000 days of nembutsu practice at the temple. It is the newest part of the temple, completed in 1972. In the five hundred years since

Saikyōji was restored by Shinzei in 1486, the sound of the nembutsu bell has never been silenced.

The *fudan* nembutsu practice is supposed to continue for one million days. If it does continue that long, that means it will end in the year 4300. I have no reason to doubt that that day will occur. Of course, it is impossible for us to know whether that day will ever occur or not, but if faith survives, I am certain someone will engrave this into the stone monument: one million days of *fudan* nembutsu.

Mankind is alienated these days from the happiness which comes from having something to believe in. I often wonder what will happen to us, where will we go?

The sound of the *fudan* nembutsu bell echoes throughout the temple grounds. It is all the evidence there is that someone is practicing the nembutsu.

Hoping that this practice will continue ceaselessly until the one million days are completed, I made my way down the path to Sakamoto on my way back home.

SECT   Headquarters of the Shinzei Branch of the Tendai sect.

ESTABLISHMENT   Founded by Shinzei in 1486.

PRINCIPAL IMAGE   Amida.

CULTURAL PROPERTIES   The images of Amida and Yakushi, the Guest Hall (Kyakuden), several sutra scrolls, and the Taima Mandala are Important Cultural Properties.

VISITING INFORMATION   The temple grounds are open to the public all year round, but the interiors of the halls and buildings can only be viewed by appointment.

OF SPECIAL INTEREST   The garden in front of the Guest Hall is very attractive. It is constructed in the *chisen kaiyū* style, which means it is to be enjoyed while walking through it. The Guest Hall and the Main Hall are the two main halls of interest to the visitor here. The *fusuma* paintings of the Kanō school in the Guest Hall date from the Momoyama period. In the Main Hall there is a wooden sculpture called Monkey Substitute, which, according to legend, intoned the sacred nembutsu chant to help protect Mount Hiei from attack.

LOCATION AND TRANSPORTATION   3210 Sakamoto Hommachi, Ōtsu-shi, Shiga Prefecture. From the Sakamoto Station of the Keihan Line it is a twenty-minute walk.

西教寺　　滋賀県大津市坂本本町 3210

43. Miidera

Miidera is formally known as Chōtōzan Onjōji, but somehow
Miidera sounds more friendly. In spring, the area around the
Kannon Hall (Kannondō) is a blur of falling blossoms. And the
view from the Moon-viewing Platform (Kangetsudai) is spectacular. Through the haze of the falling cherry blossoms, you can
see Ōtsu and a misty Lake Biwa. Before I knew it, I was beginning
to recall ancient Japan in the seventh century, when Ōtsu used to
be the imperial capital.

Jakuchō Setouchi, a Buddhist nun, recalls the time during her
childhood when she was first attracted to this area: "I think that
what fascinated me about Miidera was perhaps the fact that it is
located near Lake Biwa. And the reason I was drawn to Lake
Biwa and ended up visiting it so many times was because of the
ripples of sympathy I felt for its sad history, especially during the
time Ōtsu was the capital until the Jinshin Disturbance (667–72)."

These "ripples," a word often used in literature when describing
the ancient capital (*sazanami no Shiga no miyako*), were stirred
up because of the heartrending tales which have become, in time,
etched into the annals of Japanese history. This sense of a long
and sad history is buried deep within Miidera and gives it a peaceful, dignified appearance.

The road to Miidera, which is located at the base of Mount

Chōtō in the western part of Ōtsu, is not far from the bustle of the city. But still the grounds of the temple, which are surrounded by a moss-covered stone wall, are full of luxuriant green trees. One step into this environment is enough to know that you are not in the ordinary world anymore. The grounds of Miidera feel sanctified.

The cleanly swept visitor's path leads from the Deva Gate (Niōmon) to the Main Hall (Kondō), the Sutra Hall (Issaikyōzō), the Sect Founder's Hall (Taishibyo), the Three-storied Pagoda (Sanjū no Tō), the Library (Kangakuin), the Fire Ritual Hall (Gomadō), and the Abhiseka Hall (Kanjōdō).

In the shade of the tall, old trees, you can hear Miidera's bell.

> Biwa's seven views
> Lay hidden by the fog—
> Miidera's bell.

It somehow seems like the remaining seven famous scenes in and around Ōmi are all condensed into the eighth one here at Miidera.

Miidera was founded during the seventh century at the orders of emperors Tenchi (r. 662–71), Kōbun (r. 671–72), and Temmu (r. 673–86) after the Jinshin Disturbance. It actually got its start after Ōtomo no Yotaō, the son of Emperor Kōbun, donated all of his land to the temple upon his father's death. This is recorded as taking place in 686, or one hundred years before the founding of Enryakuji on Mount Hiei, the most influential temple center in western Japan.

It was after Enchin (d. 891) came back from Tang China and became the first head priest of Miidera that discord between the *sammon* (Hiei) and *jimon* (Miidera) factions of Tendai Buddhism broke out. This sometimes violent antagonism represented initially by Priest Jikaku (792–862) and Enryakuji on the *sammon* side and Enchin and Miidera Onjōji on the *jimon* side continued for a long time.

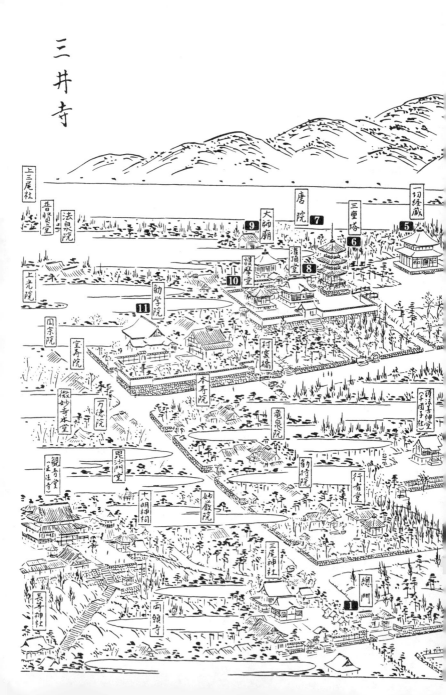

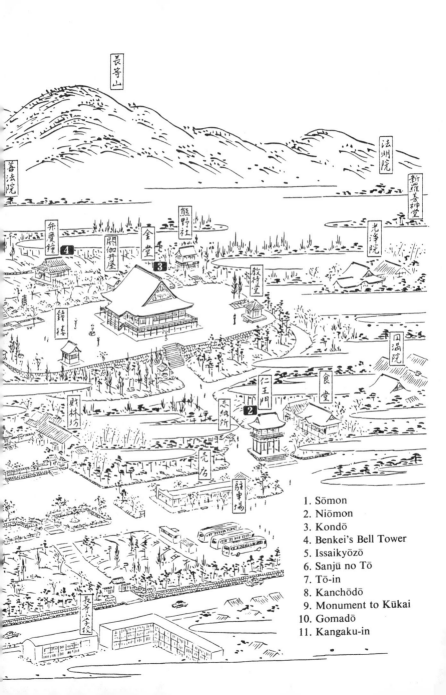

1. Sōmon
2. Niōmon
3. Kondō
4. Benkei's Bell Tower
5. Issaikyōzō
6. Sanjū no Tō
7. Tō-in
8. Kanchōdō
9. Monument to Kūkai
10. Gomadō
11. Kangaku-in

The struggle that occurred between these two sides grew into more than just the factional dispute of one sect. It was a complete involvement of Japanese Buddhism and various political conflicts: in short, a struggle for authority. These struggles continued from the time of the Taira-Minamoto Wars in the Kamakura period (1185–1333) until the Muromachi period (1336–1568). Sometimes they existed in the foreground of other political disturbances and sometimes they were in the background. Political history in Japan until the Tokugawa period is often inseparable from the history of religious wars. These wars spared nothing in their savagery. Cities and farms were burned and the country in general was laid to waste. The temple histories record innumerable burnings of Onjōji, especially from the eleventh to the fourteenth centuries. There is one article dated 1319 which says that it had been burned to the ground as many as ten times.

Of course, this also means that it was rebuilt just as many times. It came to life again and again like a phoenix rising out of the ashes. Why, I wonder, was it so strong?

There must have been something more powerful within Miidera than just enmity and antagonism. To find what that is, though, we must take a look at the hair-raising legends and tales of vengeful spirits who inhabited this area. These spirits of the dead either writhe about in an attempt to get free and seek revenge or they dance about bathed in the light of Kannon's compassion. *The Tale of the Heike* (*Heike Monogatari*) tells us much about this period, its battles, and the spirits of those sacrificed. The religious tales and temple legends also narrate this period for us with great beauty and pathos. The mysterious features of these tales, like the images of water, springs, lakes, and snakes, captivate our imaginations. They describe a world which, between Miidera's sacredness and its bloody history, feels strange but yet somehow surpasses love and revenge.

Do people who are interested in difficult Tendai philosophical doctrines make pilgrimages here? Probably not. Doctrines such as the idea of perfect harmony among the three truths or the various aspects of meditation practice will not answer our simple prayers.

> As I look at the moon
> Reflecting its beauty in the waves
> Here at Miidera
> I can hear the resonant bell
> Echo over the morning lake.

Pilgrims still come to Miiera, the fourteenth temple on the thirty-three-temple pilgrimage to western Japan. It is a beautiful temple for us to rely upon. It is best to hurry along the visitor's path to the Kannon Hall and forget about Miidera's history. Looking out at Lake Biwa in the distance from the Moon-viewing Platform, you can brush away every speck of dirt that has accumulated from your life of confusion.

SECT   Headquarters of the Jimon branch of the Tendai sect.

ESTABLISHMENT   Founded by Enchin in 672.

PRINCIPAL IMAGE   Miroku.

CULTURAL PROPERTIES   The Main Hall, image of Enchin, documents concerning Enchin, and painting of Fudō Myōō on silk are National Treasures. The Deva Gate is an Important Cultural Property.

VISITING INFORMATION   Miidera is extremely large and is open to the public all year long. There are many lovely buildings and halls and there is a direct view of Lake Biwa from the Kannon

Hall. The cherry blossom season here is particularly nice. The temple bell is considered one of the Eight Famous Views of Ōmi and its tolling in the evening is famous throughout Japan.

OF SPECIAL INTEREST   Strolling through Miidera's vast grounds will give the visitor a feeling for the noble character of this temple. The Main Hall, Deva Gate, Three-storied Pagoda, and Bishamon Hall are all worth seeing, as are the seated image of Enchin, the Eleven-faced Kannon, Thousand-armed Kannon, and Fudō Myōō images. Miidera is a treasurehouse of Buddhist sculpture.

LOCATION AND TRANSPORTATION   Onjōji-chō, Ōtsu-shi, Shiga Prefecture. Take the Ishiyama-Sakamoto Keihan Line to the Miidera Station. From there to Miidera by bus takes four minutes.

三井寺　　滋賀県大津市園城寺町

44. Ishiyamadera

Ishiyamadera is the thirteenth temple on the thirty-three-temple pilgrimage in western Japan, and one can often still see pilgrims, with their familiar bells, in the area.

It takes thirty to forty minutes to get to the station nearest Ishiyamadera from Kyoto if you take the Keihan train from Sanjō Street. This train crosses over Mount Ōsaka on its way to Ōtsu and then heads to the east along Lake Biwa from Hamaōtsu. Finally, it follows the Seta River until it arrives at Ishiyamadera Station.

The Seta River originates from Lake Biwa and heads towards Uji. From here it is called the Uji River until it joins the Kamo River from Kyoto. Where the Kizu and Ōi rivers empty into it, it is called the Yodo River and this river flows down toward Osaka.

Ishiyamadera faces the clear Seta River, while a rich plain from the southern edge of the lake stretches out in front of the temple on the opposite bank.

One can sense the rich tradition of literature surrounding Ishiyamadera as well as the long tradition of women who have spent time here.

As its name suggests, Ishiyamadera is built on top of a massive

1. Tōdaimon
2. Daikokudō
3. Rennyodō
4. Hondō
5. Murasaki Shikibu no Tō
6. Bashō's Stele
7. Tahōtō

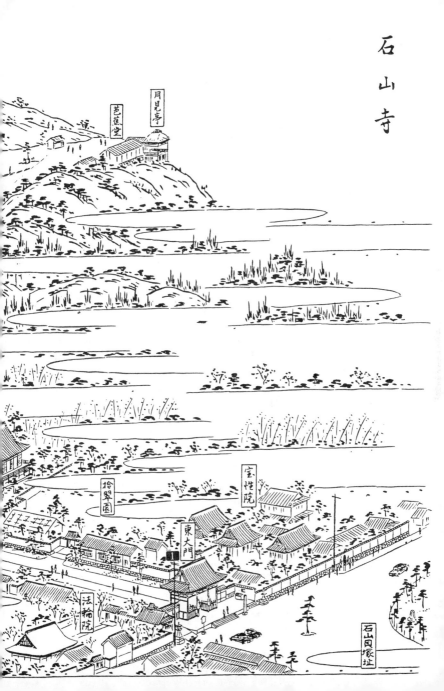

石山寺

月見亭
芭蕉堂

宝性院
拾翠園
東大門
法輪院
石山貝塚址

rock. This rock is an accumulation of layers of rocks piled together in a kind of squatting position looking like a face that has appeared right out of the earth's axis. This particular kind of rock, called wollastonite, is white, and this explains why the temple's "mountain name" is Shining Rock Mountain (Shakkōzan).

It is said that Ishiyamadera was founded during the middle of the Nara period (646–794). At the time it was established, auspicious-looking clouds are said to have concealed this rock-mountain.

What I think about when I come here is the skin-like whiteness of the rock on which Ishiyamadera is built. I also cannot help but think about how this area has become a sacred one for women, perhaps due somehow to the incredible surface of the rock which, as I mentioned above, is supposed to have appeared out of the earth's axis. It was only women, wasn't it, who took refuge and secluded themselves here?

"I wonder how many women came here to seek refuge at Ishiyamadera with a prayer in their hearts for Kannon, looking for a solution to the problems in their love lives or for the salvation of their souls or for a moment's consolation? There were many women of the nobility who crossed the distant barrier over Mount Ōsaka or who came by boat down the Seta River to forget, for even a little while, the torments of their unsatisfying marriages back in the capital," writes Takehiko Noguchi, professor at Kobe University.

Why, for example, did the mother of Fujiwara no Michitsuna, the author of the tenth-century diary *The Gossamer Years* (*Kagerō Nikki*), take refuge at Ishiyamadera? Whatever the reason, this trend during the ninth and tenth centuries added a certain charm to Heian-period literature.

Perhaps the rock at Ishiyamadera holds some secret which attracts women to it. The most elevated female visitor was certainly Murasaki Shikibu (fl. ca. 1000), the author of *The Tale of*

Genji. Her work and her presence shine above all the rest. I think it would be better to leave the details about her, though, to the literature experts.

Standing on the grounds of Ishiyamadera, I was struck by the incredible beauty of the area. This is something all the old temples have in common, but is especially true in the case of this temple. It is so beautiful that it is easy to imagine why both Murasaki Shikibu and Izumi Shikibu (late tenth–mid eleventh century) chose it as a setting for their tales.

According to temple legend, Ishiyamadera's history has been troubled. The temple was founded during the Nara period by the monk Rōben (689–773), the second head priest of the Kegon sect, in 747. This makes it more than 1,200 years old. The history of its founding is related in some detail in the *Picture Scroll of the Origins of Ishiyamadera* (*Ishiyamadera Engi Emaki*).

Its subsequent history was unfortunate. I wonder why faith and devotion did not succumb as well to misfortune? This is not so difficult to imagine if we take a look at the pilgrims who still come here today.

The old wooden placards which are on display here and which record pilgrims' visits to the temple date back to 1506. The sincere prayers of the pilgrims who sought to confirm Kannon's compassion are also recorded on these wooden fragments. These pilgrims are not the aristocratic characters who appear in Heian literature. They are the common people, and their poignant prayers reflect their status. The married couples who make this pilgrimage today are no different.

Matsuo Bashō (1644–94), the famous haiku poet, once rested here during his travels:

> Cooler than the white rock
> Here at Ishiyama
> Is the cool autumn wind.

> Falling with great force
> On the rock at Ishiyama—
> The winter hailstones!

Women as well as other travelers come here to rest at the base of this large rock.

I am not always tempted to move on to another temple the way Bashō was in his journeys, but here at Ishiyamadera, I feel that I do want to move on. Rather than stay here and seclude myself within the temple like the ancient Heian noblewomen, I felt a strong impulse to continue my journey. Perhaps that urge is one that accompanies the age we live in.

From Ishiyamadera, I climbed back up towards the Seta River. When I turned in the direction of Lake Biwa, the "Shiga Sea," as it is sometimes called, opened up in front of me and appeared vast and limitless. I could not help but think that something perhaps indescribable exists there.

On my way back from Ishiyamadera, I met a couple who were on a pilgrimage heading towards the fourteenth temple, Miidera. On the spot I improvised this poem:

> Though the pilgrim's heart,
> While longing for the next world,
> May be frivolous,
> Amida's vow to save mankind
> Is heavy as the rock at Ishiyama.

SECT   Special headquarters of the Tōji branch of the Shingon sect.

ESTABLISHMENT   Founded by Rōben in 749.

PRINCIPAL IMAGE   Nyoirin Kannon.

CULTURAL PROPERTIES   The Main Hall (Hondō or Kannondō) and the Many-Treasures Pagoda (Tahōtō) are National Treasures. The Deva Gate (Niōmon or Tōdaimon), Nyoirin Kannon, and standing Kannon image are Important Cultural Properties.

VISITING INFORMATION   The grounds and the halls are open year round to the public. It is generally believed that Murasaki Shikibu wrote part of *The Tale of Genji,* the world's first novel, here. There is a festival here in mid-September to honor her. The Ishiyama Festival (Ishiyama Matsuri) held on May 5 is also well known.

OF SPECIAL INTEREST   The view from Ishiyamadera to the Seta River is quite beautiful because the temple sits on a large mountain-like rock. The halls and buildings here are so beautiful that they have often drawn men of letters here to reflect and to write. There are many documents and manuscripts—literary and religious—dating from as far back as the Heian period here, and they can be seen in the Museum.

LOCATION AND TRANSPORTATION   1-1-1 Ishiyamadera, Ōtsu-shi, Shiga Prefecture. From Sanjō Keihan in Kyoto, take the Keihan line to Ishiyamadera Station and walk for five minutes.

石山寺　　滋賀県大津市石山寺1-1-1

45. Chikubushima Hōgonji

Chikubushima is a small, solitary island surrounded by cliffs in the middle of Lake Biwa. To get there from Kyoto, you take the Kosei Line and get off at Ōmi Imazu and then take a boat to the island. There is also a more luxurious boat from Hamaōtsu which goes around the island. There are even boats from Nagahama on the northern shore of the lake and Hikone on the eastern shore. But in the winter, service on these lines is often suspended.

The people who have lived around Lake Biwa have worshiped this island as the dwelling places of their ancestors and undoubtedly thought of it as the place where they too would go when they died. This island is the home of Chikubushima Hōgonji and is the thirtieth temple on the thirty-three-temple pilgrimage through western Japan.

> At Chikubushima
> Both the sun and the moon
> Float atop the waves—
> The treasure shop in my heart
> Amasses great fortune, thanks to Benzaiten.

The temple legends tell us that by the imperial decree of Emperor Shōmu (r. 724–49) the great priest Gyōgi (668–749) was sent here in 738 to build a temple and sculpt Buddhist images (the Four Guardian Kings who protect the four directions—measuring almost two and a half feet high) in order to promote peace and tranquility throughout the country. Even if the temple legends are incorrect and Gyōgi is not Hōgonji's founder, it is only natural that an island as isolated and mysterious as Chikubushima would attract people's devotion.

We do not need to read through *The Origins of Chikubushima* (*Chikubushima Engi*) to understand this mysterious island world which people have always sought. Because our existence is often strange and incomprehensible even to ourselves, we seek this world like the teachings themselves. That mysteriousness or incomprehensibility is also why the island has become the home of the goddess who rules over the lake. Both Kannon, the bodhisattva of compassion, and Benzaiten, a female goddess, are enshrined here at Hōgonji.

The common people relied on the power of the images they had made. In this way, the already mysterious island was made even more mysterious and people began to gather here at the dwelling place of the water nymphs. They gathered here to rely on the compassion of Kannon and the prosperous blessings of Benzaiten. People's simple prayers for longevity, wealth, and position have turned this island into one of the sacred places of the world.

Chikubushima often appears in Japanese literature. Stories in *The Tale of the Heike* (*Heike Monogatari*) which concern miracles on a sacred island and prayers for success in battle undoubtedly are connected with the myths and legends surrounding Chikubushima.

"There is a lake in this world where we live and in that lake there is a mountain covered in quartz which sprang forth from the deepest part of the earth. They say it is a place where goddesses and nymphs live. That mountain is none other than this island."

The dwelling place of the goddesses and nymphs is the Pure Land. Benzaiten holds a lute in her hands and the music she plays

宝厳寺
弁天堂
8
7

五重石塔
6

竜神堂

納経所

笠浜閣

護摩堂

鐘楼

稲荷社

御法水

本坊
1

御法水

山神笑名産

土産物店

盗賊岩

椎見足跡岩

笠岩

富士岩

屏風岩

笠岩

一写桟橋

竹生島

1. Hombō
2. Karamon
3. Honden
4. Tsukubusuma Shrine
5. Hōmotsukan
6. Gojū no Sekitō
7. Bentendō
8. Hōgonji
9. Byōbu Rock
10. Pier No. 2

can be heard by those on and around the lake. Chikubushima appears often in all kinds of literature, from *An Account of the Rise and Fall of the Genji and the Heike* (*Gempei Seisui Ki*) to the Noh play, *Chikubushima*:

> As might be expected, since there are many different kinds of prayers for salvation, these prayers sometimes manifest in the form of goddesses. The goddesses will grant the wishes of those to whom the teachings are meaningful. Also, by quelling disturbances throughout the country, they fulfill their vows to save all mankind. When they return to their palace in the lake, the dragon god stirs up the waves making the lake turbulent. Taking the shape of great snakes which swarmed around the heavens and earth, the goddesses then flew into the palace.

I am certain the play also contains a song that begins, "The green trees are darkened by shadows giving the illusion that fish are climbing up their branches."

These scenes of old men and women, fishing boats, dragon gods, and goddesses and nymphs lure us even further into the world of Chikubushima. Traditionally, the pilgrimage here has been a popular one. In fact, it was considered so holy that people felt they would just as soon die during their journey than not make it at all.

It is said that there used to be a number of lodgings available in the village of Hayasaki on the northern shore of the lake where, at one time, you could take a boat out to the island. Today, at Yōseiji, a Pure Land temple in the area, there is an obituary register that contains the names of pilgrims who have died making this final pilgrimage from here.

I wonder how many white-robed pilgrims there have been who died midway through their journey? If there were priests among them, then there were lay people as well. People of all ages with various backgrounds came to Chikubushima to rely on Kannon's compassion and pray to Benzaiten for prosperity. As long as there is suffering from poverty, illness, natural disasters, and death, the hope of salvation from that suffering will quicken our paces to this island.

The Abbot of Chikubushima Hōgonji, Kakukai Mine, wrote: "Thanks to the recent wave of development around Lake Biwa, visitors are once again making their way to Chikubushima. In terms of sightseeing, Chikubushima's spectacular landscape and picturesque scenery are the most beautiful sights there are around the northern part of the lake. A visit here will be soothing to those who feel run-down by the rat race of modern society. It might even give them spiritual sustenance for the future. . . .

"Before Chikubushima was an island for sightseeing, though, it was an island of purification. It bore the history and tradition of an island where faith was important. The happiness and tranquility of truth blessed those who prostrated themselves humbly to the gods and buddhas of the island. Hōgonji has protected the sacredness of this place ever since it was founded by Gyōgi. And together with the people who come here, it will face the challenges of the future and continue to adhere to the practicalities of the Buddhist path."

SECT   The Buzan branch of the Shingon sect.

ESTABLISHMENT   Founded by Gyōgi in 724.

PRINCIPAL IMAGE   Thousand-armed Kannon.

CULTURAL PROPERTIES   The Chinese Gate (Karamon) and sutra scrolls in the temple's possession are National Treasures. The Kannon Hall (Kannondō), painting on silk of the Buddha's sixteen disciples, and the Shakamuni trinity images are Important Cultural Properties.

VISITING INFORMATION   The grounds, Main Hall, and Museum (Hōmotsukan) are open to the public.

OF SPECIAL INTEREST   There are no gardens of special interest here, but the stairway up to the temple and the view from the temple grounds afford the visitor a beautiful view of Lake Biwa. The Chinese Gate dates from the Momoyama period (1568–1600). There are numerous documents here which relate the popularity of the pilgrimage to Chikubushima from as far back as the Heian period (794–1185). There are also many documents concerning the life of the founder of the Shingon sect of esoteric Buddhism, Kūkai (774–834).

LOCATION AND TRANSPORTATION   Chikubushima, Hayasaki, Biwa-cho, Higashi Asai-gun, Shiga Prefecture. There are ferry services from Hamaōtsu, Hikone Nagahama, and Imazu along Lake Biwa. This service is suspended from the middle of November through the middle of March.

竹生島宝厳寺　　滋賀県東浅井郡びわ町早崎竹生島

46. Eiheiji

We are no longer able to tolerate extremes in temperaure these days. We live in a kind of greenhouse whose temperature is always regulated. Much of our individuality has been lost because we are so balanced, standardized, and controlled.

Here at Eiheiji, where the temperature falls below zero every day, there were no unusually heavy snowfalls like last year, but still snow has managed to accumulate on the temple grounds. The water flowing along either side of the visitors' path is extremely cold.

From Fukui the Katsuyama highway heads east, crossing over Mount Haku on its way to Shiratori in Gifu Prefecture. If you turn off to the right and head into the mountains, you will come to Eiheiji's main gate. It is an intense cold here: the mountains themselves seem completely frozen. The rows of towering cedars soar up into the air as if they could touch the sky. How old could they be, I wonder? The stone steps up to the Main Gate (Sammon) are shining and cold. One sees almost no visitors here on a day like today.

When the snow melts and it becomes spring, Eiheiji is overrun with visitors and pilgrims, but in midwinter the coffee shops have very few customers and many of them are actually closed.

The clear water which flows through here from Mount Haku

永平寺

1. Seimon
2. Entsūmon
3. Shōrō
4. Sammon
5. Chūjakumon
6. Sōdō
7. Butsuden
8. Hattō
9. Tōsu
10. Sanshōkaku
11. Dōgen's Tomb
12. Kuin
13. Kyōzō
14. Eiheiji River

seems to have purified the whole area. And there is not a single voice to interrupt the stillness. At any one time, there are 150 *unsui,* or young monks, practicing at Eiheiji.

Standing in front of the two-story Main Gate, one of the *unsui* who was guiding me around explained the following words of Mankai Zenshi (1706–67) in a loud voice:

> Practice in the *zazen* hall is strict.
> One who does not take practice seriously is not
>   permitted to enter.
> The temple gate shall remain locked to that person.
> If there is reluctance, so it will be.
> Thus he comes one step closer to Zen.

This young monk with his round, childlike face was barefoot. Standing next to him and shaking in the cold, I felt somewhat pathetic. It was an amazing way to guide someone around in the wintertime here. Looking at the Chinese characters the *unsui* was talking about, I was amazed by their strength as well as by the two characters "Kichijō" written on a wooden tablet. It is said that the Pure Land of Kichijō, the goddess of good fortune, is obtainable only through the practice of meditation (*shikan taza*). Since these are the true teachings of the Buddha, a strict schedule of practice awaits the aspirant. If you are truly one who wants to practice, then you will not be denied that opportunity.

Snow completely surrounds Eiheiji. That is why there are wooden pathways connecting all the buildings. The roofs of those pathways are also covered with a solid layer of snow. It even seems like there is snow inside the huge shoe compartment— reaching almost a kilometer in length—where people place their shoes before entering the temple. The pathway connects all the buildings of the monastery in such a way that it seems to be crawling up the mountainside. At times on the way to the Main Hall (Butsuden), one can see into the huge kitchen where they are preparing the meals for the monks. When I was there, I saw the lunchtime preparations. These preparations, known as *sōjiki kuhai,* are apparently performed just as they were described in Dōgen's work, *Instructions for the Zen Cook (Tenzō Kyōkun),* written in 1237. Watching this incredible world of propriety, I felt like I actually got a glimpse of the severity of life these monks lead. Then suddenly, I recalled the painful time when I was a young military recruit during the war.

It is not necessary to go into all the details of how and why Dōgen founded Eiheiji. We are free, of course, to research his birthplace, his practice, and the era he lived in, but we cannot actually experience Dōgen himself except through a tireless investigation of the path he followed. Can it possibly be good for us during our lifetime to covet positions higher than our own and live our lives in a dream? Isn't it true, as we can see by looking at the life of Shakamuni, that the Buddha spent one period of his life as a beggar after he gave up his life as a king, entered the mountains and forests, and attained enlightenment? Isn't it better to abandon our homes and our villages and rely instead upon the clouds and the rivers? Following the path of the teachings must be a destitute one. To find understanding, we sever our connections with the world and practice *zazen* meditation. There is no path except that one.

Dōgen moved to Yoshiminedera in present-day Fukui Prefecture when he was forty-four years old after leaving Kōshōji in Kyoto. This was his first step in the founding of Eiheiji. By this time he had already begun giving his lectures, which were eventually collected under the title *Shōbōgenzō.* The remains of Yoshiminedera are located even further into the mountains than Eiheiji. The only way to get there is to follow a very dark road, and it takes a day to make the full trip there and back.

Why did Dōgen come to such an isolated place here in the mountains? Forty-four years old is not old age. On the other hand, Dōgen was born into the noble class and, because of that, was probably not very strong. The year after he came to the mountains, the Main Hall of Eiheiji was built on Kasamatsu Peak, and this is where he settled. It is said that that building was still over three miles away from present-day Eiheiji.

My guide read me the following, which is written on a tablet on the Main Gate:

> The great blessings of the Tathagata and various Buddhas
> Are the most splendid among all the good fortunes
>   of the world.
> The Buddhas have all come here to live and
> That is why this place is called the Mountain of Good
>   Fortune.

There is neither cold nor heat, evening nor afternoon for the *unsui* who practice and work here. This is the spiritual world of men devoted to the diligence of discipline. The business concerns of the temple are taken care of starting at one o'clock in the morning in the Shōyō Hall (Shōyōden), where Dōgen is enshrined. This sort of thing will continue as long as Dōgen is kept alive as the founder and spiritual teacher here. When I started down the mountain road and looked back at Eiheiji, snow-covered Mount Haku was shining coldly in the early evening sunset. This is the mountain as Dōgen must have revered it.

SECT   Headquarters of the Sōtō sect of Zen.

ESTABLISHMENT   Founded by Dōgen in 1244.

PRINCIPAL IMAGE   Shakamuni.

CULTURAL PROPERTIES   A copy of *Fukan Zazen Gi,* a work by Dōgen, is a National Treasure. There are many other documents and manuscripts here as well.

VISITING INFORMATION   There are extensive tours of Ei-heiji's principal buildings and halls, and also opportunities to practice *zazen* if the visitor so wishes. Winter here is particularly severe so if you want to get a taste of what it is like to live and practice here in the conditions under which the priests live and practice, try going in that season. There are plenty of rooms for guests, but it is usually necessary to make a reservation before you go.

OF SPECIAL INTEREST   All of Eiheiji's buildings are con-nected by covered corridors, measuring in all 6,000 feet in length. Buddhist images are not a main attraction at Eiheiji; what is of interest is the incredible arrangement of the buildings on the mountainside and the chance to see several hundred young priests practicing *zazen* and living in a traditional Zen monastic environ-ment.

LOCATION AND TRANSPORTATION   236 Eiheiji-chō, Yo-shida-gun, Fukui Prefecture. From Fukui City, take the Echizen Line of the Keifuku Railway to Eiheiji and board a bus for the temple at the station.

永平寺　　福井県吉田郡永平寺町 236

Calendar of Selected Events

First Day of the Tiger (variable): First Tiger Day Ceremony (Hatsu Tora Matsuri). Kuramadera.

1–15: Kichijōten image on view to the public. Jōruriji.

14: Naked Dance Festival. Hōkaiji.

15: Tōshiya. Sanjūsangendō.

FEBRUARY

3: Setsubun. Senryūji.

Near Setsubun: Onioi Ceremony. Kōfukuji.

23: Godairiki Festival. Inner Daigo (Daigoji).

MARCH

1–14: Omizutori (includes Fire Festival on evenings of 12–14). Nigatsudō, Tōdaiji.

14–16: Commemoration of Budha's Nirvana. Sen'yūji.

15: Otaimatsu (Fire Festival). Seiryōji.

21–May 20: Kichijōten image on view to the public. Jōruriji. 30–April 5: Flower Festival (Buddha's Birthday). Yakushiji.

APRIL

Flower-offering Ceremeny (Hana Kuyō). Kuramadera.

8, from 7 P.M.: Otaimatsu (Fire Festival). Shin Yakushiji.

Second weekend: Ōchamori. Saidaiji.

Weekend in the middle of the month, from 1 to 4 in the afternoon: Nembutsu Kyōgen (theatrical performance). Seiryōji.

19–25: Gyoki E (Founder's Memorial Service). Chion-in.

Mid to late: Omuro cherries in full bloom. Ninnaji.

21: Memorial Ceremony for Kūkai (Shōmieiku Nerikuyō). Muroji.

MAY

Evening of the full moon: Full Moon Festival (Mangetsu Matsuri). Kuramadera.

1–5: Airing of the items in the Shoin (Treasure Hall). Jingoji.

5: Ishiyama Festival. Ishiyamadera.

11–12: Takigi (Firelight) Noh performance. Kōfukuji.

14: Nerikuyō Ceremony. Taimadera.

19: Fan Festival (Uchiwamaki). Tōshōdaiji.

JUNE

6: Memorial Celebration for Jianzhen. Tōshōdaiji.

20, 2 P.M.: Bamboo-cutting Festival (Take Kiri Eshiki). Kuramadera.

AUGUST

8–10, 16: Mantō E (Lantern-lighting Ceremony). Rokuharamitsuji.

16: Kawa Segaki (offerings to the spirits of the drowned). Tenryūji.

SEPTEMBER

Night of the full moon: Harvest Moon-viewing Festival. Daikakuji.

Middle of month: Festival for Murasaki Shikibu. Ishiyamadera.

OCTOBER

10: Airing of the treasures of Daitokuji and its subtemples. Daitokuji.

Cow Festival (Ushi Matsuri). Kōryūji.

Second Sunday: Ōchamori. Saidaiji.

15: Dragon Festival (Ryūketsu Sai). Muroji.

22: Fire Festival (Hi Matsuri). Kuramadera.

NOVEMBER

1–30: Kichijōten image on view to the public. Jōruriji.

DECEMBER

13–31: Kuya Yuyaku Nembutsu Ceremony. Rokuharamitsuji.

Recitation of the Buddha's Names (Bubumyō E). Seiryōji.

Identification Guide to
Temple Buildings

Abhiseka Hall (Kanjōdō). A hall where the Abhiseka ceremony, a purification rite of esoteric Buddhism, is conducted.

Amida Hall (Amidadō). A hall housing an image of Amida Buddha.

Amidadō. See Amida Hall

Bell Tower (Shōrō). A towerlike structure that houses a bell or drum; a belfry. In ancient temples located opposite the sutra hall.

Butsuden. See Main Hall

Chinese Gate (Karamon). See Gates

Chokushimon (Special Gate). See Gates

Chūkondō. See Middle Main Hall

Chūmon (Middle Gate). See Gates

Daihōjō. See Priests' Quarters

Daikōdō. See Lecture Hall

Daimon (Main Gate). See Gates

Deva Gate (Niōmon). See Gates

Dining Hall (Jikidō). The refectory within the compound for the monks.

Fire Ritual Hall (Gomadō). A hall where the fire ritual known as the *goma-e* is performed.

Founder's Hall (Kaisandō, Mieidō, Taishidō, Taishibyō). "Kaisan" means the person who establishes the "mountain," or temple; a Mieidō is a hall that houses the depiction (*miei*) of the founder, usually a painting; *taishi* refers to the posthumous name of Kūkai, Kōbō Daishi. A *byō* is a tomb, in contrast to a hall (*dō*).

Gates (Chinese Gate, Deva Gate, Special Gate, Main Gate, Middle Gate, Tower Gate). Many types of gates developed in the context of Japanese Buddhist architecture. In the earliest periods, the outer gate was usually on a south axis, and so it was called the South Great Gate (Nandaimon). In later Zen temples, a gate of the same function was called a Triple Gate (Sammon). A Chinese Gate (Karamon) is one in imitation of Chinese architectural style. A Deva Gate (Niō mon) is one flanked by two of the Four Guardian Deities. The Middle Gate was inside the Main Gate, and it marked off the entrance to the inner precincts of the temple compound. A Tower Gate (or high gate, Rōmon), is a two-story gate (though it may be only one story structurally, it was constructed to look as if it were two stories). The Special Gate (Chokushimon) was a gate for receiving an imperial messenger.

General Worship Hall (Hosodono). Hosodeno literally means a long, shallow hall, specifically the hall in front of the dining hall at Hōryūji.

Godaidō. See Hall of the Five Great Dieties

Gojū no Tō (Five-storied Pagoda). See Pagodas

Gomadō. See Fire Ritual Hall

Gozasho. See Imperial Hall

Guest Hall (Kyakuden). A reception hall for lay persons arriving to worship at the temple.

Haiden. See Worship Hall

Hall of the Five Great Dieties (Godaidō). A hall in which images of the Five Great Deities of esoteric Buddhism are enshrined.

Hattō. See Lecture Hall

Hōmotsuden. See Museums

Hondō. See Main Hall

Hosodono. See General Worship Hall

Hōzōden. See Museums

Imperial Hall (Gozasho). The reception hall for the emperor or a person of the nobility.

Imperial Residence (Shinden). The living quarters of an emperor.

Inner Sanctuary (Oku no In). The innermost hall of a temple, located to the rear of the main hall. It enshrines an image of the temple's founder or the most sacred object of worship.

Issaikyōzō. See Sutra Halls

Jikidō. See Dining Hall

Kaidan'indō. See Ordination Platform Hall

Kaisandō. See Founder's Hall

Kanjōdō. See Abhiseka Hall

Kannon Hall (Kannondō). A hall that houses an image of Kannon.

Kannondō. See Kannon Hall

Karamon (Chinese Gate). See Gates

Kitchen (Kuri, Soden). In the earliest Zen temples, the kitchen was a separate building with a granary and rooms for the monks preparing the temple's vegetarian meals. Today it is one room attached to the monks' living quarters.

Kōdō. See Lecture Hall

Kohōjō. See Priests' Quarters

Kokuhōkan. See Museums

Kondō (Golden Hall). See Main Hall

Kuri. See Kitchen

Kyakuden. See Guest Hall

Kyōzō. See Sutra Halls

Lecture Hall (Daikōdō, Hattō, Kōdō). Kōdō and Daikōdō (great lecture hall) are usually large temple buildings. The Hattō is the equivalent structure in Zen temple compounds.

Main Gate (Daimon, Nandaimon, Sammon). See Gates

Main Hall (Butsuden, Hondō, Kondō). In the earliest temples, the hall that housed the main image was called the Kondō (golden hall), perhaps because the images and parts of the interior were gilded. Later the word Hondō superceded Kondō. In Zen temples, the same type of hall is usually called the Butsuden.

Mandala Hall (Mandaradō). A hall that houses a mandala.

Middle Gate (Chumon). See Gates

Middle Main Hall (Chūkondō). The hall that enshrines the images of lesser importance than those in the main hall.

Mieidō. See Founder's Hall

Museums (Hōzōden, Hōmotsuden, Hōmotsukan, Kokuhōkan, Reihōkan, Shinhōzō, Shōtenkaku, Shuhōkan). With a wide variety of names, differing from age to age and temple compound to temple compound, these structures house the treasures in a temple's keeping.

Nandaimon (Main Gate). See Gates

Niōmon (Deva Gate). See Gates

Oku no In. See Inner Sanctuary

Ordination Platform Hall (Kaidan'indō). A hall that includes a platform for carrying out ordination ceremonies.

Pagodas (Sanjū no Tō, Gojū no Tō, Tahōtō). Pagodas derived from the stupas of India, and were for enshrining relics of the Buddha. They could be in three, five, or seven stories. A Tahōtō has a distinctive architectural style and does not contain relics. It is dedicated to Prabhutaratna, a Buddha of the ancient past who appears in the Lotus Sutra from out of a bejeweled "stupa of many treasures" (*tahōtō*).

Priests' Quarters (Daihōjō, Hombō, Kohōjō, Sōbō). The Daihōjo and Kohōjō are abbots' or head priests' quarters, especially in Zen temple compounds. The Sōbō are quarters for monks in general, as is the Hombō, or main living quarters.

Reihōkan. See Museums

Reliquary Hall (Shariden). A hall enshrining a relic of the Buddha.

Rōmon (Tower Gate). See Gates

Sammon (Main Gate). See Gates

Sanjū no Tō (Three-storied Pagoda). See Pagodas

Shakamuni Hall (Shakamunidō). A hall that enshrines an image of Shakamuni.

Shakamunidō. See Shakamuni Hall

Shakyō Dōjō. See Sutra Halls

Shariden. See Reliquary Hall

Shinden. See Imperial Residence

Shinhōzō. See Museums

Shōrō. See Bell Tower

Shōtenkaku. See Museums

Shūhōkan. See Museums

Sōbō. See Priests' Quarters

Soden. See Kitchen

Special Gate (Chokushimon). See Gates

Subtemples (Tatchū). A major Zen temple often has subsidiary temples within its large complex. Subsidiary temples were built for several reasons, such as to enshrine an image of the founder or one of the head abbots; to house important works of Buddhist art; or, with their landscaped gardens, to serve as a settings for the way of tea (*chanoyu, chadō*).

Sutra Halls (Issaikyōzō, Kyōzō, Shakyō Dōjō). An Issaikyōzō is a storage house for the collection of the Buddhist scriptures, as is a Kyōzō A Shakyō Dōjō is a headquarters for the task of copying the scriptures.

Tahōtō. See Pagodas

Taishibyō. See Founder's Hall

Taishidō. See Founder's Hall

Tower Gate (Rōmon). See Gates

Worship Hall (Haiden). The hall

in a shrine where worshipers may pay their respects.

Yakushi Hall (Yakushidō). A hall where an image of Yakushi Buddha is enshrined.

Yakushidō. See Yakushi Hall

Glossary

Amida (Nyorai). S: Amitayus, Amitabha. Amida's origins are explained in the early Mahayana sutra known in English as the Larger Pure Land Sutra. He began as the bodhisattva Dharmakara (J: Hōzō), making forty-eight vows that he realized along with his enlightenment. He vowed that he would, upon attaining enlightenment, rule over a Pure Land in the west, and that all believers who sincerely thought of him and called out his name would be born there. In the Pure Land, free from the sufferings of the mundane world, the believers could then perfect their own enlightenment. In spite of the orthodox Buddhist ideas that Amida represents, he came to be worshiped by the populace as a savior figure who ruled over a pleasurable paradise to which all sought entrance. Amida is the central figure of devotion in the Pure Land sects, and he has long been included in the esoteric Buddhist pantheon as well. See also Hōnen; Jōdo sect; Jōdo Shin sect; Pure Land; Shinran

Asanga. J: Mujaku. Asanga and his younger brother Vasubandhu (J: Seshin) were fourth-century Indian Buddhist philosophers who are credited with developing the Yogacara school of Buddhist thought, one of the main premises of which is that the mind must be purified through yogic practice in order to reach enlightenment. Asanga is regarded as the founder of the Hossō sect. See also Hossō sect.

Ashuku. S: Aksobhya. A mythological Buddha said to dwell in the east. He is worshiped especially in esoteric Buddhism.

Ashura. S: Asura. In Indian mythology, the Asura were similar to the

Roman Titans, fierce warrior spirits. They came to be included in the Six Realms of Buddhist cosmology, and were often interpreted as the aggressive impulse or state of mind within the human condition. See also Six Realms.

Becoming a Buddha in this lifetime (*sokushin jōbutsu*). This is one of the core doctrines of the Shingon sect of esoteric Buddhism. By the time esoteric Buddhism developed (in ninth-century India), the possibility of actually becoming a Buddha seemed far removed from the realm of human achievement. This doctrine reaffirmed that possibility and outlined a path to realizing it. See also Shingon.

Benzaiten. S: Sarasvati. A goddess of Indian origin who was regarded as a source of intelligence and refinement, a prolonger of life, and a protector from natural disasters. She is usually represented as a beautiful female figure holding a Japanese lute, or *biwa*, and is popularly regarded as a patroness of the arts. Benzaiten is also an important figure in esoteric Buddhist practice and one of the seven gods of good fortune in Japan.

Birushana. S: Vairocana. The Buddha who preaches the Avatamsaka Sutra (J: Kegon Kyō), seated in the center of a great lotus blossom and surrounded by infinite replicas of himself.

Bishamonten. S: Vaisravana. One of the Four Guardian Kings, protectors of the Buddhist religion. Each of the Guardian Kings was designated the protector of one of the four directions. Bishamonten guarded the north. Though a fierce, martial deity, Bishamonten was also popularly regarded as a bestower of wealth, and was counted among the seven gods of good fortune. The goddess Kichijōten was regarded as his consort.

Bon Festival. In full, Urabon'e; S: Ullambana. The Festival for the Dead, observed in mid-July (mid-August in some places). It is said to be based on an incident reported in a Chinese Buddhist scripture in which one of the Buddha's disciples rescued his mother from hell. In Japan it has been celebrated since the seventh century. Families gather and visit the family grave. A spirit altar is often set up with offerings for the ancestral spirits, which are believed to descend at this time and then depart again.

Bonten. S: Brahma. The Indian creator god, in Buddhism transformed into a protector of the religion. He was regarded as reigning over the most elevated realm within the world of form in traditional Buddhist cosmology.

Bosatsu. S: Bodhisattva. A being who dedicates himself to bringing enlightenment to all other sentient beings, delaying his own enlightenment until that is achieved. The bodhisattva is the spiritual ideal of Mahayana Buddhist practice. In the popular mind, bodhisattvas were regarded as deities who assisted humankind.

Dainichi (Nyorai). S: Mahavairocana. The Great Sun Buddha and the main figure of worship in esoteric Buddhism, both Shingon and Tendai. Mahavairocana is often regarded as a symbolic representation of the cosmos. See also Shingon.

Dharma. J: Hō. A multivalent term. The main meanings are (1) constituents of existence, or facts; (2) the Buddhist teaching; and (3) the ultimate truth of existence.

Diamond-sceptre Mandala. S: Vajra-dhatu mandala; J: Kongō mandara. One of the two main mandalas of the Shingon school of esoteric Buddhism, the Diamond-sceptre mandala is primarily a depiction of a practitioner's progress and practice toward enlightenment.

Dōgen (1200–1253). The founder of the Sōtō sect of Zen Buddhism in Japan. His teachings and writings have continued to be very influential and his sect claims the majority of Zen followers in Japan today.

Eight Great Children. J: Hachi Dai Dōji. The eight attendants of Fudō Myōō. See also Fudō Myōō.

Eisai (1141–1215). The founder of the Rinzai sect of Zen in Japan. Eisai traveled to China in 1168 and again in 1187. He attempted to establish the Rinzai sect after returning from the second trip. Throughout his life he also remained deeply interested in the Lotus Sutra and esoteric Buddhism.

Ema. Pictorial votive offerings, often paintings of fortuitous objects on wooden plaques.

Engi. S: Pratituyasamutpada. Literally, "dependent origination," a Buddhist technical term that describes how phenomena arise and exist in relation to each other. In Japan, the word came to be used for the literary genre of stories and legends relating the origins of temples and shrines, often in the form of illustrated scrolls.

Enlightenment verse. Zen monks frequently composed a verse expressing their new state on the occasion of attaining enlightenment, and these verses in turn could be used by monks in training as tools in their own practice to achieve the same end.

Esoteric Buddhism. J: Mikkyō. Literally, "The Secret Teachings," a term used in Japan to refer to the Tantric tradition of Shingon and Tendai in contrast to "exoteric Buddhism" (J: Kenkyō), the sects based on texts or traditions other than Tantric. Esoteric Buddhism was first introduced to Japan by Kūkai (774–835) and Saichō (767–822) in the ninth century, and in the following centuries came to occupy the mainstream of Japanese Buddhism. Its decline was hastened by the more popular, "single-practice" sects of the Kamakura period such as Jōdo, Jōdo Shin, Nichiren, and Zen. The artistic heritage of esoteric Buddhism is especially rich.

Festival for the Dead. See Bon Festival

Five Great Kings of Light. S: Vidyaraja; J: Go Dai Myōō. Originally Hindu deities, the Great Kings of Light were regarded in Buddhism as incarnations of the powers of the cosmic Buddhas. They have fierce visages because great ferocity and strength are required to cut the ties of ignorance that bind us. Fudō Myōō (S: Acalanatha) is the most popular in Japan. The other four are Gōsanze Myōō (Trailokyavijaya), Gundari Myōō (Kundali), Daitoku Myōō (Yamantaka), and Kongoyasha Myōō (Vajrayaksa).

Five Mountains. This temple-ranking system takes its name from the designation of five major temples ("mountains" refers to temples, which were located on mountaintops) in China. The system was introduced into Japan in the fourteenth century, and strictly referred to five temples in Kamakura and five in Kyoto, though the temples so designated varied, and the number exceeded ten at times. The literary movement of the same name was a revitalization of Chinese learning and literature led by the monks of the Five Mountains temples.

Four Guardian Kings. S: Caturmaharajakayikadeva; J: Shitennō. In

Buddhist mythology, the Four Guardian Kings are the rulers of the four heavenly realms girdling the axis mundi, Mount Sumeru, and each is the guardian of the region below. Dhrtarastra (J: Jikokuten) protects the east, Virudhaka (J: Zōchōten) guards the south, Virupaksa (J: Kōmokuten) guards the west, and Vaisravana or Dhanada (J: Bishamonten or Tamonten) guards the north.

Fukukensaku Kannon. S: Amoghapasa. One of the six representations of Kannon in the Womb-store mandala. With the rope (*kensaku*) of non-emptiness (*fuku*), this bodhisattva captures all sentient beings and tosses them on the far shore of enlightenment.

Furna. S: Purna. One of the Buddha's ten major disciples.

Gakkō (Bosatsu). S: Candraprabha. Together with Nikkō, an attendant of Yakushi Nyorai. Gakkō is also depicted in the mandalas of esoteric Buddhism.

General Basara. See Twelve Divine Generals

General Indara. See Twelve Divine Generals

General Mekira. See Twelve Divine Generals

General Santera. See Twelve Divine Generals

Gozan, Gozan bungaku. See Five Mountains

Hachi Dai Dōji. See Eight Great Children

Hō. See Dharma

Hōnen (1133–1212). The founder of the Pure Land sect, the first sect to break away from the great mountain centers of Heian-period Buddhism, Mount Hiei and Mount Kōya. Hōnen taught the exclusive practice of the *nembutsu*—thinking of the Buddha or, later, reciting his name—to achieve salvation. He also believed that the world had entered an age of decline, known as *mappō*, in which saintly practices were no longer possible. See also Amida; nembutsu; *mappō*; Pure Land

Hossō sect. One of the six sects of Nara Buddhism. It is based on the Yogacara teaching of Indian Buddhism, founded by Asanga and Vasubandhu, and transmitted to Japan through China. The main thrust of the teaching was that the mind is crucial in creating karma, and that enlightenment was to be achieved by purifying the mind through yogic practice. The incomplete transmission of the teachings that reached Japan categorized living beings into six classes, one of which was eternally barred from achieving enlightenment, and this point of doctrine was later to become a major controversy in Japan, as it had been in China earlier. See also Asanga; Six Nara sects

Ippen (1239–89). The founder of the Ji sect of Pure Land Buddhism. Though educated in Tendai doctrine on Mount Hiei, Ippen adopted a wandering life and traveled around Japan preaching surrender to the power of Amida Buddha and the ecstatic chanting of the *nembutsu*. See also Ji sect; *nembutsu*.

Ji sect. The Japanese sect of Pure Land Buddhism founded by Ippen (1239–89). Ippen taught that one must surrender oneself completely to Amida's powers and that the ecstatic chanting of the *nembutsu* led to unification with the Buddha. See also Ippen; *nembutsu*

Jōdo sect. The Pure Land sect of Japanese Buddhism founded by Hōnen (1133–1212). It taught that chanting the name of Amida was the only practice necessary for salvation and emphasized that we live in a dark age (*mappō*) when the saintly practices of earlier ages are impossible for us to perfect. Birth in Amida's Pure Land, rather than achieving enlightenment, is the goal believers aspire to, and the sect's teachings are strongly devotional in emphasis. See also Amida; Hōnen; *mappō*; *nembutsu*; Pure Land

Jōdo Shin sect. The True Pure Land sect was founded by Shinran (1173–1262), Honen's disciple. Though the two sects share much, Shinran went a bit further in emphasizing that we are utterly unable to achieve enlightenment on our own, and therefore we must rely entirely on Amida's guarantee that we will be born in his Pure Land. Shinran stresses severe introspection and faith as the means of practice.

Jōjitsu sect. One of the Six Nara sects, based on a scholastic sect of Chinese Buddhism that studied a transitional early Mahayana philosophical treatise. It had little influence in Japan.

Jūni Shinsho. See Twelve Divine Generals

Kalavinka. See Kuyobutsu

Kannon. S: Avalokitesvara. In India, this bodhisattva was a male deity. His sex changed as he was introduced and popularized in China. By the time "she" reached Japan as Kannon, the deity was represented as a beautiful woman with a compassionate smile. Kannon became closely associated with women and particularly with childbirth in Japan, and has always been one of the most popular figures of worship.

Kegon sect. One of the Six Nara sects, Kegon was a very influential philosophical sect of Chinese Buddhism. Its profound philosophy was put to political use in Japan by Emperor Shōmu (r. 724–49), who built a huge image of the central deity of Kegon literature, Birushana (S: Vairocana) as a symbol of his divine authority.

Kichijōten. S: Srimahadevi. A goddess of good fortune, often depicted as a beautiful, mature woman. She was regarded as the consort of Bishamonten, and was with him one of the seven gods of good fortune. See also Bishamonten.

Kokubunji. The regional temples ordered built throughout the provinces in the tenth century. Most have fallen into ruin, and many did so soon after they were built, but they nevertheless represented an attempt to extend imperial authority and Buddhism throughout Japan, and in some cases became centers of local learning.

Kongō Mandara. See Diamond-sceptre mandala

Kūkai (774–835). The founder of the Shingon sect of esoteric Buddhism in Japan. Kūkai traveled to China in 804 and studied the esoteric doctrines with a Chinese master for three years before returning to Japan and transmitting the learning he had acquired. Kūkai, posthumously known as Kōbō Daishi, has become a folk deity in Japan and is worshiped in many forms for many achievements—including the invention of the hiragana syllabary, which he is supposed to have derived from Sanskrit phonetics.

Kusha. One of the Six Nara sects, based on the Theravada treatise known as the Abhidharma-kosa, which taught an analysis of the elements of existence (dharma) as a means of achieving enlightenment. The school had little influence in Japan.

Kuyōbutsu. S: Kalavinka.

Lotus Sutra. S: Saddharma-pundarika-sutra; J: Myōhō Renge Kyō, also Hoke Kyō. Probably the single most influential Buddhist scripture in East Asia, this is an early Mahayana work that teaches that there are many paths to salvation, but the goal is one: universal enlightenment. The sutra emphasizes the bodhisattva's practice, but it was more popular for the protection, rewards, and practical benefits it promised believers. It is the central text of the Tendai and Nichiren sects.

Mandala. J: Mandara. A visual representation of enlightenment and the path to it. Mandalas are most frequently paintings of Buddhas, bodhisattvas, deities, and symbolic forms arranged in a grid pattern that derives from a representation of an Indian castle, with the central and most powerful deity in the center and guardian deities in the surrounding corridors and halls. A mandala is used as an aid for visualizing the deities and meditating on their meanings; at the same time, it is regarded as a depiction of the ultimate truth of the cosmos.

Manjusri. See Monjushiri

Mappō. Often translated as the Latter Days of the Law. *Mappō* was the last of three periods taught in certain later Buddhist texts. The inception and duration of each period differed from source to source, but in the first period, the Buddha's law was True and enlightenment could be achieved by many; in the second period, only the shadow or image of the law remained, and few could attain enlightenment; in the last period, nothing remained, and enlightenment was impossible. Only faith—or some intense and single-minded practice—had any effect in this period at all, and even then, birth in Pure Land was the most one could hope for. The idea of *mappō* was pivotal in the growth of the new Buddhist sects of the Kamakura period.

Miroku. S: Maitreya. The Buddha of the future. Miroku dwells now in Tushita Heaven (J: Tosotsu), and he is destined to descend to earth in the future and attain enlightenment. Miroku was a focus of worship in Japan from a very early period.

Mokkenren. S: Maudgalyayana. One of the Buddha's ten major disciples.

Monjushiri. S: Manjusri. A mythological Buddha noted especially for his wisdom. Monjushiri figures in early prajna and Avatamsaka literature, and is also an important deity of the pantheon of esoteric Buddhism. He is regarded as reigning over a Pure Land in an easterly direction.

Namu Amida Butsu. The verbal formula of the *nembutsu*, meaning "Praise to Amida Buddha." See also *nembutsu*.

nembutsu. Literally, "thinking of the Buddha," this practice gradually evolved from a meditative one into the utterance of the Buddha's name. In Japan it was practiced as early as the Nara period, and was later an important part of Tendai practice, in the Heian period. It was selected by Hōnen (1133–1212) as the main practice for his Jōdo sect, and also adopted by his disciple Shinran (1173–1262), who founded the Jōdo Shin sect. Variously interpreted (many *nembutsu* must be chanted, or one was enough; *nembutsu* was a means to achieve enlightenment, or an expression of gratitude for the enlightenment proffered by Amida; as magic incantation, ritual, or private meditation), it became a mainstay of Japanese Buddhist practice.

Nichiren sect. Founded by Nichiren (1222–82) and based on the truth of the Lotus Sutra. The main practice of the sect is the chanting of the formula *Namu Myōhō Renge Kyō*: "Praise to the Lotus Sutra of the True Law."

Nikkō (Bosatsu). S: Suryaprabha. Together with Gakkō Bosatsu, an attendant of Yakushi Buddha.

Nyoirin Kannon. S: Cintamanicakra. One of the six aspects of Kannon. The figure holds a "wishing jewel" (*mani*) and a wheel, symbol of the teaching of the Buddhist law, and grants the wishes of all sentient beings. Nyoirin Kannon is depicted in the Womb-store mandala of esoteric Buddhism.

Ōbaku sect. The third-largest sect of Japanese Zen, introduced to Japan in the seventeenth century by Chinese monks. Ōbaku Zen practice included elements of *nembutsu* and esoteric Buddhist practice, as was the case with Ming-dynasty Chinese Zen.

Obon. See Bon Festival

Princess Chūjō. A legendary heroine of drama and fiction said to have lived in the eighth century and to have been the daughter of Fujiwara no Toyonari. In some sources, she is said to have entered Buddhist orders because she was persecuted by her wicked stepmother and abandoned in the mountains; in others, in her sadness at her father's exile. Princess Chūjō is credited with having woven out of lotus fibers a depiction of the Pure Land in mandala form in 763.

Pure Land. S: Sukhavati J: Jōdo, also Gokuraku Jōdo. The concept of "pure lands" in Buddhism seems to have arisen as a symbolic representation of the realm of enlightenment. Several mythological Buddhas were regarded as reigning over their own pure lands, especially Amida in the West, and Yakushi in the east. Amida's Pure Land, which played the greatest role in popular religious aspiration, was created as he perfected his vows as a bodhisattva. Though regarded by most believers as a glorious paradise in which one strove to be born after death, the religious purpose of the concept of the Pure Land was to represent a place or state of mind where the practitioner, unhindered by the sufferings and limitations of the world, could concentrate on achieving enlightenment. See Amida

Ragora. S: Rahula. One of the Buddha's ten leading disciples.

Rinzai sect. One of the two major sects of Zen in Japan, based on the Linji sect of Chinese Zen, which was introduced to Japan by Eisai (1141–1215). Rinzai monks were avidly patronized by the Kamakura, Ashikaga, and Muromachi shoguns, and the Rinzai sect is most closely associated with the flowering of "Zen culture" in the fourteenth through sixteenth centuries. Meditation on the riddle-like *kōan* is the practice most frequently associated with Rinzai Zen.

Ritsu sect. One of the Six Nara sects, based on the study of the Buddhist discipline, or Vinaya. The Ritsu sect survived long past the Nara period and enjoyed a revival of sorts in the Kamakura period, when several eminent monks rose from its ranks.

Rokudō. See Six realms

Rokuhara. See Six paramitas

Saichō (767–822). The founder of the Japanese Tendai sect. Saichō traveled to China in 804 and studied the Chinese Tiantai sect for nine months before returning to Japan and petitioning the throne for permission to establish a new sect with its own ordination platform. Until then, all monks were ordained in Nara; Saichō wished to escape the influences of the Nara clergy and reform Japanese Buddhism. While the Lotus Sutra was the scriptural core of the Tendai sect,

Saichō was also interested in Buddhist discipline, meditation practices, and esoteric scriptures. His petition to establish his own ordination platform was not granted until after his death.

Sanron sect. One of the Six Nara sects, based on three treatises propounding the Madhyamika philosophy of Indian Buddhism, which taught the Middle Way of neither affirming or rejecting reality. Madhyamika philosophy was central to all Japanese Buddhism, but the sect itself played an inconsequential role in Japanese Buddhist history.

Seishi (Bosatsu). S: Mahasthamaprapta. Together with Kannon, one of the attendants of Amida. Seishi symbolizes wisdom, and is also depicted in the mandalas of esoteric Buddhism.

Setsubun. A purification ceremony held, by the old calendar, at the New Year (now held at the start of February), in which roasted beans are thrown to drive away demons, accompanied by the cry, "Out with the demons and in with good fortune!" Setsubun festivities are carried out at temples and shrines as well as homes, and though the festival in its present form dates from no earlier than the sixteenth century, it has roots in ancient planting rites.

Shaba world. S: Saha. This world of suffering, "where patience is needed," in contrast to the realm of enlightenment.

Shakamuni. S: Sakyamuni. Literally, "The Sage of the Sakya Clan," one of the most commonly used titles of the Buddha.

Sharihotsu. S: Sariputra. One of the Buddha's ten major disciples.

Shingon sect. The Japanese incarnation of esoteric Buddhism, founded by Kūkai (774–835). Shingon means True Word, and refers to the Tantric practice of using mantras, or sacred syllables, as an aid to attaining enlightenment. Shingon practice includes mudras, or sacred gestures, and mandalas, or visual depictions of enlightenment, as well as mantras, and its aim is to allow the practitioner to achieve enlightenment in this life. Because Shingon relies heavily on visualization of deities in its practice, it has greatly encouraged the production of Buddhist art.

Shinran (1173–1262). A disciple of Hōnen (1133–1212) and the founder of the Jōdo Shin sect. Shinran was exiled at the same time as his master Hōnen, but Shinran was sent to the cold hinterlands of the provinces of Echigo and Echizen, far from the capital. He lived there as a layman, married, and sired children. Even after he was allowed to return to Kyoto he continued to wander, this time in the province of Hitachi, and spread his teachings. Shinran taught that the *nembutsu* was no act of faith or merit on our parts, but the spontaneous expression of the Buddha's compassion. He urged relentless introspection and called for an end to distinctions between cleric and lay person, high and low, and men and women.

Shitennō. See Four Guardian Kings

Six Nara sects. Actually, the Six sects were more like seminars or courses of academic Buddhist study as transmitted from China through Korea in the Nara period. They did not have separate religious hierarchies or rituals, and often existed side by side in the same temple. Though their influence declined greatly in later eras, they contributed to building the base of an understanding of Buddhist thought in Japan, at least among certain members of the clergy.

Six paramitas. The six practices that a bodhisattva must perfect to achieve enlightenment. They are (1) giving, (2) moral conduct, (3) patience, (4) vigor, (5) meditation, and (6) wisdom.

Six realms. S: *gati*. The six states through which living beings transmigrate. From the lowest to the most elevated they are (1) hell, (2) hungry ghosts, (3) beasts, (4) humans, (5) asuras, and (6) gods.

Sokushin jōbutsu. See Becoming a Buddha in this lifetime

Sōtō sect. The Japanese version of the Chinese Caodong sect of Zen, established in Japan by Dōgen (1200–1252). Sōtō is often contrasted with the other main Zen sect in Japan, Rinzai, in this fashion: while Rinzai emphasizes intellectual sharpness and stresses the solution of riddle-like *kōan* as the key to enlightenment, Sōtō teaches "just sitting" in meditation. The differences are not so clear-cut, in fact. Sōtō is the most widespread form of Japanese Zen.

Taishakuten. S: Indra. In Buddhist cosmology, the Hindu deity Indra is regarded as a protector of the Buddhist faith and the lord of a heaven that sits atop Mount Sumeru.

Taizō Mandara. See Womb-store Mandala

Tendai sect. Founded by Saichō (767–822), the Tendai sect takes its name from Mount Tiantai (Tendai in Japanese pronunciation), which is the headquarters of the Chinese sect of that name founded by Zhiyi (538–97). The Lotus Sutra is the central scripture of Tendai, but Saichō also showed great interest in Buddhist discipline, devotional practices, and esoteric Buddhism, and Tendai included all of these elements from its inception in Japan. With headquarters on Mount Hiei northwest of Kyoto, it was the main sect of Heian-period Buddhism and later, in the Kamakura period, was the womb for the new, more popularly oriented sects that developed. See also Saichō

Tenjin. The deification of the Heian-period scholar and statesman Sugawara no Michizane (845–903). Sugawara was slandered by a rival at court and banished to Dazaifu, where he died in exile. Following his death, several disasters were visited upon his enemies, and in order to still the wrath of his spirit he was enshrined as the god of literacy.

Tushita Heaven. J: Tosotsu. The heaven in which the Buddha awaited his birth into the world, and often associated with Miroku (S: Maitreya), the Buddha of the future, who is thought to be waiting there now.

Twelve Divine Generals. Twelve *yaksha* (demonic spirits) generals who protect the followers of Yakushi Buddha.

Vairocana. See Birushana

Vimalakirtinirdesa Sutra. J: Yuima Gyō. A popular Mahayana sutra that relates the story of the wise layman Vimalakirti, who had mastered the truth of emptiness.

Womb-store Mandala. S: Garbhakosadhatu mandala; J: Taizō mandara. One of the two main mandalas of the Shingon school of esoteric Buddhism, the Womb-store mandala is a depiction of the world of enlightenment, with Dainichi Nyorai at its center.

Yakushi (Nyorai). S: Bhaisajyaguru. The Buddha of Healing, who reigns over a lapis lazuli pure land in the east.

Zenzai Dōji. S: Sudhana-sresthi-daraka. The name of the bodhisattva whose story is related in a section of the Avatamsaka Sutra. Zenzai visits fifty-three teachers who lead him along the path to enlightenment, which he finally achieves.

The "weathermark" identifies this book as a production of Tanko-Weatherhill, Inc., publishers of fine books on Asia and the Pacific. Book design and typography: Miriam F. Yamaguchi. Production supervisor: Mitsuo Okado. Composition of text: Korea Textbook Co., Seoul. Printing: Shōbundō Printing Co., Tokyo. Binding: Makoto Binderies, Tokyo. The typeface used is Monotype Times New Roman.